PSI SUCCESSFUL BUSINESS

THE INSIDER'S GUIDE TO
SMALL BUSINESS LOANS

Dan M. Koehler

Edited by Camille Akin

OASIS PRESS BOOKS & SOFTWARE
PSI Research / The Oasis Press®
Grants Pass, Oregon

Published by The Oasis Press®
© 1996 by Dan Koehler

All rights reserved. No part of this publication may be reproduced or used in any form or by any means, graphic, electronic or mechanical, including photocopying, recording, taping, or information storage and retrieval systems without written permission of the publishers.

This publication is designed to provide accurate and authoritative information in regard to the subject matter covered. It is sold with the understanding that the publisher is not engaged in rendering legal, accounting, or other professional service. If legal advice or other expert assistance is required, the services of a competent professional person should be sought.
    — *from a declaration of principles jointly adopted by a committee of the American Bar Association and a committee of publishers*

Editor: Camille Akin
Assistant Editor: Erin Wait
Format and Typographic Design: Pen & Palette Unlimited
Cover Designer: Steven Burns

Please direct any comments, questions, or suggestions regarding this book to:

    Editorial Department
    The Oasis Press®/PSI Research
    300 North Valley Drive
    Grants Pass, OR 97526
    (541) 479-9464
    (800) 228-2275

The Oasis Press® is a Registered Trademark of Publishing Services, Inc., an Oregon corporation doing business as PSI Research.

Library of Congress Cataloging-in-Publication Data
Koehler, Dan M., 1933–
    The insider's guide to small business loans / Dan M. Koehler.
        p.   cm. -- (PSI successful business library)
    Includes index.
    ISBN 1-55571-373-4 (pbk.)
    1. United States. Small Business Administration. 2. Government lending--United States. 3. Small business--United States--Finance. 4. United States. Small Business Administration--Forms. I. Title. II. Series.
HG3729.U5K63 1995
332.7'42--dc20   95-40753

Printed in the United States of America
First edition 10 9 8 7 6 5 4 3 2 1

Printed on recycled paper when available.

Table of Contents

Foreword	v
Preface	vii
Acknowledgments	ix
About the Author	x
Chapter 1: Understanding the Borrowing Process	1
Chapter 2: Know Your Lender Options	13
Chapter 3: Applying for a Small Business Loan	33
Chapter 4: SBA Loan Programs	65
Chapter 5: The Application Case Histories	89
Appendix A: SBA Field Locations	147
Appendix B: U.S. Export Assistance Centers	155
Appendix C: Non-Bank Lenders	157
Appendix D: Microloan Demonstration Program	159
Appendix E: Certified and Preferred Lenders	175
Appendix F: Small Business Investment Companies	189
Glossary	233
Index	239

Forms and Worksheets in this Book

Chapter 1:	*SBA Form 641, Request for Counseling:* Sample	10
	Worksheet #1 – Estimate of Start-Up Costs (Part A)	11
	Worksheet #2 – Estimate of Start-Up Costs (Part B)	12
Chapter 2:	*SBA Form 1167, PASS Application*	30
Chapter 3:	*SBA Form 4, Application for Business Loan:* Sample	48
	SBA Form 912, Statement of Personal History: Sample	52
	SBA Form 4 Schedule A, Schedule of Collateral: Sample	53
	SBA Form 413, Personal Financial Statement: Sample	55
	SBA Form 1100, Monthly Cash Flow Projection	57
	Financial Statement Spread Sheet	60
	SBA Form 159, Compensation Agreement: Sample	62
Chapter 4:	*SBA Form 4, Application for Small Business Loan (Short Form):* Sample	86
	SBA Form 4-L, Application for Business Loan (Up to $100,000): Sample	88

Foreword

We at AT&T Capital Corporation believe *The Insider's Guide to Small Business Loans* is long overdue. For more than ten years, AT&T Capital has provided a range of financial services to the small business community. Our experience gives us a realistic, insider's view of the needs and expectations of America's small business owners.

Since December 1991, through our subsidiary AT&T Small Business Lending Corporation, SBA lending has become a cornerstone of our company's efforts to assist and support this nation's small businesses. We believe fueling the growth of the small business community is vital to America's economic health.

We believe this book is an important work that can make a significant contribution to the small business community — the contribution of knowledge and understanding. Surveys of small business borrowers show that when it comes to evaluating a lender, knowledge is a key component of customer satisfaction. Small business owners have a need and a desire to know more, and they expect the lender to be a well-informed, value-added resource. This book helps the small businessperson unravel the complexities of the lending process and understand the modus operandi of the current system. Once equipped with this information, aspiring and established small business owners will attain the comfort level and the confidence to move ahead — to apply for, and receive, the financing required to start or grow their companies.

As a non-bank lender of SBA loans, AT&T Capital prides itself on its ability to provide borrowers with in-depth information on and insight into the SBA loan programs. But we cannot reach every borrower who needs this knowledge. That is why we hope this book will help spread the word and encourage aspiring small business owners to forge ahead, to build and grow their companies and live their dreams.

SuzAnne Ridgway
National Marketing Director, Business Finance
AT&T Capital Corporation

Preface

There are no secrets to success. It is the result of preparation, hard work, learning from failure.

— General Colin Powell

People who plan to go into business for themselves face either a great adventure — or a great disaster. The outcome depends almost solely upon how well they prepare themselves by investigating and analyzing the situation they are about to enter.

Since leaving the U.S. Small Business Administration, I have taught the principles of small business lending to more than 25,000 prospective and current entrepreneurs at more than 300 seminars. These seminar attendees have ranged from those with no previous lending knowledge to well-informed professionals, such as accountants and lawyers. One of the key problems I find is the lack of understanding concerning borrowing procedures. This lack of understanding lies at the heart of why so many people don't get the loans they deserve. Without fail, I receive the same questions and comments.

- How much will I be able to borrow?
- How much equity will I need to get a loan?
- I didn't think I was eligible.
- What about all the red tape involved in getting a loan?

In the simplest of terms, this book addresses these concerns and more.

Many business owners are refused loans because they don't know what kind or how much of a loan they need. In reality, banks hesitate to lend to business owners with vague ideas of what and how much they need. As a small business owner seeking a loan, you are responsible to do your homework. Don't expect the bank to do it for you.

In other cases, some small business owners are refused a loan by banks they have been dealing with for many years. These banks may want to grant a loan to a loyal customer, but lending institutions must be certain that the borrower's business is capable of repaying the loan. Sound ridiculous? You would be surprised at how often things as simple as this cause a loan to be turned down by a lender.

Knowledge of the financial facts of business life can save you the embarrassment of having your loan denied. Even more important, proper preparation and use of correct information can help you get a loan. Putting things into the proper light can make all the difference.

Just about anyone can obtain a small business loan if three key factors are considered. You must:

- Show the ability to repay the loan.
- Have a sound business plan.
- Have the necessary collateral to support the loan.

If you can supply these three key factors, I can show you how to approach your lender with a properly prepared loan application and get the loan you need.

Dan M. Koehler
January 1996

Acknowledgments

I would like to thank the many people who offered their time and assistance during the course of preparing this book. In particular, I wish to give special acknowledgment to the following individuals:

- Linda Deak, who took the time to edit and relentlessly pursue each verb and noun and to greatly enhance the quality of this book.
- Sally Riley of the Small Business Development Center (SBDC), Thomas Nelson Community College, for her support and for her valuable suggestions.
- Barney Wilson, executive director at the University of Baltimore's SBDC for his review and recommendations.
- Carol Guthridge, CPA for the accounting firm of Rudolph, Palitz, for her professional advice on the specifics of accounting and small business.
- Don Price, Regional Account Manager for AT&T Capital Corporation in Hampton, Virginia, who shared his small business lending expertise with me as well as his insight into the entrepreneurial process.
- Jean LaForce of the Financial Institutions Branch of the U.S. Small Business Administration, Washington, D.C., for her assistance in keeping me up-to-date on the many changes in SBA programs that have taken place in the last two years.
- Camille Akin, my editor, for all the suggestions and improvements she made to the book.
- Emmett Ramey, the publisher, for recognizing the need for a book of this type and being a pleasure to work with.
- My wife, Barbara, who not only encouraged me to write this book, but assisted in its preparation.

Finally, a special thanks to all those small businesspeople who have, over the years, shared their experience and expertise with me and helped make this book possible.

About the Author

An active participant in the small business community for more than 25 years, Dan M. Koehler has owned his own small business as well as held policy-making positions in the federal government. He was director of Program Development for the U.S. Small Business Administration (SBA). Thereafter, he was appointed deputy regional director for the New York Region of the SBA. In addition, he served as chief for Community Development and Policy Analysis in the Washington, D.C. SBA office.

Mr. Koehler has been a faculty member for the National Institute of Economics and, in this capacity, has taught more than 300 seminars on small business lending programs nationwide. He has acted as a discussion leader for the American Institute of Certified Public Accountants on SBA loan programs and has written its current manual on the subject.

In 1986, Mr. Koehler was appointed by President Ronald Reagan as a delegate to the National White House Conference on Small Business. Currently, he is president of the American Alliance of Small Businesses located in Pasadena, Maryland, a suburb of Washington, D.C., and writes a newsletter that covers small business lending topics.

Chapter 1

Understanding the Borrowing Process

*Obstacles are things a person sees
when he takes his eyes off his goal.*

— E. Joseph Cossman

Know the Borrowing Basics

Many small businesspeople find it hard to understand why a lending institution refuses to lend them money. Others have no trouble getting needed funds, but may be surprised to find strings attached to their loans. Too many business owners fail to realize that banks and other lenders must operate within certain rules and regulations.

To successfully obtain a small business loan, you will need to understand essential borrowing fundamentals, including:

- Credit factors;
- Collateral requirements;
- How to apply for a loan;
- What your lender looks at when reviewing your application;
- How to avoid common mistakes;
- Types of business loans available for your particular situation; and
- Loan sources available for your type of business.

Throughout this book you are given key guidelines that will help you understand the above borrowing basics. To begin, consider your ability to repay a loan, your business' management, and any collateral or cash, or both, you can contribute. You can bet these will be your lender's primary considerations.

The Ability to Repay

Many small business owners want to know what to emphasize when putting together a business loan application. The number one factor is the ability to repay a loan from the cash flow of a business. To a lender, that means adequate historical, interim, and projected cash flows that show repayment ability. An absence of repayment ability will, in almost all cases, cause a lender to reject a loan application.

Management

Management is the second most important issue in evaluating the potential success of a business. If you already have an existing business, chances are that your lender will know you and be familiar with your business background. On the other hand, if you are just starting a business, your lender will need some assurance as to how you will successfully operate your business. This means that you will need to put additional emphasis on your management credentials in your business plan. For some helpful hints on creating a business plan, refer to Chapter 3.

Collateral

Another key element that a lender looks at is collateral. In general, the lender wants the proposed collateral for a loan to be of such a nature that, when considered with the integrity and ability of the management, and with the applicant's past and prospective earnings, repayment of the loan will be reasonably assured.

Collateral may consist of one or more of the following:

- Mortgage on land, buildings, equity in your personal residence, and equipment;
- Assignment of warehouse receipts for marketable merchandise;
- Assignment of current receivables;
- Cash value of life insurance;
- Mortgage on chattels;
- Stocks and bonds; or
- Assignment of certain types of contracts.

Your Cash Contribution

How much of your funds are you prepared to inject into the business? Ideally, your contribution should be two dollars for each dollar borrowed for a start up, and you should have excellent credit. If this is not the case, meet with your lender to explain your situation. Not everyone has the same set of circumstances, and some problems can be overcome.

Familiarize Yourself with the SBA

The U.S. Small Business Administration is a small — less than 3,500 employees — independent federal agency that was created by Congress in 1953 to assist, counsel, and champion the millions of American small businesses that are the essence and backbone of this country's competitive, free enterprise economy. Over the years, not only has its loan making capacity grown, but so has its ability to offer management assistance programs, surety bonds, government contracts, and a vast array of assistance to small businesses through more than 100 offices in all parts of the nation. (Refer to Appendix A for a complete list of SBA field locations.)

Many businesses began with, and continue to use, the assistance of SBA sponsored programs. Some of these well-known businesses include:

- Nike
- Apple Computer
- Federal Express Corporation
- Winnebago Industries
- T.J. Cinnamons
- Godfather's Pizza
- Digital Switch Corporation
- Formby's Refinishing Products
- Compaq Computers
- Stew Leonard's

Today, the SBA guarantees between 30–40% of all long-term loans to small businesses nationwide. As this percentage continues to grow, so will the chances that your loan will come through one of its agency programs.

Depending on the type of loan you need, loan approval can take one day or several months. The length of time needed to get a loan approved is almost entirely up to you, the borrower. As the prospective borrower you are responsible for correctly and accurately completing your loan application package. In fact, the most often cited reasons for acceptance delays of application packages are missing documentation and missing signatures and dates on each exhibit. (Refer to Chapter 5 for properly prepared loan applications.)

This book gives the highlights of sound business borrowing. Whether you have little or no borrowing experience, you should be able to put together a loan package that will get speedy approval, regardless of whether it is a straight bank loan or one processed by your lender with an SBA guarantee. If you are a more experienced owner-manager, you might use this book to reevaluate your borrowing operations.

SBA Equity Guidelines

The SBA uses equity (tangible) guidelines when reviewing your application. Regardless of whether you obtain a loan from a lender, with or without a government guarantee (such as an SBA loan), you will need some equity for a lender to consider your loan. Generally, the amount of money a lender will grant is based on the amount of money you can contribute upfront.

In general, the SBA uses the following guidelines when reviewing a loan application.

For a start-up business, the SBA will consider a loan ranging from two to four dollars for each dollar you put up. If you are a veteran who is starting a new business, the SBA will invest three to five dollars for each dollar you can inject. Further, as an educated and degreed professional, you can expect the SBA to invest three to four dollars for every dollar you invest.

If you are considering buying an existing business, keep in mind that the SBA will invest three to four dollars for each dollar you put upfront. In this situation, the SBA will also focus on the cash flow of the business. (Notes due seller on standby can be equity, but you must have a reasonable amount at risk.) Keep in mind, goodwill and intangibles are difficult for a lender to finance under SBA loan programs.

Finally, if yours is an existing business, the SBA will probably invest three to four dollars for each dollar you can invest. Similar to the guidelines for a loan to buy an existing business, your business' cash flow is key. The SBA will look at historical profit and loss (P&L) data, not projections. Additionally, the SBA will allow an existing business to use appraisals of fixed assets — if heavily depreciated — to improve balance sheets.

> Remember, these are only guidelines. The SBA will consider each loan on a case-by-case basis. Your equity injection is only one part of what it considers when looking at an application. As you go through the necessary steps to develop your loan application, other credit factors will be discussed in greater detail.

First Things First: Pre-Application

Your ability to get money for your business when you need it is just as important as good location or proper equipment is to your overall operation. You may be like many other people and wonder where to start.

Before you begin the application process, you can follow five key steps to get you started on the right foot.

Step 1 – Get Free Advice

The SBA, the Service Corps of Retired Executives (SCORE), and the Small Business Development Centers (SBDCs) will help with financial planning and business counseling, and act as special advocates in a variety of areas. If, for example, you feel you need counseling, call the nearest SCORE/SBDC office (the local SBA office will have the phone number) to schedule an appointment with a counselor. These counselors have a broad range of business expertise and a great willingness to help small businesses. They work closely with the SBA to provide free information and advice. You don't need to be an SBA borrower.

If you are considering going into business, or are already an experienced business owner and want to update your skills, be sure to attend one of the conferences or workshops. You will find them well worth your time. For topic and schedule information, contact the nearest SBA office or call your local chamber of commerce.

The SBA also offers volunteer counseling. This includes the previously mentioned SCORE members who have already been, or still are, active businesspeople, as well as members of such national organizations as the Federation of Business and Professional Women, the National Association of Black Accountants, the Association of Industrial Engineers, and others. All of these professionals have expressed a desire to share their experience and expertise with people just entering the small business community. What better way to learn about a business you hope to start than to consult with someone who has achieved success in the same field?

Also, the student and faculty participants in the SBA-sponsored Small Business Institute Program are helpful. They provide long-term counseling and assistance to owners of new or troubled small businesses located near the geographic area of their schools of business administration. If you are already in business and are experiencing difficulties, do not wait for things to get worse. Immediately contact your nearest SBA office. You may be eligible for free aid from the resources of an entire university, and you don't even need to be an SBA borrower.

Chapters 2 and 4 provide more details on these and other SBA programs.

One way or another, get in touch with your nearest SBA field office. On your first visit to the SBA office, you may be asked to fill out a *Request for Counseling, Form 641.* (A sample copy of *Form 641* is located at the end of this chapter.) Indicate that you want to go into business, and request the necessary initial publications that some SBA field offices call "The Starting Kit." If the office doesn't have a kit, ask for the *Resource Directory for Small Business Management, SBA Form 115C.* From the directory you can order helpful publications, including:

Step 2 – Contact Your Local SBA Office

- *Checklist for Going into Business* — Item # MP12 — $2.00
- *Business Plan for Retailers* — MP09 — 2.00
- *Business Plan for Small Service Firms* — MP11 — 2.00
- *Business Plan for Home-Based Businesses* — MP15 — 2.00
- *Business Plan for Small Construction Firms* — MP05 — 2.00
- *Business Plan for Small Manufacturers* — MP04 — 2.00
- *How to Buy or Sell a Business* — MP16 — 2.00

These publications address the most important business topics, and answer the questions most often asked by prospective and existing business owners. Of these publications, *Checklist for Going into Business* is a must if you are thinking about starting a business. The checklist highlights the important factors you should consider before starting your own business. To order the above publications, send a check or money order made payable to the U.S. Small Business Administration to:

SBA Publications
P.O. Box 46521
Denver, CO 80201-0030

Remember, even if you don't plan to use the SBA for your loan, these materials are invaluable to you. Reviewing these publications is a great way to start developing your business plan and loan package. The more you can learn, the more potential you have for success. By presenting your business in the best light, you enhance your chances of getting the financing you need.

To get started, turn to the worksheets at the end of this chapter. Review them carefully, and fill them out as accurately as you can. Do not guess. If necessary, take time to get the right answers from people who should know. When you have finished, sign the *Request for Counseling, Form 641*, and hand deliver or mail it to your nearest SBA office. Some offices have enough counseling staff to accommodate walk-ins. Most, however, will be able to give you more time if you make an appointment.

Step 3 – Prepare for Your Counseling Session

What kind of counseling do you need? What do you hope to gain from it? Study the business plan that best fits your proposed enterprise, and try to develop a specific plan for it. Can you complete the plan on your own, or do you need assistance? Make a list of questions to which you need answers. Bring the questions and your business plan — complete or incomplete — with you to the SCORE office where your first counseling session will most likely be held.

Even if your previous work experience makes you confident that your primary interest is in financing and you don't need management assistance, you would be wise to make your initial appointment with a SCORE counselor. If you have really high administrative qualifications, the counselor may tell you to proceed on your own. The SCORE/SBDC volunteer counselor will help you review and, if necessary, complete your business plan and brief you on the kinds of questions you may expect from the bank loan officer. Chapter 3 will give you helpful hints on creating a successful business plan.

Before you leave the initial counseling session, try to establish a positive and lasting relationship with your counselor. If you have been assigned to a SCORE member, make a note of his or her office schedule and a phone number where you may reach that person for additional questions or for a follow-up appointment. SCORE members have spent most of their lives running successful businesses, and their help can be invaluable to your future success. Their services are free, even if they must drive a long distance to look at your business site.

Step 4 – Attend a Pre-Business Workshop

For many prospective business owners, attending a pre-business workshop is the first step. You can learn a great deal of helpful information from formal presentations at a workshop. But, equally important, you will have the opportunity to meet with others facing the same decisions and opportunities, and to exchange ideas and experiences with them. Other participants may raise questions that you have not considered. Further, you might find assurance knowing you are not alone in your apprehensions and self-doubt. You may find, as have many others, that to ask questions in a group is a good, non-committal way to start.

Attending a pre-business workshop will probably alert you to other areas of business expertise you should explore further. Before you leave, be sure to ask for a schedule of future workshops and training sessions. If there are none immediately available, ask to be placed on a mailing list for announcements of upcoming events. You may need to wait a reasonable length of time. If nothing is forthcoming, request the information again. SBA field offices may be understaffed and overworked, but their people are glad to help those who seriously request it.

Step 5 – Locate Helpful Resources

Most communities in each state offer a great deal of help to potential business owners. Both state and local agencies can give you valuable assistance, both before you go into business and after you are established. A good place to start is with your local chamber of commerce, which should be able to supply you with names and phone numbers of agencies interested in helping small businesses.

Your local library can be a gold mine for resources. You should be able to find a copy of Robert Morris & Associates' *Annual Statement Studies.* This publication is an excellent source to find standard debt-to-equity ratios for various industries so you can compare the ones you are using to what your lender uses. In addition, review a copy of Dun and Bradstreet's *Key Business Ratios.* Both publications are excellent sources for established or larger businesses.

If yours is a new business, use trade journals or trade associations. You should find a listing at your library in the *Encyclopedia of Associations.* Another good source for some traditional businesses is the *Small Business Sourcebook.* Other helpful resources include the business guides published by The Oasis Press. For a catalog of business publications, contact:

The Oasis Press
(800) 228-2275

Some SBA offices, or the participating SCORE/SBDC chapter, will furnish you with a list of local resources. Cross-check them against each other. Not all resources suggested will be found in every community, but most potential small business owners are usually pleasantly surprised at the many kinds of assistance their libraries offer that they never knew existed.

The SBA has developed a free, on-line service that gives any person with a personal computer and a modem 24-hour access to an information-packed bulletin board. *SBA Online* will give you:

- Information on starting and operating a business;
- Listings of financial assistance;
- Help for minorities, women, and veterans;
- Information on international trade;
- Specific laws and government regulations for small business;
- State profiles for small business; and
- Government procurement assistance.

To access *SBA Online* you can use one of the following phone numbers.

(800) 697-4636
- SBA and other government agency information
- Downloadable text files

(900) 463-4636
- SBA and other government agency information
- Downloadable application software files
- Gateway
- Mail
- Internet mail and news groups
- On-line searchable data banks

To log on to *SBA Online* for the first time:

- Set the following parameters for your modem's communication program:
  - No parity
  - Eight data bits
  - One stop bit
  - VT 102 terminal emulation
- Dial 1-800-697-4636 or 1-900-463-4636, depending on the services you desire, at any modem speed (2400 to 19.2K).
- Press Control key + "C" after you see a "Connect" message. You will see the SBA logo and be prompted to type in your name and business address.

On your first call, you will need to create a password for future use. Once you have established your password, the main menu will appear allowing the following selections:

- General information
- Services available
- Local information
- Outside resources
- Quick search menu

Keep in mind, you are limited to 120 minutes per call.

Regardless of whether you are asking for a conventional bank loan or applying for an SBA guaranteed loan, there are certain steps that you need to follow before approaching your lender. Use this checklist to ensure you follow the right steps.

Quick Start Checklist

- ❏ Contact the nearest SBA office and ask for a free copy of the *Resource Directory for Small Business Management, SBA Form 115C*. Order the publications that fit your particular situation.

- ❏ Estimate your start-up costs with *worksheets #1 and #2,* located at the end of this chapter. You will complete one-year projections later. (See the *Monthly Cash Flow Projection* in Chapter 3.)

- ❏ Fill out the *SBA Request for Counseling, Form 641*. (A sample copy of *Form 641* is located at the end of this chapter.) Make an appointment with your nearest SBDC or SCORE counselor.

- ❏ Find out from the SBA office when and where the next pre-business workshop will be held and attend, even if you have had previous small business experience.

- ❏ Begin to draft your business plan. Work with your SCORE or SBDC volunteers. Show them your draft and get their advice.

> Before you take your loan package to a lender, let your local SCORE chapter or SBDC review your work. They will know what your lender is looking for in a loan application and will make suggestions and any corrections that may be necessary. Chapter 2 will go into more details on how SCORE and your local SBDC can help you.

SBA Form 641, Request for Counseling: Sample

U.S. SMALL BUSINESS ADMINISTRATION

OMB Approval No. 3245-0091
Expiration Date: 11-30-93

REQUEST FOR COUNSELING

SAMPLE

A. NAME OF COMPANY

B. YOUR NAME (Last, First, Middle)

C. TELEPHONE
(H)
(B)

D. STREET

E. CITY

F. STATE

G. COUNTY

H. ZIP

I. TYPE OF BUSINESS (Check one)
1. ☐ Retail   4. ☐ Manufacturing
2. ☐ Service   5. ☐ Construction
3. ☐ Wholesale   6. ☐ Not in Business

J. BUS. OWNSHP./GENDER
1. ☐ Male
2. ☐ Female
3. ☐ Male/Female

K. VETERAN STATUS
1. ☐ Veteran
2. ☐ Vietnam-Era Veteran
3. ☐ Disabled Veteran

L.
- INDICATE PREFERRED DATE AND TIME FOR APPOINTMENT
  DATE _____ TIME _____
- ARE YOU CURRENTLY IN BUSINESS?   YES _____ NO _____
- IF YES, HOW LONG? _____
- TYPE OF BUSINESS (USE THREE TO FIVE WORDS)
  _____

M. ETHNIC BACKGROUND
a. Race:
1. ☐ American Indian or Alaskan Native
2. ☐ Asian or Pacific Islander
3. ☐ Black
4. ☐ White

b. Ethnicity:
1. ☐ Hispanic Origin
2. ☐ Not of Hispanic Origin

N. INDICATE, BRIEFLY, THE NATURE OF SERVICE AND/OR COUNSELING YOU ARE SEEKING
_____
_____

O.
- IT HAS BEEN EXPLAINED TO ME THAT I MAY USE FURTHER SERVICES SPONSORED BY THE U.S. SMALL BUSINESS ADMINISTRATION   YES _____   NO _____
- I HAVE ATTENDED A SMALL BUSINESS WORKSHOP   YES _____   NO _____
- CONDUCTED BY _____

P. HOW DID YOU LEARN OF THESE COUNSELING SERVICES?
1. ☐ Yellow Pages   3. ☐ Radio   5. ☐ Bank   7. ☐ Word-of-Mouth
2. ☐ Television   4. ☐ Newspapers 6. ☐ Chamber of Commerce   8. ☐ Other

Q. SBA CLIENT (To Be Filled Out By Counselor)
1. ☐ Borrower   2. ☐ Applicant   3. ☐ 8(a) Client   4. ☐ COC   5. ☐ Surety Bond

R. AREA OF COUNSELING PROVIDED (To Be Filled Out By Counselor)
1. Bus. Start-Up/Acquisition   5. Accounting & Records   9. Personnel
2. Source of Capital   6. Finan. Analysis/Cost Control 10. Computer Systems
3. Marketing/Sales   7. Inventory Control   11. Internat'l. Trade
4. Government Procurement   8. Engineering R&D   12. Business Liq./Sale

I request business management counseling from the Small Business Administration. I agree to cooperate should I be selected to participate in surveys designed to evaluate SBA assistance services. I authorize SBA to furnish relevant information to the assigned management counselor(s) although I expect that information to be held in strict confidence by him/her.

I further understand that any counselor has agreed not to: (1) recommend goods or services from sources in which he/she has an interest and (2) accept fees or commissions developing from this counseling relationship. In consideration of SBA's furnishing management or technical assistance, I waive all claims against SBA personnel, SCORE, SBDC and its host organizations, SBI, and other SBA Resource Counselors arising from this assistance.

SIGNATURE AND TITLE OF REQUESTER   **DATE**

FOR USE OF THE SMALL BUSINESS ADMINISTRATION

RESOURCE   **DISTRICT**   **REGION**

SBA FORM 641 (2-91) PREVIOUS EDITION IS OBSOLETE
WHITE: COUNSELOR
YELLOW: SBI OR SCORE OR SBDC SUB.
PINK: DO OR NSO OR SBDC LEAD

Worksheet #1 – Estimate of Start-Up Costs (Part A)

WORKSHEET #1

ESTIMATED MONTHLY EXPENSES			
Item	Your estimate of monthly expenses based on sales of $_____ per year **Column 1**	Your estimate of how much cash you need to start your business. (See column 3.) **Column 2**	What to put in column 2 (These figures are typical for one kind of business. You will have to decide how many months to allow for in your business.) **Column 3**
Salary of owner-manager	$	$	2 times column 1
All other salaries and wages			3 times column 1
Rent			3 times column 1
Advertising			3 times column 1
Delivery expense			3 times column 1
Supplies			3 times column 1
Telephone and telegraph			3 times column 1
Other utilities			3 times column 1
Insurance			Payment required by insurance company
Taxes, including Social Security			4 times column 1
Interest			3 times column 1
Maintenance			3 times column 1
Legal and other professional fees			3 times column 1
Miscellaneous			3 times column 1
STARTING COSTS YOU ONLY HAVE TO PAY ONCE			Leave column 2 blank
Fixtures and equipment			Fill in **Worksheet #2** put the toal here
Decorating and remodeling			Talk it over with a contractor
Installation of fixtures and equipment			Talk to suppliers from whom you buy these
Starting inventory			Suppliers will probably help you estimate this
Deposits with public utilities			Find out from utilities companies
Legal and other professional fees			Lawyer, accountant, or other professional
Licenses and permits			Find out from city offices what you need
Advertising and promotion for opening			Estimate what you will use
Accounts receivable			What you need to buy more stock until credit customers pay
Cash			For unexpected expenses or losses, special purchases, etc.
Other			Make a separate list and enter total
TOTAL ESTIMATED CASH YOU NEED TO START WITH		$	Add up all the numbers in column 2

Worksheet #2 – Estimate of Start-Up Costs (Part B)

WORKSHEET #2
LIST OF FURNITURE, FIXTURES, AND EQUIPMENT

Leave out or add items to suit your business. Use separate sheets to list exactly what you need for each of the items below.	If you plan to pay cash in full, enter the full amount below and in the last column.	If you are going to pay by installments, fill out the columns below. Enter in the last column your downpayment plus at least one installment.			Estimate of the cash you need for furniture, fixtures and equipment.
		Price	Price	Amount of each installment	
Counters	$	$	$	$	$
Storage shelves, cabinets					
Display stands, shelves, tables					
Cash register					
Safe					
Window display fixtures					
Special lighting					
Outside sign					
Delivery equipment if needed					
TOTAL FURNITURE, FIXTURES, AND EQUIPMENT (Enter this figure also in WORKSHEET #1 under STARTING COSTS YOU ONLY HAVE TO PAY ONCE.)					$

Upon completion of these worksheets you will have determined your cash requirement for the first three months of operation:

    Monthly expenses x 3
    + One-time start-up cash
    Total estimated start-up cash (bottom of Worksheet #1)

You will then need to carry these figures over to your *Monthly Cash Flow Projection* located at the end of Chapter 3. If you have answered all the questions carefully, you have done some hard work and serious thinking. But you have probably found some things you still need to know more about or do something about.

Do all you can for yourself, but don't hesitate to ask for help from people who can tell you what you need to know. Remember, running a business takes guts! You must decide what you need and then go after it. Good luck.

Chapter 2

Know Your Lender Options

A banker: the person who lends you his umbrella when the sun is shining and wants it back the minute it rains.

— Mark Twain

Starting a business is risky, at best, but your chances of succeeding will be much better if you understand the loan application process. Regardless of whether you are applying for a conventional bank loan or one with a government guarantee (such as an SBA loan), the process starts with the lender — not the SBA.

The SBA offers a variety of financing options for small businesses. However, it rarely makes a direct loan to an individual or business. The SBA is primarily a guarantor — it guarantees loans made by banks and other private lenders to small business clients. The SBA guarantee reduces the probability of a loss to a lender and makes it easier for you — the small business client — to borrow money.

Small business lenders can come from four principal areas.

- Your bank of record is the bank where you have been doing business. Your bank can grant you either a conventional loan (no government involvement), or it can participate with the SBA in a guaranteed loan.
- A non-bank lender is a licensed private lender that has the authority to make guaranteed loans. Currently, ten non-bank lenders exist nationwide who specialize in SBA loans. They prefer loans in excess of $50,000. (See Appendix C for a complete nationwide list.)
- Microloan lenders are local development agencies that can grant SBA loans for as little as $100 to a maximum of $25,000. Call the nearest SBA office to locate the microloan lender nearest you, or use the list located in Appendix D at the end of this book.

- Venture capital companies — also known as small business investment companies (SBICs) — are privately owned and operated firms that use their capital and funds borrowed from the SBA to finance small businesses. (See Appendix F for a complete directory of SBICs.)

Your Bank of Record

You should start with your own bank, the people who know you best. Besides, all other lenders that you may approach will ask you what your bank told you. Your application package will be reviewed for its credit and management merits. The lender will then make one of three decisions. The lender can:

- Approve the loan entirely by itself with a direct bank loan without SBA involvement.
- Approve the loan subject to an SBA guarantee, in which case the SBA will also review your application and the lender's analysis (at the lender's request) before making its own determination. This is called an SBA guarantee loan.
- Decline the loan internally or in participation with the SBA, or both. For your lender to choose the SBA guarantee option, it needs to analyze the application, determine your credit and management merits, and certify that the loan will be granted if the SBA provides a guarantee.

When a lender's loan is guaranteed by the SBA, certain conditions are imposed on the lending institution to govern how the loan is closed and monitored. These conditions protect both you and the government. Other terms and conditions are imposed on you, the borrower, that pertain to the operation of your business. Also, the lender may impose additional requirements on you provided they do not conflict with the SBA's rules and regulations.

When you apply to a lender for an SBA guaranteed loan, keep in mind that it is a two-step process that will take longer than a straight bank loan. Since an SBA loan is more involved, not all lenders are immediately receptive to going through the process. The best way for you to overcome any hesitancy by your lender toward an SBA loan is for you to clearly and accurately present all the facts and figures regarding your business.

Regardless of which lender you approach, you should start by completing the steps outlined in Chapter 1. If you need assistance in completing your loan application, your lender should be able to help you — or recommend someone who can assist with your particular situation. Your local SCORE chapter or SBDC will be more than happy to help.

Non-Bank Lenders

One of the most important SBA loan sources is the non-bank lender, also known as a Small Business Lending Company (SBLC). Starting in the late 1970s, in anticipation of the increase in SBA funding for the 7(a)

Regular Loan Guarantee Program, the SBA began exploring the idea of licensing private lenders who would have the authority to make guaranteed loans. SBLCs were created at that time to ensure an industry of devoted SBA lenders.

In 1982, the SBA ceased issuing non-bank lending licenses. However, interest in acquiring non-bank lending licenses has grown significantly in recent years as SBA funding levels have increased. AT&T Small Business Lending Corporation (AT&T SBLC), a wholly owned subsidiary of AT&T Capital Corporation, acquired one of these licenses in 1991 and is now a preferred lender nationwide.

A primary advantage that a non-bank lender has over other SBA lenders is that non-bank lenders are only regulated by the SBA, whereas other lenders must report to other regulatory authorities as well. Geographic expansion is easier for the non-bank lender because it does not need to establish and maintain relationships with appropriate regulatory offices in each state it enters to conduct business. The non-bank lender only needs to maintain its regulatory relationship with the SBA. In addition, non-bank lenders are not self-restricted the way banks may be through their own charters.

The most important advantage of a non-bank lender is that, unlike banks who offer a myriad of services, non-bank lenders specialize in SBA guaranteed loans. A non-bank lender's primary source of profit comes from SBA guaranteed loans. As a result, you can be guaranteed efficient and professional handling of your loan application. In fact, non-bank lenders, such as AT&T Small Business Lending Corporation, are moving the processing of SBA loans into the twenty-first century to ensure that the words SBA and red tape are no longer synonymous.

Using AT&T SBLC as an example, a non-bank lender can help you in the following way. Suppose your business is growing and you need a loan for $500,000 to purchase an additional building. Your business has been growing rapidly, your credit is not quite strong enough to qualify for a conventional loan, and your bank of record does not grant SBA loans. Where do you turn to satisfy your company's financial needs?

You could turn to another local or regional bank that grants SBA loans, but this raises two concerns. First, when a local or regional bank makes a sizable loan, it usually wants you to place all of your business banking with it. This jeopardizes the relationship between you and your existing bank. Second, most banks have a size limitation of $1 million on SBA loans.

However, you shop around and eventually find a bank that is willing to work with you. As the transaction progresses, the bank learns that part of the collateral for the loan consists of a building in another state. The bank you were working with has restrictions in its charter that prevent it from using out-of-state collateral to support a loan. Now where do you turn to satisfy your financial requirements?

Your bank of record recommends that you talk to AT&T SBLC, a non-bank lender that offers SBA loans to borrowers nationwide. You will quickly find out that this non-bank lender has a network of professional loan officers that are prepared to deal with your situation. Unlike the bank deal, an SBA guaranteed loan through AT&T SBLC will be fully amortized for up to 25 years, if necessary, and contains no prepayment penalties, balloon payments, or call provisions. The balance sheet can be leveraged, thereby eliminating specific loan-to-value restrictions and emphasizing consideration of all business assets in collateral evaluation.

For new debt or refinancing, the representative in your area will work with you or your accountant in preparing an AT&T SBLC business loan application, and further, all paperwork with regard to the SBA application is prepared by AT&T SBLC, who wants you to focus on running your business, not on preparing government application documents.

Depending on your location, the application will be processed by one of AT&T SBLC's two processing centers, located in Denver, Colorado, or Parsippany, New Jersey. Credit underwriting, loan documentation, closing, and servicing will be handled by a team of professionals with extensive SBA lending experience — the only kind of lending it does. After closing, you will be able to call, toll-free, with servicing requests that will be handled by a team of portfolio specialists.

Once you outgrow the SBA loan programs, AT&T Capital Corporation can continue to meet the needs of your business through other conventional financing and leasing programs. AT&T Capital is one of the major lenders in the LowDoc lending program. At this time, AT&T Capital Corporation is becoming one of the biggest underwriters of LowDoc loans nationwide.

Truly, from the above scenario, you can see how a non-bank lender can become your best financial resource. See Appendix C for a complete list of non-bank lenders.

Microloan Lenders

Microloan lenders create opportunities for people to become successful entrepreneurs. These lenders include provisions for technical assistance and other support services for microbusinesses — referred to as "the smallest of the small business sector." They can be very diverse but have some common characteristics. Microbusinesses tend to:

- Have less than five employees (the entrepreneur is usually the sole employee);
- Be service or retail oriented;
- Have been in existence for less than five years;

- Be mostly home-based, such as a street vendor (operating out of a nontraditional location);
- Be an outgrowth of a hobby or primary employment;
- Require small amounts of capital ($10,000 or less);
- Require moderate to high levels of technical assistance; or
- Be the sole source of income to the entrepreneur.

Microloan lenders are community-based groups that make capital available to local entrepreneurs with feasible ideas who cannot initially access funds through traditional lenders. A complete list of microloan lenders is in Appendix D. A description of the program is in Chapter 4.

Small Business Investment Companies (SBICs)

Virtually all Small Business Investment Companies (SBICs) are profit-motivated businesses that make either loans or equity investments. Today, there are two types of SBICs: regular SBICs and Specialized Small Business Investment Companies (SSBICs). SSBICs are specifically oriented toward the needs of entrepreneurs whose opportunities to own and operate businesses have been limited by social or economic disadvantages.

History and Background

The name SSBIC is an unofficial term. Technically, such companies are known as Section 301(d) licensees because they are organized under Section 301(d) of the Small Business Investment Act of 1958 (the Act), as amended. With a few exceptions, the same rules and regulations apply to both regular SBICs and SSBICs. Therefore, unless otherwise specified, when the term SBIC is used, it refers to both types of entities.

The SBIC program was given life in the midst of the 1958 recession. The Act, with amendments, authorizes the SBA to license private sector corporations and partnerships to provide financing and management assistance to small entrepreneurial businesses in the United States, using long-term debt guaranteed by the SBA to supplement their private capital. The SBICs, in turn, use their private capital, plus SBA-guaranteed debt, to provide equity capital and long-term debt to small businesses. Private capital takes the first risk. Only after the loss of all private equity capital is the government portion at risk.

Domestically and internationally, the Act created a unique public-sector partnership in the history of economic development. On one hand, the primacy of private capital in the capital structures of SBICs insulates government funds from loss. On the other hand, private ownership and management of the SBICs ensure the investment decision making is maximally efficient in marketplace terms.

To date, SBICs have disbursed more than $12 billion to more than 100,000 small businesses. As a result, SBIC-financed businesses have far out-performed all national averages as measured by increases in assets, sales, profits, and new employment. Thousands of profitable business owners can attest to the benefits, in dollars and management counseling, they have received from SBICs during the past 37 years. In addition, SSBICs, operating since 1969, have deployed another $1.2 billion to 14,000 small businesses.

How SBIC Financing Works

An SBIC finances small businesses either by straight loans or by venture capital, equity-type investments. A major incentive for SBICs to risk their capital in small businesses is the chance to share in the profits if the businesses grow and prosper. In some cases, these investments give the SBIC actual or potential ownership of a minority of a small business' stock. However, SBICs are generally prohibited from taking a control position in a small business.

An SBIC may use several types of financing, or combination of financing, with a single small business. For example, it may purchase common stock in the business and simultaneously make a straight loan to it. If the business needs future financing, an SBIC might make a second loan, but this time it obtains warrants to purchase additional common stock.

When an SBIC grants a loan, the interest rate charged is not only governed by applicable state laws and regulations, but also by SBA regulations. Generally, financing must be for at least five years, except a borrower may elect to have a prepayment clause included in the financing agreement.

Equity-Type Investments

Typically, a small business loan applicant and an SBIC negotiate the terms of equity-type investments. Generally, interest rates are lower and collateral requirements less stringent than the rates of straight loans. In fact, collateral may not even be required. Often an SBIC will subordinate its debenture or loan to other borrowings by a small business, thereby strengthening a business' credit standing with banks or other lenders. Sometimes amortization requirements will be deferred for the early years of the debt to give a small business every chance for a good start.

The amount of equity sought by an SBIC will depend on the percentage of your business' total assets represented by the SBIC financing, your business' record of stability and growth, and a variety of other factors.

Three types of investments are commonly used by SBICs.

- Loans with warrants — In return for a loan, a small business issues warrants enabling the SBIC to purchase common stock in its business, usually at a favorable price, during a specified period of time.
- Convertible debentures — The SBIC lends a small business money and, in return, receives a debenture. The SBIC then can either accept repayment of the loan or can convert the debenture into an equivalent amount of common stock of the small business.
- Common stock — The SBIC purchases common stock from the small business.

Straight Loans

While most SBICs want an opportunity to share in the growth and potential profits of the small businesses they finance, some will make loans that involve no equity features. A small business that obtains a straight loan usually will be required to provide security, but this may take the form of a second mortgage, a personal guarantee, or some other type of collateral that may not be acceptable to banks or other conventional lending institutions.

Like an equity-type investment, an SBIC will negotiate with a small business on the interest rate for a straight loan. Collateral requirements, terms of repayment, and other parts of the loan agreement also are determined by negotiation within the boundaries of the regulations.

SBIC Eligibility

SBICs invest in a broad range of industries. Some SBICs seek out small businesses with new products or services because of the strong growth potential of such firms. Many SBICs specialize in the field in which their management has special competency. Most SBICs, however, consider a wide variety of investment opportunities.

Only businesses defined by the SBA as "small" are eligible for SBIC financing. The SBA defines a company as small when its net worth is $18 million or less, and its average net income for the preceding two years does not exceed $6 million. For businesses in industries for which the above standards are too low, alternative size standards are available. In determining whether a business qualifies, an SBIC considers all of the business' parents, subsidiaries, and affiliates.

If you own or operate a small business and would like to obtain SBIC financing, you should first identify and investigate existing SBICs that may be interested in financing your company. The Investment Division of the SBA publishes a complete listing of SBICs by state. For your convenience, a copy of this directory is included at the back of this book in Appendix F. Use the directory located in Appendix F as a first step in learning as much as possible about SBICs in your area. In choosing an SBIC, consider the types of investments it makes, how much money is available for investment, and how much might be available in the future. You should also consider whether the SBIC can offer you management services appropriate to your needs.

Plan in Advance

You should determine your business' needs and research SBICs well in advance — long before you will actually need the money. Your research will take time, as will the SBIC's research of your business.

When you have identified the SBICs you think are best suited to provide financing for your company, you will need to prepare a presentation. Your initial presentation will play a major role in your success in obtaining financing. It is up to you to demonstrate that an investment in your business is worthwhile. The best way to show worth is by presenting a detailed and comprehensive business plan. Use the guidelines for a successful business plan from Chapter 3.

> SBICs are not required to use SBA loan forms. Each SBIC will have its own specialized form.

SBIC Response Time

There are no hard and fast rules about the length of time it will take an SBIC to investigate and close a transaction. Ordinarily, an initial response is made quickly. On the other hand, the thorough study an SBIC must undertake before making a final decision can take several weeks or longer. Naturally, a well-documented presentation on your part will reduce the amount of time the SBIC will require.

If you need more information on SBICs, or need an additional directory of SBICs, contact:

Associate Administrator for Investment
U.S. Small Business Administration
409 Third Street SW
Washington, DC 20416
(202) 205-6510
FAX (202) 205-6959

The SBA Can Help You

The SBA has many services that are available to people already in small business or those considering opening a business. They include training and educational programs, advisory services, publications, financial programs, and contract assistance. The SBA also offers specialized programs for women business owners, minorities, veterans, international trade, and rural development, to name a few. These programs are free and open to those who already have an SBA loan, those considering a loan, and even to those who do not need financial assistance but have a need for management, technical, or contract assistance.

Service Corps of Retired Executives (SCORE)

SCORE is a nationwide 14,000 member volunteer program sponsored by the SBA. The program matches experienced volunteers with small businesses that need expert help. These men and women business executives, whose collective experience spans the full range of American enterprise, share their management and technical expertise with present and prospective owners/managers of small businesses. Most are retired; however, full-time, employed executives are also available. They make up about 20% of SCORE's membership.

A SCORE volunteer offers in-depth counseling and training for business owners. SCORE volunteers can help you identify basic management problems, determine the causes, and suggest solutions. The counseling can take place at an SBA field office or at your business. There is no charge for this assistance. SCORE also offers pre-business workshops and a variety of other programs concerning small business.

SCORE counselors can be located by calling the nearest SBA office or, in many cases, your local chamber of commerce.

Small Business Development Centers (SBDCs)

SBDCs provide management and technical assistance to current and prospective small business owners. They offer one-stop assistance to small businesses by providing a wide variety of information and guidance. The program is a cooperative effort of the private sector, the educational community, and federal, state, and local governments.

At present, there are 56 SBDCs — one or more in each state — with a network of more than 900 service locations. They can provide up-to-date counseling, training, and technical assistance on all aspects related to your business. Counseling services are provided free-of-charge, and training programs are offered at little or no cost.

To locate the SBDC nearest you, call your local SBA office.

Small Business Institute Program (SBI)

The SBI program gives small business owners an opportunity to receive intensive management counseling from qualified graduate and undergraduate business students working under expert faculty guidance. SBI counseling focuses on the full range of management problems and solutions, including market studies, accounting systems, personnel policies, production design, exporting, expansion feasibility, and strategic planning.

The SBI program was established in 1972 in cooperation with 36 colleges and universities. Today, more than 500 schools of business participate in the program. Annually, about 18,500 students provide help to approximately 6,000 businesses each year. To date, SBI teams have counseled more than 160,000 small businesses, and approximately 500,000 students have received "real world" experience.

To learn more about the SBI program, contact your nearest SBA office and ask for a business development officer.

Women's Business Ownership

Businesses owned by women provide more than 11 million jobs in the United States and employ more workers than the Fortune 500. Further, women make up more than half of America's population, and currently own one-third of its businesses. In response to these statistics, the SBA has initiated a special outreach effort and created counseling programs to help women become successful entrepreneurs. SBA programs designed specifically for women include the:

- Demonstration Training Program, which offers a number of training centers around the country that give financial management and technical assistance;
- Women's Network for Entrepreneurial Training, which teams seasoned entrepreneurs with less experienced women whose businesses are ready to grow; and
- Women's Pre-Qualification Loan Program, which allows the SBA to prequalify a loan guarantee for a woman business owner before she goes to a bank.

To find out how these programs can help your business, contact your local SBA office and ask for a women's business ownership representative, or call:

The Office of Women's Business Ownership
U.S. Small Business Administration
409 Third Street SW
Washington, DC 20416
(202) 205-6673
FAX (202) 205-7287

Veterans Affairs

The SBA works closely with veteran service organizations, military installations, and other federal and state agencies in developing and monitoring the delivery of business-related services to veterans. This program also includes the Defense Loan & Technical Assistance (DELTA) Program. The DELTA program provides financial and technical assistance to defense-dependent small businesses adversely impacted by defense reductions.

To learn more about the DELTA program, contact your nearest SBA office and ask for a veteran's affairs officer, or call:

Office of Veteran's Affairs
409 Third Street SW
Washington, DC 20416
(202) 205-6773
FAX (202) 205-7292

Management and Technical Assistance 7(j) Program

The 7(j) program provides management and technical aid to specific clients. As part of this program, the SBA will help with bookkeeping and accounting services, production, engineering, technical advice, feasibility studies, marketing analysis, advertising expertise, business plans, loan packaging, and limited legal services. Many of these services are free. To be eligible, you must be either a:

- Section 8(a) certified business;
- Socially and economically disadvantaged individual;
- Business operating in areas of low income or high unemployment; or
- A firm owned by low-income individuals.

Call your nearest SBA office and ask for *SBA Form 641, Request for Counseling*. (See Chapter 1 for a sample of *Form 641*.)

Export Assistance Centers (EACs)

The Export Assistance Center (EAC) Program can help you open doors to worldwide opportunities in exporting. Through its Export Assistance Centers, a full range of services are available to you, including:

- International marketing — EAC trade professionals will help you pinpoint your best prospects, develop an effective export strategy, and promote your product; and

- Trade finance programs — EACs offer numerous programs to meet your trade finance needs. Finance specialists help you determine which programs are best for you.

For more information, refer to Appendix B, or you can contact:

The Trade Information Center
U.S. Department of Commerce
HCHB, Room 7424
Washington, DC 20230
(800) 872-8723
FAX (202) 482-4473

Statewide Programs

While information from federal sources may be valuable, some small business owners need assistance from state-run entities. To learn about state assistance programs for your small business, contact one or more of the following agencies within your state:

- Governor's Office;
- Department of Commerce;
- Chamber of Commerce; or
- Tax Agency.

The SBA's Office of Advocacy publishes a book called *The States and Small Business: A Directory of Programs and Activities,* which gives more details on many of the state programs and services. To obtain a copy of this helpful book, contact:

Government Printing Office
(202) 512-1800

Another excellent source of state-specific information related to your small business is the much-praised *Starting and Operating a Business* series. Packed with the most current business issues, each state book offers a wealth of knowledge to both the current business owner as well as the burgeoning entrepreneur. To learn more about the series that *Inc.* magazine chose as top business books, contact:

The Oasis Press
(800) 228-2275

Surety Bond Guarantee Program (SBG)

The U.S. Small Business Administration can guarantee bonds for contracts of up to $1.25 million through its Surety Bond Guarantee (SBG) Program. Any contractor required to have a bid, performance, or payment bond to obtain a contract, including but not limited to construction, repair, maintenance, service, supply, and janitorial businesses, can benefit from the SBG program.

Businesses are eligible if they satisfy the SBA's size standards according to Part 121.3-10 of the SBA's *Published Rules and Regulations,* except for businesses in the construction and service industries and their affiliates, whose average annual receipts for the last three fiscal years do not exceed $5 million. There is no limit on the number of bonds that can be guaranteed for any one contractor.

Any contract bond (bid or performance, or both, or performance plus payment), is eligible if:

- There is a provision in the contract section of the rate manual of the Surety Association of America;
- A bond is required by the contract documents; and
- The bond is executed either by a surety company acceptable to the U.S. Treasury Department (Circular 570), or a surety company otherwise qualified by the SBA to participate in the SBG program.

If your business is eligible and you wish to apply for a bond under the SBG program, carefully follow the six key steps listed below.

Step 1: Contact a surety, or its representative, that participates in the SBG program. The nearest SBA office may refer you to these sureties.

Step 2: Complete the following documents and return them to the surety:

- *SBA Form 912, Statement of Personal History;*
- *SBA Form 1261, Statements Required by Laws and Executive Orders;*
- *SBA Form 994, Application for Surety Bond Guarantee Assistance;*
- *SBA Form 994F, Schedule of Uncompleted Work;* and
- Documents relating to credit information and business history that are standard to the surety industry.

Step 3: If the application is for final bonds (performance or payment, or both) include any applicable contractor fee. The check is payable to the SBA.

Step 4: Upon completion of favorable underwriting, the surety will forward all required documents, including *SBA Form 990, Guarantee Agreement* and *SBA Form 991, Surety Bond Guarantee Agreement Addendum,* to the appropriate SBA office.

Step 5: The SBG staff will review the application, make final determination, and notify the surety of its decision. The SBA returns the countersigned guarantee agreement to the surety. If the SBA declines to issue the guarantee, the check for the contractor fee is also returned to the surety.

Step 6: If any adverse information develops subsequent to the SBA's approval of the guarantee, the surety may decline to issue bonds.

The surety company processes and underwrites the application and data received from the agent in the same manner as any other contract bond application.

The surety company can decide to:

- Execute the bond without the SBA's guarantee;
- Execute the bond only with the SBA's guarantee; or
- Decline the bond even with the SBA's guarantee.

However, if the surety company decides to execute the bond on the basis of the SBA's guarantee, it prepares a Surety Bond Guarantee Underwriting Review and the Surety Bond Guarantee Agreement. The surety company then forwards these documents, with supporting data (including the contractor's fee), to the appropriate SBA office to request the SBA's guarantee.

The SBA, upon receipt of the surety company's submission, applies its own underwriting criteria. If the decision is favorable, the SBA will complete, execute, and return the guarantee agreements to the surety company; otherwise, the SBA will indicate its disapproval and return the submission to the surety company.

The cost of an SBA guarantee is paid by the contractor and the surety company. Before executing the bond, the contractor must pay the SBA a fee of 0.6% ($6.00 per $1,000.00) of the contract amount. The contractor must also pay the surety company a maximum premium charge for the bond. This varies by state. When the bond is executed, the surety company must pay the SBA 20% of its premium charge on the bond.

In consideration of the surety company paying the SBA 20% of the gross bond premium, the SBA guarantees the surety company up to 90% of any loss sustained on contracts, subject to a $500 maximum deductible to the surety company, regardless of the contract amount.

The SBA can render a variety of services to a qualifying contractor, including counseling the contractor in compiling the necessary data required by the surety company and giving certain financial management and technical assistance, either sought by the contractor or recommended by the surety.

For more information on application procedures, duties of the SBA and SBG, and cost, contact:

Office of Surety Guarantees
(202) 205-6540
FAX (202) 205-7600

Procurement Assistance Programs

The U.S. Government is the world's largest buyer of goods and services. Purchases by military and civilian installations amount to about $189 billion a year, ranging from complex space vehicles to paper clips, janitorial services to cancer research. In short, the government buys just about every category of commodities and services available.

The SBA has the responsibility of making certain that U.S. small businesses obtain a fair share of government contracts and subcontracts. This mission is spelled out in the Small Business Act of 1953. The SBA works closely with federal agencies and the nation's leading contractors. It carries out its procurement assistance responsibilities through a number of programs and makes thousands of contracts worth billions of dollars available to small businesses.

How You Can Bid on a Government Contract

Military and civilian purchasing activities, installations, or offices scattered throughout the country buy through two methods: sealed bidding and negotiation.

When soliciting for bids, a purchasing office normally sends bid invitations to firms listed on its solicitation mailing lists — or, if a given list is unduly long, the purchasing office may solicit segments of the total list. The solicitation mailing list is composed of small businesses that have advised the purchasing office that they want to make an offer on particular solicitations and have supplied data showing their ability to fulfill contracts for particular items, services, or projects.

In some cases, the purchasing installation or office will want offers from additional businesses not listed on its solicitation mailing list. These businesses are usually located through public advertisements in the *Commerce Business Daily* (*CBD*), trade papers, notices in post offices, and by SBA representatives.

Invitations for Bids (IFBs) usually include a copy of the specifications for the particular proposed purchase; instructions for preparation of bids; and the conditions of purchase, delivery, and payment. The IFB also designates the date and time of bid opening. Each sealed bid is opened in public at the purchasing office at the time designated in the invitation. Facts about each bid are read aloud and recorded. A contract is then awarded to the low bidder whose bid conforms with all requirements of the invitation and whose bid will be advantageous to the government in terms of price and price-related factors included in the invitation.

When buying by negotiation, the government uses procedures that differ from sealed bidding. Buying by negotiation is authorized in certain circumstances by law under applicable Federal Acquisition Regulations (FAR). Often, negotiated contracts cover advanced technology not widely supplied by small businesses and may include very complex areas of research and development, projects connected with highly sophisticated systems, missile programs, aircraft, and weapons systems. However, negotiation procedures also may be applied to more or less standard items when negotiation authority has been properly documented by the contracting office. For example, items or services may be purchased by negotiation when it is impossible to draft adequate specifications or to describe fully the specific item, service, or project.

When purchasing by negotiation, the purchasing office also makes use of its solicitation mailing list for the particular item or service. It may also ask for detailed statements of estimated costs or other evidence of reasonable price. These Requests for Proposals (RFPs) are sent to a number of offerors so that the purchase may be made on a competitive basis.

Requests for Quotations (RFQs) may be used in negotiated procurements to communicate government requirements to prospective contractors. A quotation received in response to an RFQ is not an offer and cannot be accepted by the government to create a binding contract. An RFQ may be used when the government does not intend to award a contract on the basis of the solicitation, but wishes to obtain price, terms of delivery, or other information for planning purposes.

After reviewing the various quotations received on the proposed purchase, a contracting officer may negotiate further with the businesses that have submitted acceptable proposals to assure the contract most advantageous to the government.

The SBA's procurement assistance effort is greatly strengthened by the Certificate of Competency (COC) Program. The SBA is authorized by Congress to certify the "capability, competency, credit, integrity, perseverance and tenacity" of a small business to perform a specific government contract. If a contracting officer proposes to reject the offer of a small business that is a low offerer because that officer questions the business' ability to perform the contract on any of the previously mentioned grounds, the case is referred to the SBA.

Certificate of Competency Program (COC)

SBA personnel then contact the company concerned to inform it of the impending decision and to offer an opportunity to apply to the SBA for a Certificate of Competency, which, if granted, would require awarding the contract to the firm in accordance with the Small Business Act. The SBA may also, at its discretion, issue a Certificate of Competency in connection with the sale of federal property if the responsibility (that is, the capability, competency, credit, integrity, perseverance, and tenacity) of the purchaser is questioned. It may also issue a Certificate of Competency for firms found ineligible by a contracting officer due to a provision of the Walsh-Healey Public Contracts Act that requires a government contractor be either a manufacturer or a regular dealer.

The COC program is carried out by a specialized SBA field staff of individuals with technical, engineering, and government procurement backgrounds in cooperation with financial specialists who are also of the SBA field staff. On receipt of a COC application, the contracting officer of the purchasing agency is notified that the prospective contractor has applied, and a team of financial and technical personnel is sent to the business to survey its potential. The SBA has access to the purchasing agency's pre-award survey, which served as the basis of the contracting officer's decision. Nonetheless, the SBA conducts a completely new survey, which evaluates the characteristics of the applicant in terms of the needs of the specific acquisition in question. Credit ratings, past performance, management capabilities, management schedules, and the prospects for obtaining needed financial help or equipment are considered.

The team's findings are presented to a COC review committee composed of legal, technical, and financial representatives, which makes a detailed review of the case and recommends approval or disapproval. If the decision is negative, the business and the purchasing agency are so informed; if affirmative, a letter certifying the responsibility of the business to perform the contract (a Certificate of Competency) is sent to the purchasing agency. By terms of the Small Business Act, the COC is conclusive on questions of responsibility, and the contract must be awarded.

A COC is valid only for the specific contract for which it is issued. A business concern that is capable of handling one contract may not be qualified to handle another. Each case is considered separately, and each case is considered only if and after the contracting officer has made a negative determination of responsibility or eligibility. Businesses may not apply for a COC until a contracting officer makes a non-responsibility determination and refers the matter to the SBA.

Procurement Automated Source System (PASS)

The SBA has developed the Procurement Automated Source System (PASS), a national database that lists the names of small businesses and their capabilities, so that federal procurement officers and private prime contractors can readily identify small firms as potential contractors and subcontractors. Many federal agencies and some of the nation's largest prime contractors access the system.

To list your small business in the PASS, you must complete *SBA Form 1167*. (A sample of this form is located at the end of this chapter.) For more information on the PASS, or to request a PASS application, contact your nearest SBA office.

Prime Contracts

The SBA works closely with federal agencies to increase the dollars and percentages of total federal procurement awards to small businesses by identifying items that small businesses supply. The SBA monitors prime contractors to ensure that small businesses receive a fair share of subcontracting opportunities.

If you think this program can help your business, contact your nearest SBA office.

National Resources Sales Assistance

The National Resources Sales Assistance Program helps small businesses obtain a fair share of government property sales and leases. As necessary, the program involves small business set-asides, and provides aid, counsel and other available assistance. The program includes timber, royalty oil, minerals, and surplus real and personal property.

For more information, contact:

Office of Procurement Assistance
U.S. Small Business Administration
409 Third Street SW
Washington, DC 20416
(202) 205-6465
FAX (202) 205-7324

The SBA provides two helpful publications for businesses looking for bid opportunities.

Helpful Publications

For $24, you can get the *U.S. Government Purchasing and Sales Directory*. The directory lists all federal agencies that purchase an item, and how to contact the appropriate purchasing office. If you do not immediately find your product or service, try looking under a broader classification. The directory is also a good source of general information about selling to the government, and provides names of government offices that also offer procurement assistance.

Printed each business day, the *Commerce Business Daily* (*CBD*) lists all major Invitations for Bids and Requests for Proposals. Government agencies are required, by law, to summarize in the *CBD* — 15 days before issuing a solicitation — any proposed contract actions expected to exceed $25,000. *CBD* is a good place to find both contract and subcontracting opportunities. Subscriptions are available for $275 per year. If you don't want to subscribe, you can find copies of *CBD* in libraries and government agencies. *America Online* carries *CBD* in its business section also.

To learn more about these publications, or to place an order, contact:

U.S. Government Printing Office
P.O. Box 371954
Pittsburgh, PA 15250
(202) 512-1800

SBA Form 1167, PASS Application

Increase your business opportunities!
List your company in SBA's Automated Directory of Small Businesses...PASS

Complete and Return this Form To:
U.S. Small Business Administration
P.O. Box 9000
Melbourne, FL 32902-9919

SBA PASS

Instructions: Complete all items on this form as accurately as possible. Key items are defined on the reverse side of the form. The form must be signed by a principal of the company as distinguished from an agent, however constituted. The completed form will constitute official self certification as to size, minority, and/or woman owned status. See certification statement at signature block. Write N/A in boxes if not applicable.

What Happens: We will notify you as soon as your company is listed in the procurement Automated Source System (PASS). Your company's capabilities are then available to many Government agencies and major corporations when they request potential bidders for contracts and subcontracts. Remember – although PASS increases your exposure, it does NOT guarantee solicitations or contracts. PASS should be just one element of your regular marketing efforts.

PASS is Free! You have nothing to lose and possibly new contracts to gain. Don't delay... Return this application today!

The following company profile is ☐ a new listing or ☐ an updated listing.

PROCUREMENT AUTOMATED SOURCE SYSTEM (PASS) – COMPANY PROFILE

Identification Section

Company Name _____
Mailing Address _____
City _____ State _____ ZIP _____
Phone Number ( ) - FAX Number ( ) -
Contact _____ Title _____

Employer Id Number _____
(EIN, Tax Id, or SS#)
DUNS Number _____
(DUN & Bradstreet)
Year Business Established _____
Average Gross Revenues _____
(Last Three Years)
Average Number of Employees _____
(Last Twelve Months)

Organizational Data

Type of Organization - ☐ Corporation ☐ S. Corporation ☐ Sole Proprietorship ☐ Partnership

Parent Company Name _____
Average Gross Revenue (Last Three Years) _____
Average No. Employees (Last Twelve Months) _____

Affiliate Name _____
Average Gross Revenue (Last Three Years) _____
Average No. Employees (Last Twelve Months) _____

Affiliate Name _____
Average Gross Revenue (Last Three Years) _____
Average No. Employees (Last Twelve Months) _____

Affiliate Name _____
Average Gross Revenue (Last Three Years) _____
Average No. Employees (Last Twelve Months) _____

Ownership Data

Check boxes appropriately if company is at least 51% owned, controlled and actively managed by any of the following. (Note: Minority Person includes Black, Hispanic, Native American, Asian Indian, or Asian Pacific.)

☐ U.S. Citizen ☐ Minority Person ☐ Woman/Women ☐ Veteran ☐ Disabled Veteran ☐ Vietnam Vet. (1964-1975)

If you checked Minority Person, check one of the following:

☐ Black American ☐ Hispanic American ☐ Native American ☐ Subcontinent Asian American ☐ Asian Pacific American

Native American includes American Indian, Eskimo, Aleut, and Hawaiian – Subcontinent Asian American includes India, Pakistan, Bangladesh, etc.* – Asian Pacific American includes Orientals, Pacific Islands, Philippines, etc.*   *For complete list, refer to 13 CFR 124.105b

Business Types

PASS is divided into 4 types of business. Please estimate the percentage of your business allocated to the following (total must equal 100) and complete the appropriate Section(s).

Manufacturing/Supplies _____%

Check Applicable Box(es)
☐ Manufacturer ☐ Dealer ☐ Wholesale Distributor
Manufacturing Facility Size _____ SQ. FT.

Research and Development _____%

Number of Engineers and Scientists _____
Expertise of Key Personnel (Limit 150 Characters) _____
_____
_____

Construction _____%

Current Aggregate Bonding Level $ _____
Current Bonding Level Per Contract $ _____
Maximum Operating Radius _____ (miles)
-Anywhere in the U.S., enter 3999 above.
-Anywhere in the World, enter 9999 above.

Services _____%

Current Aggregate Bonding Level $ _____
Current Bonding Level Per Contract $ _____
Maximum Operating Radius _____ (miles)
-Anywhere in the U.S., enter 3999 above.
-Anywhere in the World, enter 9999 above

SBA Form 1167, PASS Application (continued)

Capabilities Section (Limit 350 characters; be concise and avoid abbreviations and generalities)

List products, services, special capabilities, and important categories under which you want your business listed. The system searches businesses based on the capabilities you list in this section.

___

Standard Industrial Classification (SIC) Code(s)

If unknown, leave blank. Appropriate codes will be assigned.

Special Equipment/Materials (limit 50 characters)

List ___

CAGE Code	Manufacturing Quality Assurance	Miscellaneous		
	☐ MIL-I-45208 ☐ MIL-Q-9858 ☐ Other ___	Metric Capability Accept VISA Credit Card	☐ Yes ☐ Yes	☐ No ☐ No

Security Clearance

	Top Secret	Secret	Confidential	Other
Key Personnel	☐	☐	☐	☐
Site	☐	☐	☐	☐

If other provided description ___

Export Activity

☐ Active Experienced Export
☐ Interested And/Or New to Exporting
☐ Not Interested

If you checked Active or Interested, please check one or more of the following geographic areas.

☐ Western Europe ☐ Middle East
☐ Eastern Europe/NIS ☐ Asian Pacific
☐ The Americas ☐ Africa

Performance History (Contract References)

Contract Start Date ___ Contract Start Date ___
Dollar Value ___ Dollar Value ___
Product/Service Desc. ___ Product/Service Desc. ___

Contact Name ___ Contact Name ___
Contact Phone No. ___ Contact Phone No. ___

Contract Start Date ___ Contract Start Date ___
Dollar Value ___ Dollar Value ___
Product/Service Desc. ___ Product/Service Desc. ___

Contact Name ___ Contact Name ___
Contact Phone No. ___ Contact Phone No. ___

Definitions

SIZE OF BUSINESS – A small business concern for the purpose of Government procurement is a concern, including its affiliates, which is independently owned and operated, is not dominant in the field of operation in which it is competing for government contracts and can further qualify under the criteria concerning number of employees, average annual receipts, and other criteria as prescribed by the U.S. Small Business Administration. (See Code of Federal Regulations, Title 13, Part 121, as appended, which contains detailed industry definitions and related procedures.)

MINORITY/WOMEN/VETERAN OWNED STATUS – Qualifying firms must be at least 51% owned, controlled, and actively managed by such individuals.

CAGE Code (Commercial and Government Entity Code) This is a code assigned to contractors providing goods and services to the Federal Government. For information about CAGE codes, call (616) 961-4955.

DISASTER RESPONSE – Firm's capacity for disaster response (if any) should be included in the capability statement. Required information includes 24 hour-a-day contact and the ability to ship manufactured goods within 24 hours of receiving order.

QUALITY ASSURANCE – Information applies to manufacturing processes for the Department of Defense.

CERTIFICATION – I certify 1) that this is a small business as defined in the DEFINITION section; 2) that the characteristics of the firms ownership are accurately reflected in the OWNERSHIP section; 3) that all information supplied herein (including all attachments) is correct; and 4) that neither the applicant nor any person (or concern) in any connection with the applicants principal or officer, so far as known, is now debarred or otherwise declared ineligible by any agency of the Federal Government from making offers for furnishing materials, supplies, or services to the Government or any agency thereof.

INFORMATION IN THIS PROFILE MAY BE DISCLOSED AT THE DISCRETION OF THE U.S. SMALL BUSINESS ADMINISTRATION

Signature of Company Officer ___ Title ___ Date ___

Please Note: The estimated burden hours for the completion of this form is 15 minutes per response. If you have any questions or comments concerning this estimate or any other aspect of this information collection please contact, Chief Administrative Information Branch, U.S. Small Business Administration, 409 3rd St., SW, Washington, D.C. 20416, or Gary Waxman, Clearance Officer, Paperwork Reduction Project (3245-0024), Office of Management and Budget, Washington, D.C. 20503

SBA Form 1167 (3/93)
OMB Approved: 3245-0024 Exp: (3/31/96)
*U.S. GPO: 1993-358-240/89139

Notes

Chapter 3

Applying for a Small Business Loan

*If at first you do succeed —
try to hide your astonishment.*

— *Los Angeles Times* Syndicate

General Eligibility Requirements for SBA Loans

The SBA evaluates each application on two levels — eligibility and credit merit. For your business to be eligible for an SBA loan, the size and type of business, use of proceeds, and availability of funds from other sources must meet certain SBA guidelines.

With respect to size, the SBA defines a small business as one that is independently owned and operated. The business cannot be dominant in its field and must meet sales or employment standards developed by the SBA based on the business' standard industrial classification or size standards. Fortunately, more than 97% of all non-agricultural businesses in America are classified as small, so the chance that your business will not qualify is remote.

Further, the SBA has established criteria for different types of business to determine whether a concern qualifies as a small business. Some basic criteria for different business types are listed below.

- Wholesale businesses must not have more than 100 employees.//
- Retail or service businesses must have average three-year annual sales or receipts of not more than $3.5 to 13.5 million, depending on business type.
- Manufacturing businesses must not have more than 500 employees. This number can go up to 1,500 employees depending on business type.
- Construction businesses must have annual sales or receipts of not more than $7.0 million.

If your business does not meet these size standards, contact your nearest SBA office for a specific ruling. Numerous exceptions to the size policy exist. For example, the range of size standards for the manufacturing industries is from zero employees up to 1,500 employees depending on the type of manufacturing in question. Within the manufacturing area, there are 459 separate industries. Of these, 350 have a size standard of only 500 employees. Three industries, petroleum refining, ammunition (with the exception of small arms), and railroads (line-haul operating), have a 1,500 employee size standard. The remaining 106 industries have either a size standard of 750 or 1,000 employees. In addition, for the SBA's financial programs only, the size standards can be increased by 25% if your business is located in a labor surplus area — a term the government uses for a high unemployment area.

The Credit Decision

When a bank and the SBA consider a loan request, they explore a number of major areas: your financial statement, your business plan, and you. In making the credit decision, your lender also needs to get to know you, because you play such an important role in the performance of your business. A resumé and a personal financial statement should be completed for each owner of your business.

Your banker will use this information to formulate a complete picture of your business. Based on the information you provide, a lender will make a credit decision. It is important to remember that every lender evaluates a loan package differently. The way it is evaluated depends greatly upon the current situation within the lending institution and its current lending policies. If a lender is comfortable with your business and decides to grant a loan, terms and conditions of the loan will be negotiated. If your request has merit, but your company is undercapitalized (as many new businesses are), the lender may enlist the assistance of one of the many government programs available to assist small businesses.

If for some reason your request is declined, don't be discouraged. Ask questions that will help your future financing efforts, such as:

- Where is my company or business plan lacking?
- Are there any specific problems I should address?
- What can I improve upon?

Be persistent, and learn from the experience.

Other SBA Eligibility Requirements

The SBA cannot lend money if a business can borrow money on reasonable terms:

- From a financial institution;
- By selling assets that it does not need in order to grow;

- From the personal credit or resources of the owners, partners, or principal stockholders without causing undue personal hardship;
- By selling a portion of ownership in the company through a public offering or a private placing of securities;
- From other government agencies that provide credit specifically for the applicant's type of business, or for the purpose of the required financing; or
- From other known sources of credit.

Further, the SBA cannot fund a loan if the direct or indirect purpose or result of granting a loan would be to:

- Pay off a creditor or creditors of the applicant who are inadequately secured and in a position to sustain a loss.
- Provide funds for distribution or payment to the owner, partners, or shareholders.
- Replenish working capital funds previously used to pay the owner, partners, or shareholders.
- Cause a change in the ownership of the business. Under certain circumstances, loans may be authorized for this purpose if the result would be to aid in the sound development of a small business or keep it in operation. (See the discussion on change of ownership later in this chapter.)
- Provide or free funds for speculation in any kind of property, real or personal, tangible or intangible, or to finance the construction, acquisition, conversion, or operation of recreational or amusement facilities, unless the facilities contribute to the health or general well-being of the public.

In addition, an applicant is ineligible if the business is a charitable organization, social agency, society, or other nonprofit enterprise. However, the SBA may consider a loan for a cooperative if it carries on a business activity, and the purpose of the activity is to obtain financial benefit for its members in the operation of its otherwise eligible small business concerns.

Ineligible Businesses

Several types of business are ineligible for an SBA guaranteed loan. Review the following discussions to make sure your business doesn't fall into one of the ineligible categories.

Real Estate Investment Firms. These are firms that hold real property for investment purposes, as opposed to otherwise eligible small business concerns, for the purpose of occupying the real estate being acquired.

Other Speculative Activities. Firms that develop profits from fluctuations in price rather than through the normal course of trade — such as wildcatting for oil and dealing in commodities futures — fall into this category when such activities are not part of the regular activities of the business. Also, dealers of rare coins and stamps are not eligible.

Academic Schools. Schools that teach academic subjects are ineligible for SBA loans. The restriction does not cover technical, secretarial, vocational or trade schools, or nursery and pre-kindergarten schools.

Lending Activities. Such businesses include banks, finance companies, factors, leasing companies, insurance companies (not agents), and any other firm whose stock-in-trade is money.

Pyramid Sales Plans. Pyramid sales plans are characterized by endless chains of distributors and subdistributors where a participant's primary incentive is based on the sales made by an ever-increasing number of participants. Such products as cosmetics, household goods, and other soft goods lend themselves to this type of business.

Illegal Activities. For SBA loan purposes, illegal activities are, by definition, those that are against the law within the jurisdiction of the business location. Those activities include the production, servicing, or distribution of otherwise legal products for use in connection with an illegal activity, such as the selling of drug paraphernalia or operating a motel that permits illegal prostitution. Prudent discretion will be exercised in determining whether taxpayer funds should be used to finance questionable enterprises.

Gambling Activities. Gambling activities include any business whose principal activity is gambling. While this precludes loans to race tracks, casinos, and similar enterprises, the rule does not restrict loans to otherwise eligible businesses that obtain less than one-third of their annual gross income from either:

- The sale of official state lottery tickets under a state license; or
- Legal gambling activities licensed and supervised by a state authority.

The one-third limitation applies both as a point of eligibility and as a condition to be met during the term of the loan.

Conditional Eligibility

Certain types of businesses are eligible under specific conditions. Review the following discussions to ensure your business meets these conditions for eligibility, if necessary.

Franchises. Franchises are eligible, except in situations where a franchisor retains power to control operations to such an extent as to be tantamount to an employment contract. The franchisee must have the right to profit from efforts that are commensurate with ownership. A copy of the franchisor's FTC-required disclosure statement must be submitted with the loan application, and consideration should be given to require the franchisor to guarantee the loan or standby on royalty payments, or both, when the SBA guaranteed loan becomes delinquent. Those requirements would generally prevail when the franchisor is not well-known or when credit factors warrant.

Recreational Facilities and Clubs. Recreational facilities and clubs are eligible if:

- Facilities are open to the general public; and
- In "membership only" situations, membership is not selectively denied any particular group of individuals, and the number of memberships is not restricted either as a whole or by establishing maximum limits for particular groups.

Change of Ownership Loans. Loans for this purpose are eligible provided the business benefits from the change. In most cases, this benefit should be seen as promoting the sound development of the business or, perhaps, in preserving its existence. Loans may not be made when proceeds would enable a borrower to purchase either part of a business in which it has no present interest, or part of an interest of a present and continuing owner. Loans to cause a change of ownership among members of the same family are discouraged under SBA programs, both because it can be difficult to ensure an arm's length transaction, and because this type of transaction should generally be easily financed within the family. There are exceptions to this rule. For more details, refer to the discussion later in this chapter on SBA special situations.

Farms and Agricultural Businesses. Farms and agricultural businesses are eligible. However, these applicants should first be referred to the Consolidated Farm Service Agency, particularly if the applicant has a prior or existing relationship with the USDA. For more information, contact:

Consolidated Farm Service Agency
(202) 720-1632

Fishing Vessels. Fishing vessels are eligible. However, those seeking loans for construction or reconditioning of vessels with a cargo capacity of five tons or more must first request financing from the National Marine Fisheries Service (NMFS), a part of the U.S. Department of Commerce. Loans for another purpose may be considered without the applicant having first applied to NMFS.

Medical Facilities. Hospitals, clinics, emergency outpatient facilities, and medical and dental laboratories are eligible. Convalescent and nursing homes are eligible, provided they are licensed by the appropriate government agency, and their services go beyond those of room and board.

Aliens. Aliens are eligible. However, an alien's residency status should be considered in determining the degree of risk relating to the continuity of an applicant's business. Excessive risk may be offset by the ability to fully collateralize the loan. Check with your local SBA office regarding the various types of visas.

Probation or Parole. Applications will not be accepted from businesses where a principal has indicated on a *Statement of Personal History, Form 912,* that he or she:

- Is currently incarcerated, on parole, or on probation.
- Is a defendant in a criminal proceeding.
- Has had the probation or parole lifted expressly because it prohibits an SBA loan. This restriction would not necessarily preclude a loan to a business where a principal had responded in the affirmative to any of the questions on the *SBA Statement of Personal History*. These judgments are made on a case-by-case evaluation of the nature, frequency, and timing of the offenses.

Fingerprint cards (available from your local SBA office) are required anytime a question on the form is answered in the affirmative.

SBA Loan Amount and Terms

The maximum dollar amount the SBA can guarantee is $750,000. Under its 7(a) program, the SBA can guarantee up to 75% of the amount for loans that exceed $100,000. Loans for less than $100,000 are eligible for an 80% guarantee. SBA direct loans are limited to $150,000.

In the 1995 fiscal year, the SBA has only one type of direct loan program — the Handicapped Assistance Loan (HAL) program. For more information on the HAL program, refer to Chapter 4.

The maximum SBA loan maturity is 25 years. However, the SBA expects all loans to be repaid as soon as possible. Therefore, maturity is based on the cash flow and ability of your business to repay without hardship. Generally, the maturity will vary with the purpose of the loan and can be up to:

- Seven years for working capital;
- Ten years for machinery and equipment; and
- Twenty-five years for purchase or construction of plant facilities.

Repayment is usually on a monthly installment basis requiring principal and interest, although variations may be negotiated to meet the start-up phase, seasonal cycles, or other unique business amortization needs.

Interest rates on conventional bank loans will vary with the lending institution. However, they will be in excess of the prime rate, and may range from three to five points over that rate. In addition, the term of the loan may be less than five years. Interest rates on SBA guaranteed loans are negotiated between the applicant and lender based on the terms and credit merits of the application. The SBA establishes the maximum rate lenders may charge depending on the maturity period, and banks are permitted to allow fluctuation of the rate when the prime rate changes.

The maximum initial rates for SBA loans are:

- For loans with a maturity of less than seven years, the maximum rate is the prime rate as published in the money rate section of the *Wall Street Journal,* plus two-and-one-quarter percent (2.25%).
- For loans with a maturity of seven years or more, the maximum rate can be up to the prime rate as published in the money rate section of the *Wall Street Journal,* plus two-and-three-quarters percent (2.75%).

These are the maximum rates a lender can charge, but they may be negotiated at a lower rate. After all, the lender is getting a federal government guarantee on the loan. For example, on a $50,000 loan, the SBA guarantees to repay the lender up to 80% of the unpaid balance if the borrower defaults. The lender's liability is 20%, or $10,000, on a loan of this amount. This is one of the primary reasons lenders prefer to go through the SBA on business loans.

Interest rates on SBA direct loans are established each calendar quarter by the U.S. Treasury based on the federal government's cost of borrowing. All SBA direct loans are on a fixed amortization basis.

Collateral Considerations

While collateral is not the primary credit consideration, the SBA requires that all business assets be pledged to secure a loan. In addition, you may be required to personally guarantee the loan by securing specific assets or by requiring the corporate guarantees of affiliated or associated companies, or both.

Processing Time

The time involved for the SBA to process a loan is directly related to the quality of the application it receives. If the loan package you submit to the SBA by the bank is complete, the SBA will usually have a decision for your lender in two weeks. Direct loan applications generally take longer, but an answer should be available within four weeks.

Keep in mind, as previously discussed in Chapter 1, the most often cited reasons for delays of loan applications are missing or incomplete documentation and missing signatures and dates on each exhibit. Working closely with an SBDC can help eliminate this problem.

Closing Costs

You will be responsible for paying certain closing costs, including:

- Surveys;
- Title reports;
- Appraisals; and
- Photocopy, filing, and recording fees.

The SBA does not require you to use accountants or attorneys. However, depending on the type and size of the loan, you may want to consider getting professional advice.

Starting the Application Process

You are now ready to begin the application process. The process will focus on you completing several forms and including key documents. You will want to start by completing *Form 4, Application for Business Loan.* The SBA will not consider a loan without a completed *Form 4*.

Use the sample application form located at the end of this chapter. Carefully follow its instructions and the supplemental instructions that offer valuable insight for accurate form completion. Further, you are given two application case histories in Chapter 5. The two examples, one for a start-up business and one for an existing business, will assist you in preparing your package.

Include Important Exhibits

After you complete the first one-and-one-half pages of the application, you will be asked to include several key exhibits.

Following the management section of the application, you will find a list of exhibits, numbered 1–20. For the purpose of your SBA loan application package, an exhibit is any document submitted as part of your loan application package. This includes each exhibit listed in paragraphs 1–20, as well as each individual and business income tax return, and all financial statements. Personal exhibits, such as statements of personal history, personal financial statements, resumés, and individual income tax returns should be signed and dated by each respective individual. All application packages must include exhibits outlined in paragraphs 1–6.

If applicable to your business situation, you must provide the exhibits outlined in paragraphs 7–20. Carefully review these paragraphs to determine if they apply to you or your business. If any of these exhibits do not apply, indicate not applicable with an "n/a" next to the paragraph or answer "no" in paragraphs 9–11 and 18–20.

At least the first page of each exhibit submitted as part of your package must be signed and dated by the person signing *Form 4* for the business.

Personal History Statement

A *Statement of Personal History, SBA Form 912* is located at the end of this chapter for your use. Completely fill in all blanks, including your middle name. If you answer yes to any of questions 6–8, provide specific details in an attached statement. For example, you will need to specify the date of the offense, what you were charged with, and what sentence you received.

Collateral Schedule

You may use the *Schedule of Collateral, SBA Form 4 Schedule A,* or provide your own exhibit detailing the collateral you intend to offer. If real estate is to be offered, you must provide one of the following on the property:

- A current tax assessment;
- An appraiser's opinion of the value range; or
- A current appraisal.

Personal Financial Statement

You may use the *Personal Financial Statement, SBA Form 413* located at the end of this chapter to meet this requirement. If you prefer, you may provide your own statement as long as that statement contains the information outlined on *Form 413*. This exhibit should be as of the same date as the current business financial statement, but in no event can it be more than 90 days old. In addition, a copy of each individual's most recent *Form 1040, U.S. Individual Federal Income Tax Return* must accompany each *Personal Financial Statement*.

Financial Information

If yours is a start-up business, submit projections of your business' income and expenses with assumptions for:

- The first two years of operation; and
- The first twelve months after loan approval on a monthly cash flow basis. For your convenience, a monthly cash flow projection form is located at the end of this chapter.

If yours is an existing business, submit copies of individual income tax returns for the last three years from all stockholders owning 20% or more of the applicant business. Submit all statements requested in paragraph 4 of the application, and copies of federal income tax returns for the business for the last three years. Prepare a current financial statement (balance sheet) listing all assets and liabilities of your business. Do not include personal items. To assist you, use the Financial Statement Spread Sheet at the end of this chapter. Have an earnings (profit and loss) statement for the previous full year and for the current period to the date of the balance sheet. Financial and earnings statements should not be more than 90 days old when they reach the SBA.

History of the Business/Business Plan

Regardless of whether you have an existing or start-up business, you will need to write a business plan. (See the discussion on creating your business plan later in this chapter.) At a minimum, the plan should provide sufficient information detailing the nature and structure of the business so the feasibility of your proposal can be determined. New business start-up loans will not require IRS verification. However, existing businesses will require IRS verification. To save you valuable processing time, have your lender submit the proper IRS form when it sends in the application. Typically, the IRS takes ten business days to respond.

As an existing business, you need to provide a summary of your business' history since its inception, as well as an explanation of how the loan will benefit your business.

If you are purchasing an existing business, explain why the present owner is selling and why the change of ownership is necessary to preserve the existence of the business or to promote the sound growth and development of the business. Also, provide a copy of the proposed Buy/Sell Agreement and indicate the total financing sources. Once a loan guaranty is approved, the SBA field office will send a letter to your lender explaining

Resumé

All applicant businesses must provide a resumé, or a description of the educational, technical, and business background, for all proprietors, partners, officers, directors, or any persons with 20% or more stock ownership. Also submit resumés for all employees with any stock ownership, and any others you feel would be beneficial, such as managers or technical personnel. As a reminder, this exhibit should be signed and dated by each respective individual.

Declination Letters – Direct Loans Only

Your declination letter(s) — letters from banks that have already turned you down — must reflect an amount less than or equal to the SBA's request, or the bank must indicate that your request was considered at that level and was also turned down. Be sure that the letters contain all the information requested on *Form 4,* including a statement as to whether the bank is or is not willing to participate with the SBA. If your business is located in a city with more than 200,000 people, you will need to provide two bank declination letters.

Get All Appropriate Signatures

The last page of your application will ask for the applicant's certification. Each proprietor, general partner, limited partner, or stockholder owning 20% or more, as well as each guarantor, must sign *Form 4*. Each person should sign only once.

Make sure each person signs in the appropriate block. Proprietorships or partnerships sign in the first block. Corporations sign in the second block. Be sure each signature includes a date.

Guaranty Loan Applicants. Submit your completed loan application package to your lender, who will then forward it to the SBA.

Contract Loan Applicants. A *Monthly Cash Flow Projection, SBA Form 1100* or its equivalent is required for the loan contract period. You will need to use *SBA Form 74B* for a line of credit under the Contract Loan Program. If you do not have a copy of these forms, contact the nearest SBA office. For more information on the Contract Loan Program, see Chapter 4.

Direct Loan Applicants. The SBA may not provide direct financing if credit is available on reasonable terms elsewhere. The credit standards for direct loans are the same as those for guaranty loans. If you are applying for a direct loan, you should submit your completed application package to the nearest SBA office serving your area.

Disabled Veterans. If you are a disabled veteran, provide a copy of your *DD214* showing your disability discharge or a letter providing a disability percentage certification (current within 30 days) from the U.S. Department of Veterans Affairs.

Physically Disabled. If you are physically disabled, provide a letter from your physician or other credible source, such as the Veterans Administration, a Social Security Act Assistance Program, or State Rehabilitation Service Agency, describing your disability. The letter should specify whether your disability is permanent, and how your disability limits you from engaging in the proposed business activity on an even basis with non-disabled competitors. To be eligible for a direct loan, a business must be owned 100% by disabled individual(s) whose disability is of a permanent nature and limits the person(s) from engaging in the business activity on an even basis with non-disabled individuals.

To qualify, you must meet the "credit elsewhere" test, which means that you have tried but have been unsuccessful in obtaining a commercial loan from a lender, either directly or in participation with the SBA (the guaranteed loan). If the SBA accepts your application for a direct loan, understand that the credit standards are the same as for the agency's guaranty program.

Seeking Professional Assistance

Accountants, attorneys, loan packagers, or other professionals or representatives may assist you with your loan package, if you desire. However:

- The SBA does not require that you obtain such assistance.
- Any compensation or monies paid or to be paid to anyone for assisting you in applying for a loan must be reported to the SBA on *SBA Form 159*. (A sample of this form is located at the end of this chapter.)
- Fees paid for this assistance must be fair and reasonable. Loan brokerage fees are not allowed. Fees must be for services actually performed. Neither the SBA, nor its employees, receive any portion of such fees.

Further, you are not required to purchase other services from persons who provide you with assistance in obtaining a loan.

Writing Your Business Plan

A business plan can benefit both you and your business in many ways. A business plan:

- Makes it easier for your lender to gain realistic insight into your business.
- Can be used as a communications tool when you need to familiarize sales personnel, suppliers, and others about your operations and goals.
- Can help you develop as a manager. For example, it gives you practice in thinking about competitive conditions and promotional opportunities. It will give you an insight into your business operations and help to increase your ability to make sound business decisions.

Guidelines for a Successful Business Plan

A universal format for a business plan doesn't exist. However, you can follow certain guidelines to ensure a professional and presentable plan. Select your words carefully. Write your plan in a clear and concise manner. Make sure it is typed with double spacing to make it easier on the reader's eyes.

Ask someone who knows you and your business to provide an objective opinion. Also, review your plan with your local SBDC first. Remember, your business plan is a door opener. You want it to lead to a positive interview with a loan officer. Use the outline at the end of this chapter to create your business plan.

Remember, this business plan outline is a guideline; circumstances may vary. It can be used either for a start-up business or one that is already in operation. Tailor your plan's outline to fit your situation and stress both your strengths and your business' strengths. Regardless of the style used, your business plan is basically a written portrayal of where your business is going, how it intends to get there, and what the enterprise will look like when it arrives.

For a comprehensive resource on how to prepare a winning business plan, you may be interested in *The Successful Business Plan* by Rhonda M. Abrams. For more information on this best-selling book, contact:

The Oasis Press
(800) 228-2275

Once you are satisfied that your business plan and loan application are finished, it will be time to set up an appointment with your lender.

SBA Special Situations

Some SBA loan applications will require additional details before they can be approved. Some examples include:

- Change of ownership;
- A close buyer/seller relationship; and
- Business relocations.

Change of Ownership

If your purpose in applying for financial assistance is to cause a change of ownership in a business, you will need to cover some important additional points in your business plan. You need to point out that the change of ownership will:

- Promote the sound development or preserve the existence of the small business; or
- Contribute to a well-balanced national economy by facilitating ownership of small business concerns by persons whose participation in the free enterprise system has been prevented or hampered because of economic, physical, or social disadvantage, or because of disadvantages in the business or residential locations.

Further, in your application you will need to include:

- The reason the owner is selling the business;
- A copy of the proposed Buy/Sell Agreement;
- Income tax returns for the past three years for the seller;
- Independent appraisal(s) of assets changing hands, if value cannot be readily determined from the other submitted material; and
- A balance sheet dated within 90 days for the business being sold. If the tax returns are more than 90 days old, a current operating statement for the seller, dated within 90 days of application submission, is required. Statements that are not older than 45 days may be more realistic. By the time your loan application works its way through the system, the statements may be 90 days old when they reach the SBA loan officer's desk.

A Close Buyer/Seller Relationship

If a close relationship between the buyer and seller exists, such as members of the same family, the SBA loan officer is required to scrutinize the application. In the absence of rare and extraordinary circumstances, such as the family member is in poor health, this loan will not be approved. You must be able to show a substantial reason for using SBA funds for the buy-out.

Business Relocations

Financing the relocation of your business is permitted only when it will accomplish a sound business purpose, but will not be approved if the move would:

- Cause serious unemployment in its present location.
- Nullify a labor union contract or a commitment to negotiate a collective bargaining agreement.
- Involve a substantial loss or expense to either party to an outstanding lease.

Where doubts exist regarding the legal effect of a business relocation, your attorney would be required to provide a statement of all obligations or commitments that would be affected by the move.

Business Plan Outline

I. Title Page

II. Table of Contents

III. Executive Summary — Write the summary last. Briefly describe your plan and what it contains. Explain your purpose for writing the plan and state the amount of the loan requested and the desired term.

IV. General Company Description — The description should tell the history and background of the business and list its management and achievements. You can include this in your executive summary, if you wish.

V. Products and Services — Go into detail here. Be sure to include names and addresses of your suppliers.

VI. Operations — If your operations are complicated, explain how you do what you do. If not, you can include this explanation in the general company description.

VII. Management and Organizational Structure — Is your business incorporated? Who are the principals? Give a brief biographical summary. Depending on the type and size of your business, include an organizational chart.

VIII. Marketing Plan — What is the market for your product or service? First, describe the broad market. Trade publications have good quotations you can use such as, "Americans spend $10 million per year on . . . ." Then, narrow the description to the area you serve, whether it is geographic, income level, or targeted age group. If you have more than one market, discuss each one separately.

IX. Competitive Analysis — List your competitors and describe their strengths and weaknesses.

X. Marketing Strategy — Here you need to explain your past, present, and future marketing plans. Give examples of your advertising, promotions, and public relations. Explain the media you will use and how often. Discuss your location and signage. Describe your pricing strategy and how you arrived at those figures.

XI. Financial Plan — Give a statement of the amount requested and the time requirements for those funds. Describe the benefits you expect your business to gain from the financing, such as improvement in financial position, expense reduction, or increase in efficiency.

XII. Appendices — Here you can include resumés, examples of past advertising (if appropriate), and articles from trade journals. You can also include pictures of products and professional references.

Supplemental Instructions for *SBA Form 4*

Do not leave any area of the application or the attached forms blank. If something does not apply to you or your business, indicate not applicable with an "n/a."

'Current' is defined by the SBA as not older than 90 days from receipt of your application package by the SBA. A good rule of thumb is to provide information that is not more than 45 days old. Therefore, if the application is processed slowly by your lender, it won't be outdated when it reaches the SBA.

Use the following supplemental instructions to complete the first page-and-a-half of *SBA Form 4, Application for Business Loan.* For more details on completing the bottom portion of page 2 through page 4 of *Form 4,* refer to the discussion titled Include Important Exhibits located on pages 40–42.

Individual and Full Address: List the principal contact of the business from whom additional information can be obtained.

Name of Applicant Business: List name of the existing or the proposed business.

Tax I.D. No. or SSN: For an existing business, list its Federal Tax I.D. Number. For a proposed business, list the principal contact's social security number.

Full Street Address, City, County, State, and Zip Code of Business: For an existing business, list its current address. For a proposed business, list the proposed business address. Be sure to include the zip code and the county/independent city in which your business is or will be located.

Type of Business: Be as specific as possible. (For example: retail/florist or wholesale/florist.)

Date Business Established: List the original date (month and year), the corporation, partnership, or proprietorship opened, or the proposed date of opening.

Number of Employees: For both blanks, list the number of paid full-time employees, including the owners.

Use of Proceeds: If applicable, list purchase of an existing building under **Land Acquisition.** For land and building construction or acquisition, provide one of the following: (a) a current tax assessment; (b) an appraiser's opinion of the value range; or (c) a current appraisal. A full, current appraisal will be required before loan closing. For proceeds listed under **Working Capital,** provide an explanation or justification in the **History of the Business.** Refer to Exhibit D in the case histories presented in Chapter 5. For proceeds listed under **All Other,** detail the proposed usage.

Business Indebtedness: If you have more than four obligations, attach a separate exhibit reflecting the additional debts.

Management: Fill in all information for each person listed. If something is not applicable, put "n/a" in the space. Be sure the ownership of the business listed adds up to 100%. Also, be sure to list all officers and directors regardless of stock ownership, even if they do not own stock.

SBA Form 4, Application for Business Loan: Sample

U.S. Small Business Administration
APPLICATION FOR BUSINESS LOAN

OMB Approval No. 3245-0016
Expiration Date: 6-30-94

Individual	Full Address		
Name of Applicant Business		Tax I.D. No. or SSN	
Full Street Address of Business		Tel. No. (inc. A/C)	
City	County	State	Zip	Number of Employees (Including subsidiaries and affiliates)
Type of Business		Date Business Established	
Bank of Business Account and Address		At Time of Application _____
		If Loan is Approved _____
		Subsidiaries or Affiliates (Separate from above) _____

SAMPLE

Use of Proceeds: (Enter Gross Dollar Amounts Rounded to the Nearest Hundreds)	Loan Requested		Loan Requested
Land Acquisition		Payoff SBA Loan	
New Construction/Expansion Repair		Payoff Bank Loan (Non SBA Associated)	
Acquisition and/or repair of Machinery and Equipment		Other Debt Payment (Non SBA Associated)	
Inventory Purchase		All Other	
Working Capital (Including Accounts Payable)		Total Loan Requested	
Acquisition of Existing Business		Term of Loan – (Requested Mat.)	_____ Yrs.

PREVIOUS SBA OR OTHER FEDERAL GOVERNMENT DEBT: If you or any principals or affiliates have 1) ever requested Government financing or 2) are delinquent on the repayment of any Federal Debt complete the following:

Name of Agency	Original Amount of Loan	Date of Request	Approved or Declined	Balance	Current or Past Due
	$			$	
	$			$	

ASSISTANCE   List the name(s) and occupations of any who assisted in the preparation of this form, other than applicant.

Name and Occupation	Address	Total Fees Paid	Fees Due
Name and Occupation	Address	Total Fees Paid	Fees Due

PLEASE NOTE: The estimated burden hours for the completion of the form is 19.8 hours per response. If you have any questions or comments concerning this estimate or any other aspect of this information collection please contact Chief Administrative Information Branch, U.S. Small Business Administration, Washington, D.C. 20416 and Gary Waxman, Clearance Officer, Paperwork Reduction Project (3245-0016), Office of Management and Budget, Washington, D.C. 20503.

SBA Form 4 (1-93) Previous Edition is Obsolete   Page 1

SBA Form 4, Application for Business Loan: Sample (continued)

ALL EXHIBITS MUST BE SIGNED AND DATED BY PERSON SIGNING THIS FORM

BUSINESS INDEBTEDNESS: Furnish the following information on all installment debts, contracts, notes, and mortgages payable. Indicate by an asterisk (*) items to be paid by loan proceeds and reason for paying same (present balance should agree with the latest balance sheet submitted).

To Whom Payable	Original Amount	Original Date	Present Balance	Rate of Interest	Maturity Date	Monthly Payment	Security	Current or Past Due
Acct. #	$		$			$		
Acct. #	$		$			$		
Acct. #	$		$			$		
Acct. #	$		$			$		

MANAGEMENT (Proprietor, partners, officers, directors all holders of outstanding stock – <u>100% of ownership must be shown.</u>) Use separate sheet if necessary.

Name and Social Security Number and Position Title	Complete Address	% Owned	*Military Service From	*Military Service To	*Race	*Sex

*This data is collected for statistical purpose only. It has no bearing on the credit decision to approve or decline this application.

THE FOLLOWING EXHIBITS MUST BE COMPLETED WHERE APPLICABLE. ALL QUESTIONS ANSWERED ARE MADE A PART OF THE APPLICATION.

For Guaranty Loans please provide an original and one copy (Photocopy is Acceptable) of the Application Form, and all Exhibits to the participating lender. For Direct Loans submit one original copy of the application and Exhibits to SBA.

1. Submit SBA Form 912 (Personal History Statement) for each person, e.g., owners, partners, officers, directors, major stockholders, etc.; the instructions are on SBA Form 912.

2. If your collateral consists of (A) Land and Building, (B) Machinery and Equipment, (C) Furniture and Fixtures, (D) Accounts Receivable, (E) Inventory, (F) Other, please provide an itemized list (labeled Exhibit A) that contains serial and identification numbers for all articles that had an original value greater than $500. Include a legal description of Real Estate offered as collateral.

3. Furnish a signed current personal balance sheet (SBA Form 413 may be used for this purpose) for each stockholder (with 20% or greater ownership), partner, officer, and owner. Social Security number should be included on personal financial statement. It should be as of the same date as the most recent business financial statements. Label this Exhibit B.

4. Include the statements listed below: 1,2,3 for the last three years; also 1,2,3,4 as of the same date, which are current within 90 days of filing the application; and statement 5, if applicable. This is Exhibit C (SBA has Management Aids that help in the preparation of financial statements). All information must be **signed and dated**.

1. Balance Sheet   2. Profit and Loss Statement
3. Reconciliation of Net Worth
4. Aging of Accounts Receivable and Payable
5. Earnings projects for at least one year where financial statements for the last three years are unavailable or where requested by District Office.
   (If Profit and Loss Statement is not available, explain why and substitute Federal Income Tax Forms.)

5. Provide a brief history of your company and a paragraph describing the expected benefits it will receive from the loan. Label it Exhibit D.

6. Provide a brief description similar to a resume of the education, technical and business background for all the people listed under Management. Please mark it Exhibit E.

SBA Form 4 (1-93) Previous Edition is Obsolete

SBA Form 4, Application for Business Loan: Sample (continued)

ALL EXHIBITS MUST BE SIGNED AND DATED BY PERSON SIGNING THIS FORM

7. Do you have any co-signers and/or guarantors for this loan? If so, please submit their names, addresses, tax Id Numbers, and current personal balance sheet(s) as Exhibit F.

8. Are you buying machinery or equipment with your loan money? If so, you must include a list of equipment and cost as quoted by the seller and his name and address. This is Exhibit G.

9. Have you or any officer of your company ever been involved in bankruptcy or insolvency proceedings? If so, please provide the details as Exhibit H. If none, check here: ☐ Yes ☐ No

10. Are you or your business involved in any pending lawsuits? If yes, provide the details as Exhibit I. If none, check here: ☐ Yes ☐ No

11. Do you or your spouse or any member of your household, or anyone who owns, manages, or directs your business or their spouses or members of their households work for the Small Business Administration, Small Business Advisory Council, SCORE or ACE, any Federal Agency, or the participating lender? If so, please provide the name and address of the person and the office where employed. Label this Exhibit J. If none, check here: ☐ Yes ☐ No

12. Does your business, its owners or majority stockholders own or have a controlling interest in other businesses? If yes, please provide their names and the relationship with your company along with a current balance sheet and operating statement for each. This should be Exhibit K.

13. Do you buy from, sell to, or use the services of any concern in which someone in your company has a significant financial interest? If yes, provide details on a separate sheet of paper labeled Exhibit L.

14. If your business is a franchise, include a copy of the franchise agreement and a copy of the FTC disclosure statement supplied to you by the Franchisor. Please include it as Exhibit M.

CONSTRUCTION LOANS ONLY

15. Include a separate exhibit (Exhibit N) the estimated cost of the project and a statement of the source of any additional funds.

16. Provide copies of preliminary construction plans and specifications. Include them as Exhibit O. Final plans will be required prior to disbursement.

DIRECT LOANS ONLY

17. Include two bank declination letters with your application. (In cities with 200,000 people or less, one letter will be sufficient.) These letters should include the name and telephone number of the persons contacted at the banks, the amount and terms of the loan, the reason for decline and whether or not the bank will participate with SBA.

EXPORT LOANS

18. Does your business presently engage in Export Trade?
Check here: ☐ Yes ☐ No

19. Do you have plans to begin exporting as a result of this loan?
Check here: ☐ Yes ☐ No

20. Would you like information on Exporting?
Check here: ☐ Yes ☐ No

AGREEMENTS AND CERTIFICATIONS

Agreements of non-employment SBA Personnel: I agree that if SBA approves this loan application I will not, for at least two years, hire as an employee or consultant anyone that was employed by the SBA during the one year period prior to the disbursement of the loan.

Certification: I certify: (a) I have not paid anyone connected with the Federal Government for help in getting this loan. I also agree to report to the SBA office of the Inspector General, Washington, D.C. 20416 any Federal Government employee who offers, in return for any type of compensation, to help get this loan approved.

(b) All information in this application and the Exhibits are true and complete to the best of my knowledge and are submitted to SBA so SBA can decide whether to grant a loan or participate with a lending institution in a loan to me. I agree to pay for or reimburse SBA for the cost of any surveys, title or mortgage examinations, appraisals, credit reports, etc., performed by non-SBA personnel provided I have given my consent.

(c) I understand that I need not pay anybody to deal with SBA. I have read and understand SBA Form 159 which explains SBA policy on representatives and their fees.

(d) As consideration for any Management, Technical, and Business Development Assistance that may be provided, I waive all claims against SBA and its consultants.

If you make a statement that you know to be false or if you over value a security in order to help obtain a loan under the provisions of the Small Business Act, you can be fined up to $5,000 or be put in jail for up to two years, or both.

If Applicant is a proprietor or general partner, sign below.

By: _____
                                                        Date

If Applicant is a Corporation, sign below:

Corporate Name and Seal   Date

By: _____
           Signature of President

Attested by: _____
           Signature of Corporate Secretary

SBA Form 4 (1-93) Previous Edition is Obsolete   Page 3

SBA Form 4, Application for Business Loan: Sample (continued)

APPLICANT'S CERTIFICATION

By my signature I certify that I have read and received a copy of the "STATEMENTS REQUIRED BY LAW AND EXECUTIVE ORDER" which was attached to this application. My signature represents my agreement to comply with the approval of my loan request and to comply, whenever applicable, with the hazard insurance, lead-based paint, civil rights or other limitations in this notice.

Each Proprietor, each General Partner, each Limited Partner or Stockholder owning 20% or more, and each Guarantor must sign. Each person should sign only once.

Business Name _____

SAMPLE

Date	By Signature and Title
Date	Signature and Title
Date	Signature and Title
Date	Signature and Title
Date	Signature and Title

SBA Form 4 (1-93) Previous Edition is Obsolete   * U.S. GOVERNMENT PRINTING OFFICE: 1993 0—347-226   Page 4

SBA Form 912, Statement of Personal History: Sample

United States of America
SMALL BUSINESS ADMINISTRATION
STATEMENT OF PERSONAL HISTORY

Return Executed Copies 1, 2, and 3 to SBA

OMB Approval No.: 3245-0178
Expiration Date: 2-28-97

Please Read Carefully – Print or Type
Each member of the small business concern or the development company requesting assistance must submit this form in TRIPLICATE for filing with the SBA application. This form must be filled out and submitted by:

1. If a sole proprietorship by the proprietor.
2. If a partnership by each partner.
3. If a corporation or a development company, by each officer, director, and additionally by each holder of 20% or more of the voting stock.
4. Any other person including a hired manager, who has authority to speak for and commit the borrower in the management of the business.

Name and Address of Applicant (Firm Name)(Street, City, State, and Zip Code)

SBA District/Disaster Area Office

Amount Applied for: Loan Case No.

1. Personal Statement of: [State name in full, if no middle name, state (NMN), or if initial only, indicate initial]. List all former names used, and dates each name was used. Use separate sheet if necessary.

   First   Middle   Last

Name and Address of participating bank (when applicable)

SAMPLE

2. Date of Birth: (Month, day, and year)
3. Place of Birth: (City & State or Foreign Country)

1. Give the percentage of ownership or stock owned or to be owned in the small business concern or the Development Company

Social Security No.

U.S. Citizen? ☐ YES ☐ NO
If no, give alien registration number: _____

5. Present residence Address:
   From: To: Address: City   State

   Home Telephone No. (Include A/C):   Business Telephone No. (Include A/C):

   Immediate past residence address:
   From: To: Address

BE SURE TO ANSWER THE NEXT 3 QUESTIONS CORRECTLY BECAUSE THEY ARE IMPORTANT.

THE FACT THAT YOU HAVE AN ARREST OR CONVICTION RECORD WILL NOT NECESSARILY DISQUALIFY YOU. BUT AN INCORRECT ANSWER WILL PROBABLY CAUSE YOUR APPLICATION TO BE TURNED DOWN.

IF YOU ANSWER "YES" TO 6, 7, OR 8, FURNISH DETAILS IN A SEPARATE EXHIBIT. INCLUDE DATES; LOCATION; FINES, SENTENCES, ETC.; WHETHER MISDEMEANOR OR FELONY; DATES OF PAROLE/PROBATION; UNPAID FINES OR PENALTIES; NAMES UNDER WHICH CHARGED; AND ANY OTHER PERTINENT INFORMATION.

6. Are you presently under indictment, on parole or probation?
   ☐ Yes   ☐ No   (If yes, indicate date parole or probation is to expire.)

7. Have you ever been charged with or arrested for any criminal offense other than a minor motor vehicle violation? Include offenses which have been dismissed, discharged, or nolle prosequi. (All arrests and charges must be disclosed and explained on an attached sheet.)
   ☐ Yes   ☐ No

8. Have you ever been convicted, placed on pretrial diversion, or placed on any form of probation, including adjudication withheld pending probation, for any criminal offense other than a minor motor vehicle violation?
   ☐ Yes   ☐ No

9. ☐ Fingerprints Waived   Date   Approving Authority
   ☐ Fingerprints Required
       Date Sent to FBI   Date   Approving Authority

10. ☐ Cleared for Processing   Date   Approving Authority
    ☐ Request a Character Evaluation Date   Approving Authority

The information on this form will be used in connection with an investigation of your character. Any information you wish to submit that you feel will expedite this investigation should be set forth.

CAUTION: Knowingly making a false statement on this form is a violation of Federal law and could result in criminal prosecution, significant civil penalties, and a denial of your loan. A false statement is punishable under 18 USC 1001 by imprisonment of not more than five years and/or a fine of not more than $10,000; under 15 USC 645 by imprisonment of not more than two years and/or a fine of not more than $5,000; and, if submitted to a Federally insured institution, under 18 USC 1014 by imprisonment of not more than twenty years and/or a fine of not more than $1,000,000.

Signature   Title   Date

It is against SBA's policy to provide assistance to persons not of good character and therefore consideration is given to the qualities and personality traits of a person, favorable and unfavorable, relating thereto, including behavior, integrity, candor and disposition toward criminal actions. It is also against SBA's policy to provide assistance not in the best interests of the United States, for example, if there is reason to believe that the effect of such assistance will be to encourage or support, directly or indirectly, activities inimical to the Security of the United States. Anyone concerned with the collection of this information, as to its voluntariness, disclosure of routine uses may contact the FOIA Office, 409 3rd St. S.W., and a copy of 9 "Agency Collection of Information" from SOP 40 04 will be provided.

SBA Form 912 (12-93) SOP 9020 USE 5-87 EDITION UNTIL EXHAUSTED   Copy 1 - SAB File Copy

PLEASE NOTE: The estimated burden hours for the completion of this form is 15 minutes per response. If you have any questions or comments concerning this estimate or any other aspect of this information collection please contact, Chief Administrative Information Branch, U.S. Small Business Administration, 409 Third St. S.W. Washington, D.C. 20416 or Gary Waxman, Clearance Officer, Paperwork Reduction Project (3245-0201), Office of Management and Budget, Washington, D.C. 20503.

Federal Recycling Program   Printed on Recycled Paper

SBA Form 4 Schedule A, Schedule of Collateral: Sample

U.S. Small Business Administration
SCHEDULE OF COLLATERAL
Exhibit A

OMB Approval No.: 3245-0016
Expiration Date: 6/30/94

Applicant	
Street Address	
City	State	Zip Code

SAMPLE

LIST ALL COLLATERAL TO BE USED AS SECURITY FOR THIS LOAN

Section I—REAL ESTATE

Attach a copy of the deed(s) containing a full legal description of the land and show the location (street address) and city where the deed(s) is recorded. Following the address below, give a brief description of the improvements, such as size, type of construction, use, number of stories, and present condition (use additional sheet if more space is required).

LIST PARCELS OF REAL ESTATE

Address	Year Acquired	Original Cost	Market Value	Amount of Lien	Name of Lienholder

Description(s):

SBA Form 4 Schedule A (8-91) Use 4-87 Edition until exhausted

SBA Form 4 Schedule A, Schedule of Collateral: Sample (continued)

All items listed herein must show manufacturer or make, model, year, and serial number. Items with no serial number must be clearly identified (use additional sheet if more space is required).

Description – Show Manufacturer Model, Serial No.	Year Acquired	Original Cost	Market Value	Current Lien Balance	Name of Lienholder

SAMPLE

All information contained herein is TRUE and CORRECT to the best of my knowledge. I understand that FALSE statements may result in forfeiture of benefits and possible fine and prosecution by the U.S. Attorney General (Ref. 18 U.S.C. 100).

_____ Date _____

_____ Date _____

SBA Form 4 Schedule A (8-91) Use 4-87 edition until exhausted   *U.S. Government Printing Office: 1991 — 282-429/45515

Chapter 3: Applying for a Small Business Loan   55

SBA Form 413, Personal Financial Statement: Sample

OMB Approval No. 3245-0188

PERSONAL FINANCIAL STATEMENT

U.S. SMALL BUSINESS ADMINISTRATION

As of _____, 19____

Complete this form for: (1) each proprietor, or (2) each limited partner who owns 20% or more interest and each general partner, or (3) each stockholder owning 20% or more of voting stock, or (4) any person or entity providing a guaranty on the loan.

Name	Business Phone ( )
Residence Address	Residence Phone ( )
City, State, & Zip Code	
Business Name of Applicant/Borrower	

ASSETS	Omit Cents	LIABILITIES	Omit Cents
Cash on hands & in Banks	$ _____	Accounts Payable	$ _____
Savings Accounts	$ _____	Notes Payable to Banks and Others	$ _____
IRA or Other Retirement Account	$ _____	(Describe in Section 2)	
Accounts & Notes Receivable	$ _____	Installment Account (Auto)	$ _____
Life Insurance–Cash Surrender Value Only	$ _____	Mo. Payments $ _____	
(Complete Section 8)		Installment Account (other)	$ _____
Stocks and Bonds	$ _____	Mo. Payments $ _____	
(Describe in Section 3)		Loan on Life Insurance	$ _____
Real Estate	$ _____	Mortgages on Real Estate	$ _____
(Describe in Section 4)		(Describe in Section 4)	
Automobile–Present Value	$ _____	Unpaid taxes	$ _____
Other Personal Property	$ _____	(Describe in Section 6)	
(Describe in Section 5)		Other Liabilities	$ _____
Other Assets	$ _____	(Describe in Section 7)	
(Describe in Section 5)		Total Liabilities	$ _____
		Net Worth	$ _____
Total	$ _____	Total	$ _____

Section 1.   Source of Income   **Contingent Liabilities**

Salary	$ _____	As Endorser or Co-Maker	$ _____
Net Investment Income	$ _____	Legal Claims & Judgments	$ _____
Real Estate Income	$ _____	Provision for Federal Income tax	$ _____
Other Income (Describe below)*	$ _____	Other Special Debt	$ _____

Description of Other Income in Section 1.

*Alimony or child support payments need not be disclosed in "Other Income" unless it is desired to have such payments counted toward total income.

Section 2.   Notes Payable to Bank and Others.   (Use attachments if necessary. Each attachment must be identified as part of this statement and signed.)

Name and Address of Noteholder(s)	Original Balance	Current Balance	Payment Amount	Frequency (monthly, etc.)	How Secured or Endorsed Type of Collateral

SBA Form 413 (2-94) Use 5-91 Edition until stock is exhausted. Ref: SOP 50-10 - and 50-30   (tumble)

SBA Form 413, Personal Financial Statement: Sample (continued)

Section 3. Stocks and Bonds. (Use attachments if necessary. Each attachment must be identified as part of this statement and signed.)

Number of Shares	Name of Securities	Cost	Market Value Quotation/Exchange	Date of Quotation/Exchange	Total Value

Section 4. Real Estate Owned. (List each parcel separately. Use attachments if necessary. Each attachment must be identified as a part of this statement and signed.)

	Property A	Property B	Property C
Type of Property			
Address			
Date Purchased			
Original Cost			
Present Market Value			
Name & Address of Mortgage Holder			
Mortgage Account Number			
Mortgage Balance			
Amount of Payment per Month/Year			
Status of Mortgage			

Section 5. Other Personal Property and Other Assets. (Describe, and if any is pledged as security, state name and address of lien holder, amount of lien, terms of payment, and if delinquent, describe delinquency.)

Section 6. Unpaid Taxes. (Describe in detail, as to type, to whom payable, when due, amount, and to what property, if any, a tax lien attaches.)

Section 7. Other Liabilities. (Describe in detail.)

Section 8. Life Insurance Held. (Give face amount and cash surrender value of policies – name of insurance company and beneficiaries.)

I authorize SBA/Lender to make inquiries as necessary to verify the accuracy of the statements made and to determine my creditworthiness. I certify the above and the statements contained in the attachments are true and accurate as of the stated date(s). These statements are made for the purpose of either obtaining a loan or guaranteeing a loan. I understand FALSE statements may result in forfeiture of benefits and possible prosecution by the U.S. Attorney General (Reference 18 U.S.C. 1001).

Signature _____ Date: _____ Social Security Number _____

Signature _____ Date: _____ Social Security Number _____

PLEASE NOTE: The estimated average burden hours for the completion of this form is 1.5 hours per response. If you have questions or comments concerning this estimate or any other aspect of this information, please contact Chief, Administrative Branch, U.S. Small Business Administration, Washington, D.C. 20416, and Clearance Office, Paper Reduction Project (3245-0188), Office of Management and Budget, Washington, D.C. 20503.

Federal Recycling Program — Printed on Recycled Paper

… Chapter 3: Applying for a Small Business Loan 57

SBA Form 1100, Monthly Cash Flow Projection

MONTHLY CASH FLOW PROJECTION

NAME OF BUSINESS _____ ADDRESS _____ OWNER _____ TYPE OF BUSINESS _____ PREPARED BY _____ DATE _____

Form Approval
OMB No. 3245-0012
EXPIRES: 8-31-91

YEAR _____ MONTH: Pre-Start-up Position, 1, 2, 3, 4, 5, 6, 7, 8, 9, 10, 11, 12, TOTAL Columns 1–12 (Estimate/Actual columns for each)

1. CASH ON HAND (Beginning of Month)
2. CASH RECEIPTS
   (a) Cash Sales
   (b) Collections from Credit Accounts
   (c) Loan or Other Cash Injection (specify)
3. TOTAL CASH RECEIPTS (2a + 2b + 2c = 3)
4. TOTAL CASH AVAILABLE (Before cash out) (1 + 3)
5. CASH PAID OUT
   (a) Purchases (Merchandise)
   (b) Gross Wages (Excludes withdrawals)
   (c) Payroll Expenses (Taxes, etc.)
   (d) Outside Services
   (e) Supplies (Office and operating)
   (f) Repairs and Maintenance
   (g) Advertising
   (h) Car, Delivery, and Travel
   (i) Accounting and Legal
   (j) Rent
   (k) Telephone
   (l) Utilities
   (m) Insurance
   (n) Taxes (Real estate, etc.)
   (o) Interest
   (p) Other Expenses (Specify each)
   (q) Miscellaneous (Unspecified)
   (r) Subtotal
   (s) Loan Principal Payment
   (t) Capital Purchases (Specify)
   (u) Other Start-up Costs
   (v) Reserve and/or Escrow (Specify)
   (w) Owner's Withdrawal
6. TOTAL CASH PAID OUT (Total 5a thru 5w)
7. CASH POSITION (End of month) (4 minus 6)

ESSENTIAL OPERATING DATA (Non-cash flow information)
A. Sales Volume (Dollars)
B. Accounts Receivable (End of month)
C. Bad Debt (End of month)
D. Inventory on Hand (End of month)
E. Accounts Payable (End of month)
F. Depreciation

Signature _____ Date _____

See Reverse Side for Instructions and Public Comment Information

SBA Form 1100 (1-83) REF: SOP 60 10 Previous Editions are Obsolete

SBA Form 1100, Monthly Cash Flow Projection Guidelines

GUIDELINES

GENERAL

Definition: A cash flow projection is a forecast of cash funds* a business anticipates receiving, on the one hand, and disbursing on the other hand, throughout the course of a given span of time, and the anticipated cash position at specific times during the period being projected.

Objective: The purpose of preparing a cash flow projection is to determine deficiencies or excesses in cash from that necessary to operate the business during the time for which the projection is prepared. If deficiencies are revealed in the cash flow, financial plans **must** be altered either to provide more cash by, for example, more equity capital, loans, or increased selling prices of products, or to reduce expenditures including inventory, or allow less credit sales until a proper cash flow balance is obtained. If excesses of cash are revealed, it might indicate excessive borrowing or idle money that could be "put to work." The objective is to **finally** develop a plan which, if followed, will provide a well-managed flow of cash.

The Form: The cash flow projection form provides a systematic method of recording estimates of cash receipts and expenditures, which can be compared with actual receipts and expenditures as they become known—hence the two columns, Estimate and Actual. The entries listed on the form will not necessarily apply to every business, and some entries may not be included which would be pertinent to specific businesses. It is suggested, therefore, that the form be adapted to the particular business for which the projection is being made, with appropriate changes in the entries as may be required. Before the cash flow projection can be completed and pricing structure established, it is necessary to know or to estimate various important factors of the business, for example: What are the direct costs of the product or services **per unit?** What are the monthly or yearly costs of the operation? What is the sales price per unit of the product or service? Determine that the pricing structure provides this business with reasonable breakeven goals (including a reasonable net profit) when conservative sales goals are met. What are the available sources of cash, other than income from sales; for example, loans, equity capital, rent, or other sources?

Procedure: Most of the entries for the form are self-explanatory; however, the following suggestions are offered to simplify the procedure:
(A) Suggest even dollars be used rather than showing cents.
(B) If this is a new business, or an existing business undergoing significant changes or alterations, the cash flow part of the column marked "Pre-start-up Position" should be completed. (Fill in appropriate blanks only.) Costs involved here are, for example, rent, telephone, and utilities deposits before the business is actually open. Other items might be equipment purchases, alterations, the owner's cash injection, and cash from loans received before actual operations begin.
(C) Next fill in the pre-start-up position of the essential operating data (non-cash flow information), where applicable.
(D) Complete the form using the suggestions in the partial form below for each entry.

CHECKING

In order to insure that the figures are properly calculated and balanced, they must be checked. Several methods may be used, but the following four checks are suggested as a minimum:

CHECK #1: Item #1 (Beginning Cash on Hand—1st Month) plus Item #3 (Total Cash Receipts—Total Column) minus Item #6 (Total Cash Paid Out—Total Column) should be equal to Item #7 (Cash Position at End of 12th Month).

CHECK #2: Item A (Sales Volume—Total Column) plus Item B (Accounts Receivable—Pre-start-up Position) minus Item 2(a) (Cash Sales—Total Column) minus Item 2(b) (Accounts Receivable Collection—Total Column) minus Item C (Bad Debt—Total Column) should be equal to Item B (Accounts Receivable at End of 12th Month).

---
* Cash funds, for the purpose of this projection, are defined as cash, checks, or money order, paid out or received.

CHECK #3: The horizontal total of Item #6 (Total Cash Paid Out) is equal to the vertical total of all items under Item #5 (5(a) through 5(w) in the total column at the right of the form.

CHECK #4: The horizontal total of Item #3 (Total Cash Receipts) is equal to the vertical total of all items under #2 (2(a) through 2(c) in the total column at the right of the form.

ANALYZE the correlation between the cash flow and the projected profit during the period in question. The estimated profit is the **difference** between the estimated change in assets and the estimated change in liabilities before such things as any owner withdrawal, appreciation of assets, change in investments, etc. (The change may be positive or negative.) This can be obtained as follows:
The **change in assets** before owner's withdrawal, appreciation of assets, change in investments, etc., can be computed by adding the following:
(1) Item #7 (Cash Position—End of Last Month) minus Item #1 (Cash on Hand at the Beginning of the First Month).
(2) Item #5(t) (Capital Purchases—Total Column) minus Item F (Depreciation—Total Column).
(3) Item B. (Accounts Receivable—End of 12th Month) minus Item B (Accounts Receivable—Pre-start-up Position).
(4) Item D. (Inventory on Hand—End of 12th Month) minus Item D (Inventory on Hand—Pre-start-up Position).
(5) Item #5(w) (Owner's withdrawal—Total Column) or dividends, minus such things as an increase in investment.
(6) Item #5(v) (Reserve and/or Escrow—Total Column).
The **change in liabilities** (before items noted in "change in assets") can be computed by adding the following:
(1) Item 2(c) (Loans—Total Column) minus 5(s) (Loan Principal Payment—Total Column).
(2) Item E (Accounts Payable—End of 12th Month) minus E (Accounts Payable—Pre-start-up Position).

ANALYSIS

A. The cash position at the end of each month should be adequate to meet the cash requirements for the following month. If too little cash, then additional cash will have to be injected or cash paid out must be reduced. If there is too much cash on hand, the money is not working for your business.
B. The cash flow projection, the profit and loss projection, the breakeven analysis, and good cost control information are tools which, if used properly, will be useful in making decisions that can increase profits to insure success.
C. The projection becomes more useful when the estimated information can be compared with actual information as it develops. It is important to follow through and complete the actual columns as the information becomes available. Utilize the cash flow projection to assist in setting new goals and planning operations for more profit.

SBA Form 1100, Monthly Cash Flow Projection Guidelines (continued)

1. CASH ON HAND (Beginning of month)	Cash on hand same as (7), Cash Position Previous Month.
2. CASH RECEIPTS	
(a) Cash Sales	All cash sales. Omit credit sales unless cash is actually received.
(b) Collections from Credit Accounts	Amount to be expected from all credit accounts.
(c) Loan or Other Cash injection	Indicate here all cash injections not shown in 2(a) or 2(b) above. See "A" of "Analysis".
3. TOTAL CASH RECEIPTS (2a + 2b + 2c = 3)	Self-explanatory.
4. TOTAL CASH AVAILABLE (Before cash out) (1 + 3)	Self-explanatory.
5. CASH PAID OUT	
(a) Purchases (Merchandise)	Merchandise for resale or for use in product (paid for in current month).
(b) Gross Wages (Excludes withdrawals)	Base pay plus overtime (if any).
(c) Payroll Expenses (Taxes, etc.)	Include paid vacations, paid sick leave, health insurance, unemployment insurance, etc. (this might be 10 to 45% of 5(b).
(d) Outside Services	This could include outside labor and/or material for specialized or overflow work, including subcontracting.
(e) Supplies (Office and operating)	Items purchased for use in the business (not for resale).
(f) Repairs and Maintenance	Include periodic large expenditures such as painting or decorating.
(g) Advertising	This amount should be adequate to maintain sales volume—include telephone book yellow page cost.
(h) Car, Delivery, and Travel	If personal car is used, charge in this column—include parking.
(i) Accounting and Legal	Outside services, including, for example, bookkeeping.
(j) Rent	Real estate only (See 5(p) for other rentals).
(k) Telephone	Self-explanatory.
(l) Utilities	Water, heat, light, and/or power.
(m) Insurance	Coverages on business property and products, e.g., fire, liability; also workman's compensation, fidelity, etc. Exclude "executive life"(include in "5W").
(n) Taxes (Real estate, etc.)	Plus inventory tax—sales tax—excise tax, if applicable.
(o) Interest	Remember to add interest on loan as it is injected (See 2(c) above).
(p) Other Expenses (Specify each)	Unexpected expenditures may be included here as a safety factor.
	Equipment expenses during the month should be included here (Non-capital equipment).
	When equipment is rented or leased, record payments here.
(q) Miscellaneous (Unspecified)	Small expenditures for which separate accounts would not be practical.
(r) Subtotal	This subtotal indicates cash out for operating costs.
(s) Loan Principal Payment	Include payment on all loans, including vehicle and equipment purchases on time payment.
(t) Capital Purchase (Specify)	Non-expensed (depreciable) expenditures such as equipment, building, vehicle purchases, and leasehold improvements.
(u) Other Start-up Costs	Expenses incurred prior to first month projection and paid for after the "start-up" position.
(v) Reserve and/or Escrow (Specify)	Example: insurance, tax, or equipment escrow to reduce impact of large periodic payments.
(w) Owner's Withdrawal	Should include payment for such things as owner's income tax, social security, health insurance, "executive" life insurance premiums, etc.
6. TOTAL CASH PAID OUT (Total 5a thru 5w)	Self-explanatory.
7. CASH POSITION (End of month) (4 minus 6)	Enter this amount in (1) Cash on Hand following month—See "A" of "Analysis."
ESSENTIAL OPERATING DATA (Non-cash flow information)	This is basic information necessary for proper planning and for proper cash flow-projection. In conjunction with this data, the cash flow can be evolved and shown in the above form.
A. Sales Volume (Dollars)	This is a very important figure and should be estimated carefully, taking into account size of facility and employee output as well as realistic anticipated sales. (Actual sales performed—not orders received.)
B. Accounts Receivable (End of month)	Previous unpaid credit sales plus current month's credit sales, less amounts received current month (deduct "C" below).
C. Bad Debt (End of month)	Bad debts should be subtracted from (B) in the month anticipated.
D. Inventory on Hand (End of month)	Last month's inventory plus merchandise received and/or manufactured current month minus amount sold current month.
E. Accounts Payable (End of month)	Previous month's payable plus current month's payable minus amount paid during month.
F. Depreciation	Established by your accountant, or value of all your equipment divided by useful life (in months) as allowed by Internal Revenue Service.

SBA Form 1100 (1-83)

* U.S. GOVERNMENT PRINTING OFFICE: 1993 0—347-226

Note: This is a reduced size version of *Form 1100*. If you wish, you may obtain an actual size version of this form. Call your nearest SBA office and request your free copy of *Form 1100*.

Financial Statement Spread Sheet

FINANCIAL STATEMENT SPREAD SHEET

Name		Business									SIC#	
Type Statement		Review		Review								
Statement Date			%		%		%		%			%
Cash	1											
Marketable Securities	2											
Receivables – Trade	3											
Less: Allow for Bad Debts	4											
Notes Receivable	5											
Inventories	6											
	7											
	8											
All Other Current	9											
TOTAL CURRENT ASSETS	10											
Fixed Assets – Net	11											
Due From Officers/Affiliates	12											
Investments/Inv. In Affiliates	13											
	14											
All Other Noncurrent	15											
TOTAL NONCURRENT ASSETS	16											
Intangible Assets	17											
TOTAL ASSETS	18		100		100		100		100			100
Notes Payable – Bank	19											
	20											
Due Officers/Affiliates	21											
Accounts Payable – Trade	22											
Taxes	23											
Current Maturities of L.T. Debt	24											
	25											
All Other Current	26											
TOTAL CURRENT DEBT	27											
Long Term Debt	28											
	29											
All Other Noncurrent	30											
TOTAL NONCURRENT DEBT	31											
	32											
Deferred Income Taxes	33											
Subordinated Debt	34											
TOTAL LIABILITIES	35											
	36											
Capital – Preferred Stock	37											
Capital – Common Stock	38											
Paid-In (Capital) Surplus	39											
Retained Earnings	40											
NET WORTH	41											
TOTAL LIABILITIES & NET WORTH	42		100		100		100		100			100
WORKING CAPITAL (10–27)	43											
TANGIBLE NET WORTH (41–17)	44											
Ratios Current	45											
Quick	46											
(Days) Sales to Receivables	47											
(Days) Cost of Sales to Inv.	48											
Sales to Working Capital	49											
E.B.I.T. to Interest	50											
Cash Flow to Cur. Mat. L.T.D.	51											
Total Debt to T.N.W.	52											
%Profit Before Taxes to Sales	53											
%Profit Before Taxes to T.N.W.	54											
%Profit Before Taxes to T.A.	55											
Sales to Total Assets	56											
CONTINGENT LIABILITIES	57											

Financial Statement Spread Sheet (continued)

Date of Statement										
Operations Period										
NET SALES	58		100		100		100		100		100
Materials used	59									
Labor	60									
Manufacturing Expenses	61									
	62									
COST OF GOODS SOLD	63									
GROSS PROFIT	64									
Selling Expenses	65									
General & Adm. Expenses	66									
	67									
TOTAL OPERATING EXPENSES	68									
OPERATING PROFIT	69									
Other Income	70									
	71									
Other Expense	72									
	73									
NET PROFIT BEFORE TAX	74									
Income Taxes	75									
	76									
NET PROFIT AFTER TAX	77									
Depreciation & Amortization	78									
	79									
Gross Cash Flow (77 + 78 + 79)	80									
	81									
RECONCILIATION OF NET WORTH										
Net Worth – Beginning	82									
Add: Net Profit Less: (Net Loss)	83									
Less: Dividends	84									
	85									
	86									
	87									
	88									
Net Worth – Ending	89									
Change in Net Worth (89–82)	90									
SOURCE & APPLICATION OF FUNDS										
Sources of Funds:										
Net Profit After Tax	91									
Depr., Amort., Depletion	92									
	93									
	94									
Increase – Noncurrent Debt	95									
	96									
	97									
	98									
	99									
Other Accounts – Net	100									
Decrease Net Working Capital	101									
TOTAL SOURCES	102									
Application of Funds:										
Dividends Paid	103									
	104									
	105									
Purchase of Fixed Assets	106									
Decrease – Noncurrent Debt	107									
	108									
	109									
	110									
	111									
Other Accounts – Net	112									
Increase in Working Capital	113									
TOTAL APPLICATIONS	114									

SBA Form 159, Compensation Agreement: Sample

OMB Approval No 3245-0201

SBA LOAN NUMBER

COMPENSATION AGREEMENT FOR SERVICES IN CONNECTION WITH APPLICATION AND LOAN FROM (OR IN PARTICIPATION WITH) SMALL BUSINESS ADMINISTRATION

The undersigned representative (attorney, accountant, engineer, appraiser, etc.) hereby agrees that the undersigned has not and will not, directly or indirectly, charge or receive any payment in connection with the application for or the making of the loan except for services actually performed on behalf of the Applicant. The undersigned further agrees that the amount of payment for such services shall not exceed an amount deemed reasonable by the SBA (and, if it is a participation loan, by the participating lending institution), and to refund any amount in excess of that deemed reasonable by SBA (and the participating institution). This agreement shall supersede any other agreement covering payment for such services.

A general description of the services performed, or to be performed, by the undersigned and the compensation paid or to be paid are set forth below. <u>If the total compensation in any case exceeds $1,000 (or $300 for: (1) regular business loans of $15,000 or less; or (2) all disaster home loans) or if SBA should otherwise require, the services must be itemized on a schedule attached showing each date services were performed, time spent each day, and description of service rendered on each day listed.</u>

The undersigned Applicant and representative hereby certify that no other fees have been charged or will be charged by the representative in connection with this loan, unless provided for in the loan authorization specifically approved by SBA.

GENERAL DESCRIPTION OF SERVICES

Paid Previously $ _____

Additional Amount to be Paid $ _____

Total Compensation $ _____

(Section 13 of the Small Business Act (15 USC 642) requires disclosures concerning fees. Parts 103, 108 and 120 of Title 13 of the Code of Federal Regulations contain provisions covering appearances and compensation of persons representing SBA applicants. Section 103.13-5 authorizes the suspension or revocation of the privilege of any such person to appear before SBA for charging a fee deemed unreasonable by SBA for services actually performed, charging of unreasonable expenses, or violation of this agreement. Whoever commits any fraud, by false or misleading statement or representation, or by conspiracy, shall be subject to the penalty of any applicable Federal or State statute.)

Dated _____, 19 _____

_____
(Representative)

By _____

The Applicant hereby certifies to SBA that the above representations, description of services and amounts are correct and satisfactory to Applicant.

Dated _____, 19 _____

_____
(Applicant)

By _____

The participating lending institution hereby certifies that the above representations of service rendered and amounts charged are reasonable and satisfactory to it.

Dated _____, 19 _____

_____
(Lender)

By _____

NOTE: Foregoing certification must be executed, if by a corporation, in corporate name by duly authorized officer and duly attested; if by a partnership, in the firm name together with signature of general partner.

PLEASE NOTE: The estimated burden hours for the completion of SBA Form 147, 148, 159, 160, 160A, 529B, 928 and 1059 is 6 hrs. per response. If you have any questions or comments concerning this estimate or any other aspect of this information collection please contact, Chief Administrative Information Branch, U.S. Small Business Administration, 409 3rd St. S.W. Washington, D.C. 20416 and Gary Waxman, Clearance Officer, Paperwork Reduction Project (3245-0201), Office of Management and Budget, Washington, D.C. 20503.

SBA FORM 159 (2-93) REF SOP 70 50 Use 7-89 Edition Until Exhausted

SBA Form 159, Compensation Agreement: Sample (continued)

SMALL BUSINESS ADMINISTRATION

POLICY AND REGULATIONS CONCERNING REPRESENTATIVES AND THEIR FEES

An applicant for a loan from SBA may obtain the assistance of any attorney, accountant, engineer, appraiser or other representative to aid him in the preparation and presentation of his application to SBA; however, such representation is not mandatory. In the event a loan is approved, the services of an attorney may be necessary to assist in the preparation of closing documents, title abstracts, etc. SBA will allow the payment of reasonable fees or other compensation for services performed by such representatives on behalf of the applicant.

There are no "authorized representatives" of SBA, other than our regular salaried employees. Payment of any fee or gratuity to SBA employees is illegal and will subject the parties to such a transaction to prosecution.

SBA Regulations [Part 103, Sec. 103.13-5(c)] prohibit representatives from charging or proposing to charge any contingent fee for any services performed in connection with an SBA loan unless the amount of such fee bears a necessary and reasonable relationship to the services actually performed; or to charge for any expenses which are not deemed by SBA to have been necessary in connection with the application. The Regulations (Part 120, Sec. 120.104-2) also prohibit the payment of any bonus, brokerage fee or commission in connection with SBA loans.

In line with these Regulations SBA will not approve placement or finder's fees for the use or attempted use of influence in obtaining or trying to obtain an SBA loan, or fees based solely upon a percentage of the approved loan or any part thereof.

Fees which will be approved will be limited to reasonable sums of services actually rendered in connection with the application or the closing, based upon the time and effort required, the qualifications of the representative and the nature and extent of the services rendered by such representatives. Representatives of loan applicants will be required to execute an agreement as to their compensation for services rendered in connection with said loan.

It is the responsibility of the applicant to set forth in the appropriate section of the application the names of all persons or firms engaged by or on behalf of the applicant. Applicants are required to advise the Regional Office in writing the names and fees of any representatives engaged by the applicant subsequent to the filing of the application. This reporting requirement is approved under OMB Approval Number 3245-0016.

Any loan applicant having any questions concerning the payments of fees, or the reasonableness of fees, should communicate with the Field Office where the application is filed.

SAMPLE

U.S. GOVERNMENT PRINTING OFFICE : 1993 - 348-097

Notes

Chapter 4

SBA Loan Programs

The will to win is not nearly as important as the will to prepare to win.

— Bobby Knight

Primary SBA Lending Programs

The U.S. Small Business Administration (SBA) has opened the doors of opportunity for thousands of small businesses by helping them secure capital through loan guarantees. The Small Business Act authorizes the SBA to make and guarantee loans to small business, where the necessary financing is unavailable on reasonable terms through normal lending channels. The SBA generally does not make loans; the SBA guarantees loans submitted and made by financial institutions. The SBA's basic guaranty program is generally used to fund the varied long-term capital needs of small businesses, as seen by the fact that 96% of loans made in recent years were approved, with maturities of more than three years. In fact, a recent study by Price-Waterhouse reports that businesses getting these loan guarantees show higher growth than comparable businesses.

In 1995, the SBA approved more than 55,590 loans to small businesses across the country — amounting to more than $8 billion. This figure is expected to increase to $10 billion in 1996.

You may use an SBA loan to:

- Purchase inventory and materials;
- Purchase furniture, fixtures, machinery, and equipment;
- Purchase or construct a business premises;
- Construct leasehold improvements;
- Purchase a business;
- Repay existing payables or other debt, or both; and
- Provide working capital.

An SBA guaranteed loan can be in any amount; however, the guarantee is limited to $750,000 except for:

- Export Working Capital Loans; and
- Pollution Control Loans, which have a maximum of $1,000,000.

The U.S. Small Business Administration offers a variety of financing programs for small business. However, it rarely makes a direct loan to an individual or company due to the shortage of funds allocated by Congress. The SBA is primarily a guarantor — it guarantees loans made by banks and other private lenders to small business clients.

Whether you are starting a home-based, family-owned quilt company or you are the president of a high-tech company with 400 employees, the SBA can probably help you with financing through one of its many programs.

7(a) Regular Loan Guarantee Program

The 7(a) Regular Loan Guarantee Program represents 90% of the SBA's total lending and for this reason, it is referred to as the primary lending program. The 7(a) program is designed to stimulate small business activity and promote small business contribution to economic growth. Overall, the program is designed to reduce the risk to lenders who make loans and thereby increase the availability of capital for small business use.

In this program, interest rates are negotiated between the borrower and the lender, and are subject to SBA-imposed maximum rates that may be fixed or variable. Both your lender and the SBA analyze the loan application, so loan processing time can take three to four weeks. Remember, the primary reasons for delays in loan processing are due to incomplete loan packages with missing necessary signatures or documents. To remain within the normal processing time, make sure you submit a complete package.

In an effort to speed up loan processing in the 7(a) program, the SBA created two lending programs that, if you qualify, will save you valuable time. Better known as the Preferred Lenders Program and Certified Lenders Program, both programs are for applicants who have well-established businesses and require funds for growth. These programs benefit the loan applicant, the lender, and the SBA. Loan applicants and lenders receive faster service, and the SBA is able to leverage its resources to provide better assistance to more small businesses.

Preferred Lenders Program

The Preferred Lenders Program (PLP) allows certain banks to approve your loan application without going through an SBA loan officer. The SBA allows those banks in the Preferred Lenders Program to determine things like eligibility and credit-worthiness. The SBA will guarantee up to 80% of a loan of $100,000 or less, and up to 75% for a loan of more than $100,000. This is a guarantee given to lenders that has the full faith and credit of the United States behind it — a key reason why most lenders prefer the SBA route. This program represents about 14% of SBA guaranteed loans. The PLP has a quick processing turnaround time of one week. A complete list of preferred lenders is located in Appendix E.

To apply for a loan under this program, submit a complete loan package to a PLP lender. The lender will forward only the *Application for Business Loan, SBA Form 4, Lender's Application for Guaranty, SBA Form 4-1,* and your *Statement of Personal History, SBA Form 912* to the SBA. These documents are submitted primarily because they contain information needed by the SBA to:

- Maintain a current accounting of its obligations.
- Obtain a computer-generated loan number.
- Update its loan base.

The system provides for local SBA employees to conduct on-site reviews of PLP portfolios and methods.

The Certified Lenders Program (CLP) was established to recognize that the SBA was duplicating analytical efforts made by all participants, regardless of their activity level or success rate, as measured by the number of loans purchased by the SBA under the guarantee. Guarantees can run up to 75%. Like the PLP, the CLP has a speedy processing time because of less red tape. Once your lender has reviewed your loan application and has made its recommendation, your completed package is forwarded to the nearest SBA office. An SBA loan officer will have an answer for the bank within three working days. This program represents about 30% of SBA guaranteed loans. You can find a complete list of certified lenders in Appendix E located at the back of the book.

Certified Lenders Program

If you already have an SBA loan, you must meet the following requirements before you can submit a loan application under the Certified Lenders Program:

- Your business' ownership and management, or both, must not have changed since approval of your existing loan.
- Any existing SBA loan must be current at the time of receipt of your application. Your lender is expected to make full disclosure of all adverse factors of significant relationships with the borrower that could have a bearing on the granting of additional credit. For example, if a participant is a senior lienholder on any property to be acquired or improved by the loan, a full explanation of the situation is required with prior lienholders and amounts identified in your application.

Loans to businesses with any apparent conflict of interest — such as where any principal is associated with either the lender or the SBA — are not eligible.

Secondary Loan Programs

Although the 7(a) Regular Loan Guarantee Program makes up 90% of all SBA loans, other SBA loans are available to you. Even though the following list of SBA loan programs are not eligible under the PLP or CLP, these specialized programs can be used for specific lending situations. Note that these programs are listed by the least amount of available funds to the maximum amount and include:

- Microloans
- Small Loans
- Fast-Track Loans
- LowDoc Loans
- Contract Loans
- Small General Contractor Loans
- Seasonal Lines of Credit
- Pollution Control Loans
- Handicapped Assistance Loans
- Small Business Energy Loans
- Export Working Capital Loans
- International Trade Loans
- CAPLines Short-Term Working Capital Lines of Credit

For the purpose of this book, these programs are called secondary programs. On the following pages, you will find a brief description of each program with regard to available amounts, loan purpose, type of financing, eligibility, uses, use restrictions, terms, interest rate, collateral, and application process. Check to see if any of the following secondary programs apply to your business.

Microloans

Amount:	From $100 to $25,000
Purpose:	Microloans provide financing for emerging and growing small businesses unable to obtain credit through conventional sources. A microloan can be for a part-time business or one operated from your home.
Type of Financing:	Loans should be repaid in the shortest term possible and cannot exceed six years.
Eligibility:	Varies. Contact the lender nearest you.
Uses:	Start-up and operating capital.
Use Restrictions:	Varies by lender.
Terms:	One to six years, depending on the specific need.

Interest Rate:	Varies, depending on loan structure and level of funding.
Collateral:	Varies according to lender; however, liens must be placed on any assets bought with the microloan.
Application Process:	Contact the nearest lender for details. (See Appendix D for a complete list.)

Small Loan Program

Amount:	Up to $50,000
Purpose:	SBA started the Small Loan Program to meet the ever-growing need for loans of $50,000 or less.
Type of Financing:	SBA guaranteed loans.
Eligibility:	A business must be independently owned, operated for profit, and not dominant in its field. This program also applies to businesses unable to obtain private financing on reasonable terms, but that have a good chance of succeeding.
Uses:	Working capital or to purchase fixed assets.
Use Restrictions:	Loans may not be used for debt payments.
Terms:	Usually five to seven years for working capital loans.
Interest Rate:	For loans of less than $25,000 with original maturities of less than seven years, the maximum allowable rate cannot exceed 4.25% over the lowest prime rate. For loans of less than $25,000 with original maturities of seven years or more, the maximum allowable rate cannot exceed 4.75% over the prime rate. For loans between $25,000 and $50,000, the maximum interest rate is at least 1 percentage point lower than those stated above (3.25% and 3.75%).
Collateral:	Considered on a case-by-case basis.
Application Process:	See a sample of *SBA Form 4, Application for Small Business Loan (Short Form)*, located at the end of this chapter for complete instructions.

Fast-Track Loan Program

Amount:	Up to $100,000
Purpose:	The Fast-Track Loan Program is for small businesses needing up to $100,000.
Type of Financing:	Intermediate and long-term financing for working capital and fixed assets.

	Eligibility:	Must meet the SBA's size and policy standards.
	Uses:	Start-up and operating capital.
	Use Restrictions:	Only selected lenders have authority to approve these loans. Check with the SBA office nearest you for an available lender.
	Terms:	The SBA guarantee cannot exceed 50%.
	Interest Rate:	Pegged at up to 2.25% over the lowest prime rate for loans of seven years or less. Loans for more than seven years have a 2.75% rate. Interest rates may be fixed or variable.
	Collateral:	Varies according to lender.
	Application Process:	If your lender is in this program and decides to grant your loan, it will fax the necessary information to a central SBA loan processing center. The center will review your application for eligibility and provide a loan number within one business day. Your lender can use its own application and necessary loan documentation.

LowDoc Loan Program

Amount:	Up to $100,000
Purpose:	A Low Documentation (LowDoc) Loan Guarantee Program is available for business loans of $100,000 or less. This program is designed to reduce the paperwork involved in the SBA loan programs for smaller loan requests. LowDoc simplifies the application process and provides a rapid response from the SBA — usually only two or three days. LowDoc focuses on character, credit, and experience.
Type of Financing:	Intermediate and long-term financing for working capital and fixed assets.
Eligibility:	Eligible candidates include: • Entrepreneurs starting a new business. • Businesses whose average annual sales for the preceding three years do not exceed $5 million and have 100 or fewer employees, including affiliates. • Businesses that satisfy other statutory criteria.
Uses:	Start-up and operating capital.
Use Restrictions:	Determined by financial institution.

Terms:	Term may not exceed 25 years for real estate, 15 years for all other uses, and 7 years for working capital.
	All loans must be adequately secured, but loans generally are not declined where inadequate collateral is the only unfavorable factor.
	Normally, business assets are pledged, and occasionally, personal assets are pledged.
	Personal guarantees of the principals are required.
Interest Rate:	For loans of less than seven years, up to 2.25% over the prime rate.
	For loans of seven years or more, up to 2.75% over the prime rate.
	Loans under $50,000 may be subject to slightly higher rates.
Collateral:	Varies according to lender.
Application Process:	Complete the front page of *SBA Form 4-L, Application for Business Loan (Up to $100,000)*; lender completes the back page of *Form 4-L*. A sample of this form is located at the end of this chapter. Lender may require additional information depending on bank policy. For loans of more than $50,000, the bank must provide the SBA with:

- A copy of U.S. Income Tax Schedule C or the front page of the corporate or partnership returns for the past three years;
- Personal financial statements and credit reports for all guarantors; and
- An internal bank analysis, cash flow, and pro forma balance sheets.

Contract Loan Program

Amount:	Up to $750,000
Purpose:	The Contract Loan Program is available to assist in the short-term financing of the labor and material costs of a specific, assignable contract.
Type of Financing:	Line of credit loans.
Eligibility:	A business must be for-profit and must qualify as small under SBA's standard size criteria.

In addition, the business must have been in continuous operation for twelve months immediately preceding the application date.

Contractors and subcontractors in the construction, manufacturing, and service industries may apply.

Applicants must provide a specific product or service under an assignable contract; this program is designed to provide the funds necessary to perform on such contracts.

Uses:	Costs of labor and materials needed to perform a specific contract.
Use Restrictions:	The program is not intended to provide money to finance receivables or inventory on-hand.
Terms:	Loan maturity may not exceed 12 months from the date of disbursement, except in cases of large contracts that may go up to 18 months. Any request for longer periods require special approval from the SBA.

The business must be current on payroll and operate a depository plan for the payment of future withholding taxes. This protects the SBA and the lender from the Federal Tax Lien of 1966, which holds lenders liable for unpaid income taxes when loan proceeds are used for payroll purposes.

Interest Rate:	Pegged at up to 2.25% over the lowest prime rate for loans of seven years or less. Loans for more than seven years have a 2.75% rate. Interest rates may be fixed or variable.
Collateral:	Assignment of contract proceeds, including pledge of company assets, outside assets, and personal guarantees.
Application Process:	Applicant applies to the lender before or after a contract has been received; however, detailed information on the bid or contract must be available at the time of the application.

Applicants must submit a projected cash flow for all business operations over the term of the contract and the loan. The cash flow must provide for anticipated needs, as well as fixed obligations. You are required to use *SBA Form 74B* when applying for a contract loan.

Small General Contractor Loan Program

Amount: Up to $750,000

Purpose: You can get a loan through the Small General Contractor Loan Program to finance the construction or renovation of residential and commercial buildings that will be offered for sale.

Type of Financing: Loan guaranty.

Eligibility: Construction contractors and homebuilders must have already demonstrated the managerial and technical ability to build or renovate projects comparable in size to those for which they are seeking SBA financing.

Uses: Loan proceeds can be used only for direct expenses for the building project.

Renovations must be "prompt and significant" to be eligible. Construction must begin within a reasonable time after loan approval. The renovation is considered "significant" if the cost meets or exceeds one-third of the purchase price of the property.

Use Restrictions: Not more than 5% of the loan can be used for streets, curbs, and other developmental costs that benefit properties other than the one being built or rehabilitated.

Terms: Principal repayment will be required in a single payment when the project is sold or within 36 months after completion, whichever occurs first.

Interest Rate: Pegged at up to 2.25% over the lowest prime rate for loans of seven years or less. Loans for more than seven years have a 2.75% rate. Interest rates may be fixed or variable.

Interest payments, however, are required at least twice a year and must be paid from the applicant's own resources, not from loan proceeds.

Collateral: Collateral must, at a minimum, include a second on the property to be constructed or renovated, and may include a pledge of outside assets and personal guarantees.

Application Process: To apply, you will need to submit several documents, including:

- History of the business, including the purpose of the loan.

- Financial statements for three years (balance sheets and income statements) for an existing business.
- Schedule of term debts (for existing businesses).
- Aging of accounts receivable and payable.
- Amount you have invested in the business.
- Projections of income, expenses, and cash flow.
- Signed personal financial statements and resumés.

Also, you must submit three letters, including:

- A letter from a mortgage lender doing business in the area affirming that permanent mortgage financing for qualified purchasers of comparable real estate is normally available in the project area.
- A letter from an independently-licensed real estate broker with three years of experience in the project area. The letter must state whether a market for the proposed structure exists and whether it is compatible with other buildings in the neighborhood.
- A letter from an independent architect, appraiser or engineer, confirming availability of construction inspection and certification at intervals during the project. The writer of this letter cannot be affiliated with the applicant in any way.

Seasonal Line of Credit Program

Amount: Up to $750,000

Purpose: The Seasonal Line of Credit Program offers short-term, guaranteed loans to help small businesses get past cash crunches attributable to seasonal changes in business volume.

Type of Financing: Short-term guaranteed loans.

Eligibility: To be eligible, your business must:

- Have been in operation for the preceding twelve months;
- Have a definite pattern of seasonal activity; and
- Meet the SBA's size and policy standards.

Keep in mind, loans cannot be made to businesses engaged in speculation or investment in rental real estate.

Uses:	Loans may be used for working capital or to purchase fixed assets. For example, the loan can be used to finance increases in trading assets, such as receivables and inventory, required as a result of seasonal upswings in business.
Use Restrictions:	The loan amount cannot exceed the amount necessary to overcome working capital deficiencies arising from the seasonal swings in business activity.
Terms:	With the exception of agricultural enterprises, only one seasonal line of credit may be outstanding at any time, and each loan must be followed by an out-of-debt period of at least 30 days. Further, the loan must be structured to be repaid from the company's cash flow in the shortest possible time.
Interest Rate:	Pegged at up to 2.25% over the lowest prime rate for loans of less than seven years.
Collateral:	Primarily, liens on all inventory and accounts receivable are needed. Additional collateral, including the pledge of outside assets and personal guarantees, may also be required.
Application Process:	You are asked to state the reason you need the loan and, depending on your situation, will need to include:

- History of your business;
- Financial statements for three years (balance sheets and income statements) for existing businesses;
- Schedule of term debt (for existing businesses);
- Aging of accounts receivable and payable (for existing businesses);
- Lease details (if applicable);
- Amount you have invested in the business along with personal resumés;
- Projections of income, expenses, and cash flow; and
- Signed personal financial statements.

Pollution Control Loan Program

Amount:	Up to $1,000,000
Purpose:	The Pollution Control Loan Program is designed to assist in the planning, design, or installation a "pollution control facility" for the applicant's own business.

Type of Financing: Loan guaranty.

Eligibility: Eligible businesses must be for-profit operations and must meet the SBA's size and policy standards.

Uses: Must be used to finance the planning, design, or installation of a "pollution control facility" only. Such a facility is defined as:

- Real or personal property that is likely to help prevent, reduce, abate, or control noise, air or water pollution, or contamination by removing, altering, disposing, or storing pollutants, contaminants, wastes, or heat; or
- Any related recycling property that a local, state, or federal environmental regulatory agency says will be useful for pollution control.

Terms: The SBA determines whether your business can repay the loan by evaluating whether it can generate sufficient cash flow to meet repayment obligations and the other fixed obligations of the business.

Loan maturity depends upon your ability to repay, subject to prudent lending practices and agency maximums.

Machinery and equipment cannot be financed for periods longer than their conservative economic life.

Real estate and construction loans may not exceed 25 years.

Interest Rate: Pegged at up to 2.25% over the lowest prime rate for loans of seven years or less. For loans of more than seven years, the rate is 2.75%. Interest rates may be fixed or variable.

Collateral: Primary collateral will be all inventory and accounts receivable. You may be asked to pledge outside assets and personal guarantees as well.

Application Process: To apply, you will need to state the purpose of the loan and include:

- History of your business;
- Financial statements for three years (balance sheet and income statements) for existing businesses;
- Schedule of term debts (for existing businesses);
- Aging of accounts receivable and payable;

- Lease details (if applicable);
- Amount of your investment in the business;
- Projections of income, expenses, and cash flow;
- Signed personal financial statements; and
- Personal resumés.

Handicapped Assistance Loan Program

Amount: Up to $750,000

Purpose: The Handicapped Assistance Loan (HAL) Program is available for disabled individuals and public or private nonprofit organizations for the employment of the disabled who can get financing for starting, acquiring, or operating a small business. For the purpose of this loan program, a handicapped individual is a person who has a permanent physical, mental or emotional impairment, defect, ailment, disease, or major disability. Two types of handicapped assistance loans exist — HAL-1 loans and HAL-2 loans. HAL-1 loans are for public or private nonprofit organizations. HAL-2 loans are for disabled individuals only.

Type of Financing: Guaranty loans. Also, direct loans limited to $150,000.

Eligibility: To be eligible for a loan for your public or private nonprofit organization (HAL-1), your business must meet the following criteria:

- Financial assistance is available to state and federally chartered organizations that employ disabled individuals.
- Nonprofit organizations must have the capability and experience to successfully produce or provide marketable goods and services.
- An evaluation of the experience, competency, and ability of the owners and operators of the small business must indicate that they can operate it successfully and can repay the loan from business earnings.
- Eligibility rules specify that the applying organization's net income cannot benefit any stockholder or other individual, and that at least 75% of the direct work involved must be done by disabled persons.

- Applicants must provide evidence that the business is operated in the interest of disabled individuals. The evidence may consist of copies of by-laws, incorporation papers, a certification of tax-exempt status as determined by the Internal Revenue Service, or recognition and approval by the U.S. Secretary of Labor or a state vocational rehabilitation agency.

To be eligible for loans under the HAL-2 program, disabled individuals must provide evidence that:

- Their business is a for-profit operation and qualifies as small under the SBA's size standard criteria;
- The business is 100% owned by one or more disabled individuals;
- Their disability keeps them from competing on a par with non-disabled competitors; and
- The disabled owner(s) actively participate in managing the business.

Applications that propose absentee ownership are not eligible.

Uses: HAL-2 loan proceeds may be used for most business purposes, such as starting, acquiring, or operating a small business.

Use Restrictions: Loans cannot be made to businesses engaged in speculation or investment in rental real estate.

Direct loans will not be provided if a guaranteed loan is available.

The SBA will not provide financial assistance if funds are otherwise available from the applicant's own resources, from a private lending institution, or through another government agency.

HAL-1 loan proceeds may not be used for supportive service expenses, such as subsidized wages of low producers, health and rehabilitation services, management, training, education, and housing of disabled workers and other such uses.

Terms: The loan maturity depends on the business' ability to repay, subject to the requirements of prudent lending practices and the SBA's regulatory maximums.

Machinery and equipment cannot be financed for periods longer than their conservative economic life.

Real estate and construction loan maturities generally cannot exceed 25 years.

Working capital maturities generally cannot exceed seven years.

Collateral: Collateral is required to the extent that it is available and sufficiently valuable to secure the loan.

Interest Rate: Interest rates on direct loans are 3% per year; interest rates on guaranteed loans are set by the lender and must be within the SBA's guidelines.

Application Process: To apply, you will need to provide your lender with the:

- Purpose of the loan;
- History of your business;
- Financial statements for three years (balance sheet and income statements) for existing businesses;
- Schedule of term debts (for existing businesses);
- Aging of accounts receivable and payable (for existing businesses);
- Lease details (if applicable);
- Amount of your investment in the business;
- Projections of income, expenses, and cash flow;
- Signed personal financial statements; and
- Personal resumés.

Small Business Energy Loan Program

Amount: Up to $750,000

Purpose: Financing is available for small businesses engaged in ways to conserve the nation's energy resources through the Small Business Energy Loan Program.

Type of Financing: Loan guaranty.

Eligibility: Small businesses engaged in the following energy production or conservation activities are eligible:

- Wind energy conversion equipment;
- Solar thermal energy equipment;
- Photovoltaic cells and related equipment;

- Hydroelectric power equipment;
- Equipment primarily used to produce energy from wood, biological waste, grain, or other bio-mass sources;
- Equipment for industrial cogeneration of energy, heating, or production of energy from industrial waste; or
- Products or services that use devices that increase the energy efficiency of existing equipment, or improve operation of systems that use fossil fuels and are on the *Energy Conservation Measures List* of the U.S. Secretary of Energy or approved by the SBA. These include insulation procedures and procedures involving heating, cooling, and lighting in residential, commercial, and industrial buildings.

Uses: Financing is available for small businesses engaged in engineering, manufacturing, distributing, marketing, installing, or servicing products or services designed to conserve energy resources. Loans can also be used to buy land for plant construction; convert or expand existing facilities; purchase machinery, equipment, furniture, fixtures, facilities, supplies and materials; or provide working capital for entry or expansion into eligible conservation project areas.

Further, up to 30% of loan proceeds can be used for research and development if a business plan shows strong repayment ability, or when a product or service already being marketed needs further development.

Use Restrictions: Businesses installing or undertaking energy conservation measures in their own plants or offices are not eligible under this program, although they can apply under the SBA's regular business loan program.

Terms: The maximum maturity for fixed assets is 25 years. Maturities for the loans are set according to the borrower's ability to repay and the proposed use of proceeds.

Interest Rate: Same as the 7(a) Regular Loan Guarantee Program.

Collateral: Primary collateral will be all inventory and accounts receivable. You may be asked to pledge outside assets and personal guarantees as well.

Application Process: To apply, you will need to include:

- Purpose of the loan;
- History of your business;
- Financial statements for three years (balance sheet and income statements) for existing businesses;
- Lease details (if applicable);
- Schedule of term debts (for existing businesses);
- Aging of accounts receivable and payable (for existing businesses);
- Amount of investment in the business by the owner;
- Projections of income, expenses, and cash flow;
- Signed personal financial statements; and
- Personal resumés.

Export Working Capital Loan Program

Amount: Up to $833,333

Purpose: The Export Working Capital Loan Program is for small businesses involved in the manufacturing of goods or the purchase of goods or services for export. The program also can be used to support standby letters of credit used as bid bonds, performance bonds, or payment of guarantees to foreign buyers.

Type of Financing: Guaranty loans.

Eligibility: A business is eligible if it is:

- Independently owned and operated for-profit and not dominant in its field; and
- Unable to obtain private financing on reasonable terms, but with a good chance of succeeding.

Uses: A loan can support a single export transaction or multiple transactions on a revolving basis, during the term of the loan.

Use Restrictions: There are no use restrictions on this program.

Terms: Maturity generally does not exceed 12–18 months for a single transaction — depending on the use of proceeds — and 3 years for a revolving line of credit.

Interest Rate: Interest rates are negotiated between the lender and borrower and may be fixed or variable. The SBA does not impose interest rate ceilings or maximum fee limitations on lenders. However, the SBA reviews rates and fees charged to borrowers.

Collateral: In general, collateral must cover 100% of the loan disbursement and may include export inventory, foreign receivables, and assignments of contract and letter of credit proceeds. Personal guarantees by principals who have 20% ownership in a closely held company generally will be required. Other guarantees and export credit insurance may also be required.

Application Process: Submit your application to your lender along with:

- Purpose of the line of credit;
- History of your business;
- Financial statements for three years (balance sheets and income statements) for existing businesses;
- Schedule of term debts (for existing businesses);
- Aging of accounts receivable and payable (for existing businesses);
- Lease details (if applicable);
- Amount of your investment in the business;
- Projections of income, expenses, and cash flow;
- Signed personal history statements; and
- Personal resumés.

If your loan request exceeds the SBA maximum of $833,333, apply directly to the Export-Import Bank's Working Capital Program. For more information, contact:

Business Development
Export-Import Bank of the United States
811 Vermont Avenue NW
Washington, DC 20571
(800) 565-EXIM
FAX (202) 565-3380
(202) 565-3835 (Electronic Bulletin Board)

Refer to Appendix B for more details.

International Trade Loan Program

Amount: Up to $1,250,000

Purpose: The International Trade Loan Program was established for small businesses that are engaged or preparing to engage in international trade, and small businesses adversely affected by competition from imports.

Type of Financing: Loan guaranty.

Eligibility: An applicant's business generally must be operated for-profit and meet the SBA's size standards. Also, an applicant business cannot be engaged in speculation or investment in rental real estate.

Uses: Loans can be used to finance labor and materials for manufacturing or wholesaling for export, to develop foreign markets, or to finance foreign accounts receivable. Foreign business travel and participation in trade shows are also among the eligible uses.

Use Restrictions: There are no use restrictions on this program.

Terms: Maturities cannot exceed 25 years, excluding the working capital portion of the financing. The SBA's maximum share for facilities or equipment loans is $1 million, plus $250,000 for working capital.

Interest Rate: Pegged at up to 2.25% over the lowest prime rate for loans of seven years or less. Loans for more than seven years have a 2.75% rate. Interest rates may be fixed or variable.

Collateral: The SBA requires that a first position on those items financed be taken along with any other security considered appropriate. It must be located in the United States or its territories and possessions.

Application Process: If your small business is eligible, submit a business plan that includes a profit and loss projection and a narrative that substantiates the development of new, or expansion of existing, export markets. Further, you will need to give a narrative explanation and financial statements demonstrating how directly competitive imported items have made an important contribution to a decline in your business' competitive position.

CAPLines Short-Term Working Capital Lines of Credit Program

Amount:	Up to $750,000
Purpose:	To supply capital to cover cyclical, recurring, and short-term financing needs.
Type of Financing:	Under CAPLines, the SBA can provide financial assistance on a guaranteed basis to credit-worthy small businesses needing any of four types of working capital, including seasonal, contract, builder, and asset-based.
Eligibility:	This program has the same guidelines as the SBA 7(a) Regular Loan Guarantee Program. However, a CAPLines loan cannot be processed under CLP or PLP programs.
Uses:	Eligible uses of the financing include operating capital, inventory, and consolidation.
Use Restrictions:	This program was not designed to finance long-term assets, such as real estate, land, and equipment.
Terms:	Maximum maturity is five years.
	Advances can be made at any time before loan maturity.
	The amount advanced against an eligible receivable typically ranges between 70 and 80% of the face value of the pledged receivable.
	Advance rates for inventory typically range between 25 and 50% of either cost or market value, whichever is less.
	For service, contract, and manufacturing businesses, advances generally will not exceed the sum of the cost of material, plus labor.
	Revenues from the cash cycle of a business operation — when inventory is sold, a service is provided, or receivables are collected — will constitute the primary source of repayment.
Collateral:	The CAPLine must be secured by a first lien on the assets being financed, such as inventory, receivables, or contracts.
	Personal guarantees are required. Secondary liens on machinery and equipment, real estate, and personal assets may be required, where necessary.
Interest Rate:	The rate will be negotiated between the borrower and the lender, but may not exceed the prime rate plus 2.25%.

Application Process: Follow the same steps as for the SBA 7(a) Regular Loan Guarantee Program.

Small Business Innovation Research Grants

Under the Small Business Innovation Research (SBIR) Program, agencies of the federal government with the largest research and development budgets are required to set aside a legislated percentage each year for the competitive award of SBIR funding agreements to qualified small business concerns. The SBA has unilateral authority and responsibility for coordinating and monitoring the government-wide activities of the SBIR program and reporting its results annually to Congress.

Currently, ten federal government agencies participate in the SBIR program, including:

- Department of Agriculture
- Department of Commerce
- Department of Defense
- Department of Education
- Department of Energy
- Department of Health & Human Services
- Department of Transportation
- Environmental Protection Agency
- National Aeronautics & Space Nuclear Regulatory Commission
- National Science Foundation

The SBIR program is a competitive federal award system consisting of three key phases.

Phase I is to evaluate the scientific technical merit and feasibility of an idea. Awards are for periods of up to six months in amounts up to $100,000. Only Phase I awardees are eligible for consideration of a Phase II award.

Phase II is to expand on the results and further pursue the development of Phase I. Awards are for periods of up to two years in amounts up to $750,000.

Phase III is for the commercialization of the results of Phase II and requires the use of private sector or non-SBIR federal funding. SBIR funds may not be utilized in Phase III.

To learn more about the SBIR Program, contact:

SBIR
(202) 205-6450
(800) 697-4636 (SBA OnLine Bulletin Board)
FAX (202) 205-7754
Internet: Telnet SBAONLINE.SBA.GOV

SBA Form 4, Application for Small Business Loan (Short-Form): Sample

U.S. Small Business Administration
Application for Small Business Loan
(Short Form)
(May be used for Participation Loans of $50,000 and under)

OMB Approval No. 3245-0016
Expiration Date: 9/30/92

Applicant	Address
Name of Business	Tax I.D. No.
Street Address	Tel. No. (Include A/C) ( )
City / County / State / Zip	No. of Employees (including subsidiaries and affiliates)
Type of Business / Date Business Established	At Time of Application ____
	If Loan is Approved ____
Bank of Business Account and Address	Subsidiaries or Affiliates (Separate from Above) ____
Amount Requested	Show how the proceeds are to be used (round to the nearest hundreds)
Term Requested ___ yrs.	

SAMPLE

The following schedules must be completed and submitted as a part of the loan application. (Applicant's name and address need only be provided once.) <u>ALL SCHEDULES MUST BE SIGNED AND DATED BY THE PERSON SIGNING THIS FORM:</u>

1. Include financial statements of the applicant as listed below: <u>ALL FINANCIAL STATEMENTS MUST BE SIGNED AND DATED.</u>

   a. For an <u>existing</u> business, include yearend financial statements composed of a balance sheet, income statement and reconciliation of net worth for each year in business up to three years. (Federal tax returns may be substituted for income statements.) In addition, submit a balance sheet and income statement for the current period (within 90 days of filing of the application) together with an aging of accounts receivable and payable. A projection of income and expenses for one year after the proposed loan is most helpful and may be requested by SBA.

   b. For a <u>new</u> business, prepare a balance sheet reflecting the assets, liabilities and net worth of the business assuming the loan is approved and disbursed. In addition, provide a projection of income and expenses for one year after the loan is disbursed.

2. List all assets to be pledged as collateral.

   a. For machinery and/or equipment, provide an itemized list that contains identification numbers for all items with an original value greater than $500.

   Collateral lists additionally should contain the year acquired, original cost, present market value, current balance owed, and name of lienholders. Mark this <u>Schedule A</u>. (SBA Form 4, Schedule A, or a computer-generated facsimile, <u>may</u> be used for this purpose.)

3. The following SBA forms must be submitted by each owner (20% or more ownership), partner, or officer:

   a. A current personal financial statement (SBA Form 413 may be used for this purpose),

   b. SBA Form 912, Personal History Statement. (This also may be required of hired managers with authority to commit the applicant.)

4. Please provide the following information (in the order shown below) for all members of management including owners, partners, officers and directors:

   <u>Name</u>, <u>Social Security Number</u>, <u>Position held</u>, <u>Home Address</u>, <u>Percentage Ownership (Total 100%)</u>, *<u>Date of Entry/Discharge from Military Service</u>, *<u>Race</u>, *<u>Sex</u> (*This data is collected for statistical purposes and has no bearing on the credit decision.)

   In addition, provide a brief description of the educational, technical and business background for all people listed under management. Mark this <u>Schedule B</u>.

5. Please supply the following information (in the order shown below) on all the applicant's short-term and long-term debt. Indicate by an asterisk (*) items to be paid by loan proceeds and give reasons for payments.

   <u>Orig. Date</u>, <u>Orig. Amt ($)</u>, <u>Lender</u>, <u>Present Bal ($)</u>, <u>Rate of Int.</u>, <u>Maturity Date</u>, <u>Monthly Pmt ($)</u>, <u>Collateral</u>, <u>Current or Past Due</u>

   (Principal balance shown should agree with the amounts on the latest balance sheet submitted.) Mark this <u>Schedule C</u>.

6. Please sign and date SBA Form 1624 regarding certification of debarment and suspension.

PLEASE NOTE: The estimated burden hours for the completion of SBA Forms 4 (short form) and 4I is 19.5 hours per response. If you have any questions or comments concerning this estimate or any other aspect of this information collection please contact, Chief Administrative Information Branch, U.S. Small Business Administration, Washington, D.C. 20416 and Gary Waxman, Clearance Officer, Paperwork Reduction Project (3245-0016), Office of Management and Budget, Washington, D.C. 20503.

SBA Form 4 (7-91) Short Form

SBA Form 4, Application for Small Business Loan (Short-Form): Sample (continued)

COMPLETE THE FOLLOWING INFORMATION ONLY IF IT APPLIES TO YOUR APPLICATION

7. If you have any co-signers and/or guarantors for this loan, please submit their names, tax identification number, addresses, and personal financial statements. Mark this Schedule E.
8. If you are buying machinery and/or equipment with the loan, you must include a list of the equipment and cost (as quoted by the supplier) and the supplier's name, address and telephone number. Mark this Schedule F.
9. If you, your business, or any of the officers of your business, or have been, involved in pending lawsuits, bankruptcy, insolvency proceedings, please provide the details. Mark this Schedule G.
10. If you or your spouse or any member of your household, or anyone who owns, manages or directs your business or their spouses or members of their households, work for the Small Business Administration, Small Business Advisory Council, SCORE, ACE, any Federal agency, or the participating lender, please provide the name and address of the person and the office where employed. Mark this Schedule H.
11. If the applicant, its owners or majority stockholders own or have a controlling interest in other businesses, please provide their names and the relationship with your company along with the most recent yearend financial statements for each affiliate. Mark this Schedule I.
12. If the applicant buys from, sells to, or uses the services of any concern in which someone in your company has a significant financial interest, please provide details. Mark this Schedule J.
13. If the applicant or any principals or affiliates have ever requested previous SBA or other Government financing, or are delinquent on the repayment of any Federal debt, supply the following information: identify the applicant, name the Government agency, date of request, whether approved or declined, original amount of the loan, present balance, monthly payments, whether current or past due, and purpose of the loan. Mark this Schedule K.
14. If anyone assisted in the preparation of this application other than the applicant please list the name(s), occupation(s), their address(es), total fees paid and fees due. Mark this Schedule L.

FRANCHISE LOANS ONLY

15. If the applicant is a franchise, include a copy of the Franchise Agreement and a copy of the Federal Trade Commission disclosure statement available from the Franchisor (by law). Mark this Schedule M.

FOR CONSTRUCTION AND/OR RENOVATIONS OVER $10,000

16. Include as a separate schedule (schedule N) the estimated cost of the project as well as a statement of the source of any additional funds beyond the loan requested. Mark this Schedule N.
18. Provide copies of preliminary construction plans and specifications. Include them as Schedule O. Final plans will be required prior to disbursements.

EXPORT LOANS ONLY

19. If loan proceeds will be used for exporting, check here_____

TO BE COMPLETED BY ALL APPLICANTS
AGREEMENTS AND CERTIFICATIONS

Agreements of Nonemployment of SBA Personnel: I agree that if SBA approves this loan application, I will not, for at least two years, hire as an employee or consultant anyone that was employed by SBA during the one year period prior to the disbursement of the loan.

Certification: I certify:

(a) I have not paid anyone connected with the Federal government for help in getting this loan. I also agree to report to the SBA Office of Inspector General, Washington, D.C. 20416, any Federal government employee who offers, in return for any type of compensation, to help get this loan approved.
(b) All information in this application and the schedules is true and complete to the best of my knowledge and is submitted to SBA so that SBA can decide whether to grant a loan or to participate with a lending institution in a loan to me. I agree to pay for or reimburse SBA for the cost of any surveys, title or mortgage examinations, appraisals, credit reports, etc., performed by non-SBA personnel provided I have given my consent.
(c) I understand that I need not pay anybody to deal with SBA. I have read and understand Form 159 which explains SBA policy on representatives and their fees.
(d) If I make a statement that I know to be false or if I overvalue a security in order to help obtain a loan under the provisions of the Small Business Act, I can be fined up to $5,000 or be put in jail for up to two years or both.
(e) As consideration for any management, technical, and Business Development Assistance that may be provided, I waive all claims against SBA and its consultants.
(f) I have read and received a copy of the "STATEMENTS REQUIRED BY LAWS AND EXECUTIVE ORDER" which was attached to this application.

If Applicant is a proprietor or general partner, sign below:

By: _____ Dated: _____

If Applicant is a corporation, sign below:

_____ Dated: _____
Corporate Name and Seal

By: _____
Signature of President

Attested by: _____
Signature of Corporate Official

The Proprietor, each General Partner (or Limited Partner owning 20% or more), each Guarantor, each Corporate officer, each Director, each Stockholder owning 20% or more, and, where appropriate, the spouses of each of these must sign. The person signing on behalf of the business must also sign individually.

_____ Date: _____
Signature

_____ Date: _____
Signature

SBA Form 4-L, Application for Business Loan (Up to $100,000): Sample

SBA Form 4-L (6/3/94)

U.S. SMALL BUSINESS ADMINISTRATION
APPLICATION FOR BUSINESS LOAN (UP TO $100,000)
It is not necessary to hire outside assistance for preparation of the application.

Corporate Name (If any) _____
Trade Name & Street Address _____
Home Phone (___) _____
Bus. Phone (___) _____
Ownership in any other business? Yes ___ No ___
#Employees (Including Subsidiaries & Affiliates)
Include Owners & Managers
Before Loan _____ After Loan _____
Bank of Business Account: _____

City _____ County _____ State _____ Zip _____
Mailing Address (if different) _____
Type of Business _____ Date Established _____
IRS Tax ID # _____

SAMPLE

MANAGEMENT (Proprietor, partners, officers, directors owning 20% or more of the company)—Must account for 100% of ownership of the business.

Name	SOCIAL SECURITY #	Complete Address	% Owned	Y/N	*Military Service From / To	*Race	*Sex

*This data is collected for statistical purposes only. It has no bearing on the credit decision to approve or decline this application. Disclosure is voluntary.

U.S. Citizen? Yes ___ No ___ If no, include a copy of Alien Registration Card (Form I 151 or I 551) Alien Registration # _____

Are any of the above individuals (a) presently under indictment, on parole or probation, or have they ever been (b) charged for any criminal offense other than a minor vehicle violation or (c) convicted, placed on pretrial diversion, or placed on any form of probation including adjudication withheld pending probation for any criminal offense other than a minor vehicle violation? Yes ___ No ___ If yes, loan request must be submitted under regular 7(a) loan program.

Have you employed anyone to prepare this application? Yes ___ No ___ If yes, how much have you paid? $_____ How much do you owe? $_____

Have you or any officer of your company ever been involved in bankruptcy or insolvency proceedings? Yes ___ No ___ If yes, provide details to bank.
Are you or your business involved in any pending lawsuits? Yes ___ No ___ If yes, provide details to bank.

DESCRIBE YOUR BUSINESS OPERATION:

IS BUSINESS ENGAGED IN EXPORT TRADE? Yes ___ No ___ DO YOU INTEND TO BEGIN EXPORTING AS A RESULT OF THIS LOAN? Yes ___ No ___

SUMMARY OF MANAGEMENT'S BUSINESS EXPERIENCE, EDUCATION, AND TRAINING:

LOAN REQUEST: HOW MUCH, FOR WHAT, WHY IT IS NEEDED

INDEBTEDNESS: Furnish information on ALL BUSINESS debts, contracts, notes, and mortgages payable. Indicate by an (*) items to be paid with loan proceeds.

To Whom Payable	Original Amount	Original Date	Present Balance	Rate of Interest	Maturity Date	Monthly Payment	Collateral	Current or Past Due
	$		$			$		
	$		$			$		
	$		$			$		
	$		$			$		

PREVIOUS SBA OR OTHER GOVERNMENT FINANCING: If you or any principals or affiliates have ever requested Government Financing complete the following:

Name of Agency	Loan Number	Date Approved	$ Amount	Loan Balance	Status

If you knowingly make a false statement or overvalue a security to obtain a guaranteed loan from SBA you can be fined up to $10,000 or imprisoned for not more than five years or both under 18 USC 1001.

I hereby certify that all information contained in this document and any supporting information provided to the lender or SBA is true and correct to the best of my knowledge.

If applicant is a proprietor or general partner, sign here: By:_____ Title_____ Date_____

If corporation sign below: Corporate Name_____

By:_____ Date:_____ Attested By:_____
Signature of President   Signature of Corporate Secretary

Chapter 5

The Application Case Histories

What the world really needs is more love and less paperwork.

— Pearl Bailey

In this chapter, you will find two samples of properly prepared SBA guaranteed loan application packages. Carefully study these case histories and use them as reference points when applying for your loan. Pay close attention to details and how each applicant submitted the appropriate documentation and correct signatures and dates on each exhibit. Each package is thorough and complete — an excellent example of applications that will avoid loan processing delays.

The first case history is of a new business situation in which John A. Doe is starting a franchise restaurant, Hamburger Delight. As presented in his Statement of Purpose, he is applying for an SBA guaranteed loan in the amount of $128,000 to purchase equipment and inventory, perform renovations to an existing restaurant, and provide cash reserves for the start up. **A New Business**

The second case history is of an existing business, Acme Sheet Metal, owned by two partners, Timothy G. Wilson and John B. Smith. They are applying for an SBA guaranteed loan to acquire new machinery and equipment and to expand their operation by building a new facility. Their required loan amount is $400,000. **An Existing Business**

Each application package begins with a Statement of Purpose, followed by a Table of Contents.

Hamburger Delight: Financing Proposal

Financing proposal for Hamburger Delight – a fast-food restaurant

Statement of Purpose

- I, John A. Doe, am seeking a loan to establish a **Hamburger Delight** restaurant in Anytown, MD.
- Funds of $128,000 are needed to purchase equipment and inventory, perform necessary renovations and improvements, maintain sufficient cash reserves, and provide adequate working capital to successfully operate the restaurant.
- These sums, together with the $44,000 equity invested by me, will be sufficient to finance the transition through the start-up phase so this new business can establish itself as a profitable enterprise.

Signature _John A. Doe_ Date _12-1-xx_

Hamburger Delight: Table of Contents

	Page
Financing proposal for Hamburger Delight — Statement of Purpose	xx

SBA Documents
Application for Business Loan (SBA Form 4)	xx
Personal Financial Statement (SBA Form 413)	xx
Personal History Statement (SBA Form 912)	xx

Exhibits

Exhibit A1:	Sources and Application of Funds	xx
Exhibit A2:	Application and Expected Effect of Loan	xx
Exhibit A3:	Collateral	xx
Exhibit C1:	Balance Sheet	xx
Exhibit C2:	Debts of the Business	xx
Exhibit C3 (a):	Pro Forma Profit & Loss	xx
Exhibit C3 (b):	Pro Forma Cash Flow	xx
Exhibit C4:	Explanation of Profit & Loss and Cash Flow Items	xx
Exhibit D:	Description of the Business	xx
Exhibit E:	Resumés of Management	xx
Exhibit G:	Capital Equipment List	xx
Exhibit M:	Copy of Franchise Agreement	xx
Exhibit T:	Cost of Leasehold Improvements	xx
Exhibit V:	Preliminary Construction Plans	xx
Exhibit W:	Preliminary Copy of Lease	xx
Exhibit Y:	Income Tax Returns	xx
Exhibit Z:	Compensation Agreement	xx
Appendix F:	Letters of Recommendation	xx

Signature _John A. Doe_ Date _12-1-xx_

Note: When you prepare your loan application package, it is wise to identify page numbers for the documents and exhibits you have included. This sample table of contents gives you an idea of how to properly structure and present your material.

OMB Approval No. 3245-0016
Expiration Date: 6-30-94

U.S. Small Business Administration
APPLICATION FOR BUSINESS LOAN

Individual	Full Address
John A. Doe	77 Howard Street, Anytown, MD 00002

Name of Applicant Business	Tax I.D. No. or SSN
Hamburger Delight	01-2345678

Full Street Address of Business	Tel. No. (inc. A/C)
62 Highway #2	(410) 555-1112

City	County	State	Zip	Number of Employees (Including subsidiaries and affiliates)
Anytown	Any	MD	00002	

Type of Business	Date Business Established	
Food/Restaurant	1-1-XX	At Time of Application __0__

Bank of Business Account and Address	
Bank of Anytown 64 Main Street Anytown, MD 00001	If Loan is Approved __8__ Subsidiaries or Affiliates __0__ (Separate from above)

Use of Proceeds: (Enter Gross Dollar Amounts Rounded to the Nearest Hundreds)	Loan Requested		Loan Requested
Land Acquisition	N/A	Payoff SBA Loan	None
New Construction/Expansion Repair	38,000	Payoff Bank Loan (Non SBA Associated)	None
Acquisition and/or repair of Machinery and Equipment	40,000	Other Debt Payment (Non SBA Associated)	None
Inventory Purchase	10,000	All Other	22,000
Working Capital (Including Accounts Payable)	18,000	Total Loan Requested	128,000
Acquisition of Existing Business	N/A	Term of Loan – (Requested Mat.)	7 Yrs.

PREVIOUS SBA OR OTHER FEDERAL GOVERNMENT DEBT: If you or any principals or affiliates have 1) ever requested Government financing or 2) are delinquent on the repayment of any Federal Debt complete the following:

Name of Agency	Original Amount of Loan	Date of Request	Approved or Declined	Balance	Current or Past Due
N/A	$			$	
N/A	$			$	

ASSISTANCE List the name(s) and occupations of any who assisted in the preparation of this form, other than applicant.

Name and Occupation	Address	Total Fees Paid	Fees Due
Carlyle & Vincent, CPAs,	1 Main Street, Anytown, MD	$1,800	-0-
Name and Occupation	Address	Total Fees Paid	Fees Due

PLEASE NOTE: The estimated burden hours for the completion of the form is 19.8 hours per response. If you have any questions or comments concerning this estimate or any other aspect of this information collection please contact Chief Administrative Information Branch, U.S. Small Business Administration, Washington, D.C. 20416 and Gary Waxman, Clearance Officer, Paperwork Reduction Project (3245-0016), Office of Management and Budget, Washington, D.C. 20503.

SBA Form 4 (1-93) Previous Edition is Obsolete

ALL EXHIBITS MUST BE SIGNED AND DATED BY PERSON SIGNING THIS FORM

BUSINESS INDEBTEDNESS: Furnish the following information on all installment debts, contracts, notes, and mortgages payable. Indicate by an asterisk (*) items to be paid by loan proceeds and reason for paying same (present balance should agree with the latest balance sheet submitted).

To Whom Payable	Original Amount	Original Date	Present Balance	Rate of Interest	Maturity Date	Monthly Payment	Security	Current or Past Due
Anytown Bank Acct. # 012759	$10,500	11/XX	$10,324	7%	11/XX	$263	Lien on car	-0-
Anytown Bank Acct. # 012761	$10,000	8/XX	$9,450	7%	8/XX	$239	Lien on car	-0-
Acct. #	$		$			$		
Acct. #	$		$			$		

MANAGEMENT (Proprietor, partners, officers, directors all holders of outstanding stock – <u>100% of ownership must be shown</u>.) Use separate sheet if necessary.

Name and Social Security Number and Position Title	Complete Address	% Owned	*Military Service From	To	*Race	*Sex
John A. Doe 400-11-0000	77 Howard Street Anytown, MD 00002	100	10/XX	12/XX	W	M

*This data is collected for statistical purpose only. It has no bearing on the credit decision to approve or decline this application.

THE FOLLOWING EXHIBITS MUST BE COMPLETED WHERE APPLICABLE. ALL QUESTIONS ANSWERED ARE MADE A PART OF THE APPLICATION.

For Guaranty Loans please provide an original and one copy (Photocopy is Acceptable) of the Application Form, and all Exhibits to the participating lender. For Direct Loans submit one original copy of the application and Exhibits to SBA.

1. Submit SBA Form 912 (Personal History Statement) for each person, e.g., owners, partners, officers, directors, major stockholders, etc.; the instructions are on SBA Form 912.

2. If your collateral consists of (A) Land and Building, (B) Machinery and Equipment, (C) Furniture and Fixtures, (D) Accounts Receivable, (E) Inventory, (F) Other, please provide an itemized list (labeled Exhibit A) that contains serial and identification numbers for all articles that had an original value greater than $500. Include a legal description of Real Estate offered as collateral.

3. Furnish a signed current personal balance sheet (SBA Form 413 may be used for this purpose) for each stockholder (with 20% or greater ownership), partner, officer, and owner. Social Security number should be included on personal financial statement. It should be as of the same date as the most recent business financial statements. Label this Exhibit B.

4. Include the statements listed below: 1,2,3 for the last three years; also 1,2,3,4 as of the same date, which are current within 90 days of filing the application; and statement 5, if applicable. This is Exhibit C (SBA has Management Aids that help in the preparation of financial statements). All information must be **signed and dated**.

1. Balance Sheet   2. Profit and Loss Statement
3. Reconciliation of Net Worth
4. Aging of Accounts Receivable and Payable
5. Earnings projects for at least one year where financial statements for the last three years are unavailable or where requested by District Office.
   (If Profit and Loss Statement is not available, explain why and substitute Federal Income Tax Forms.)

5. Provide a brief history of your company and a paragraph describing the expected benefits it will receive from the loan. Label it Exhibit D.

6. Provide a brief description similar to a resume of the education, technical and business background for all the people listed under Management. Please mark it Exhibit E.

SBA Form 4 (1-93) Previous Edition is Obsolete

ALL EXHIBITS MUST BE SIGNED AND DATED BY PERSON SIGNING THIS FORM

7. Do you have any co-signers and/or guarantors for this loan? If so, please submit their names, addresses, tax Id Numbers, and current personal balance sheet(s) as Exhibit F.

8. Are you buying machinery or equipment with your loan money? If so, you must include a list of equipment and cost as quoted by the seller and his name and address. This is Exhibit G.

9. Have you or any officer of your company ever been involved in bankruptcy or insolvency proceedings? If so, please provide the details as Exhibit H. If none, check here: [ ] Yes [x] No

10. Are you or your business involved in any pending lawsuits? If yes, provide the details as Exhibit I. If none, check here: [ ] Yes [x] No

11. Do you or your spouse or any member of your household, or anyone who owns, manages, or directs your business or their spouses or members of their households work for the Small Business Administration, Small Business Advisory Council, SCORE or ACE, any Federal Agency, or the participating lender? If so, please provide the name and address of the person and the office where employed. Label this Exhibit J. If none, check here: [ ] Yes [x] No

12. Does your business, its owners or majority stockholders own or have a controlling interest in other businesses? If yes, please provide their names and the relationship with your company along with a current balance sheet and operating statement for each. This should be Exhibit K.

13. Do you buy from, sell to, or use the services of any concern in which someone in your company has a significant financial interest? If yes, provide details on a separate sheet of paper labeled Exhibit L.

14. If your business is a franchise, include a copy of the franchise agreement and a copy of the FTC disclosure statement supplied to you by the Franchisor. Please include it as Exhibit M.

CONSTRUCTION LOANS ONLY

15. Include a separate exhibit (Exhibit N) the estimated cost of the project and a statement of the source of any additional funds.

16. Provide copies of preliminary construction plans and specifications. Include them as Exhibit O. Final plans will be required prior to disbursement.

DIRECT LOANS ONLY

17. Include two bank declination letters with your application. (In cities with 200,000 people or less, one letter will be sufficient.) These letters should include the name and telephone number of the persons contacted at the banks, the amount and terms of the loan, the reason for decline and whether or not the bank will participate with SBA.

EXPORT LOANS

18. Does your business presently engage in Export Trade? Check here: [ ] Yes [x] No

19. Do you have plans to begin exporting as a result of this loan? Check here: [ ] Yes [x] No

20. Would you like information on Exporting? Check here: [ ] Yes [x] No

AGREEMENTS AND CERTIFICATIONS

Agreements of non-employment SBA Personnel: I agree that if SBA approves this loan application I will not, for at least two years, hire as an employee or consultant anyone that was employed by the SBA during the one year period prior to the disbursement of the loan.

Certification: I certify: (a) I have not paid anyone connected with the Federal Government for help in getting this loan. I also agree to report to the SBA office of the Inspector General, Washington, D.C. 20416 any Federal Government employee who offers, in return for any type of compensation, to help get this loan approved.

(b) All information in this application and the Exhibits are true and complete to the best of my knowledge and are submitted to SBA so SBA can decide whether to grant a loan or participate with a lending institution in a loan to me. I agree to pay for or reimburse SBA for the cost of any surveys, title or mortgage examinations, appraisals, credit reports, etc., performed by non-SBA personnel provided I have given my consent.

(c) I understand that I need not pay anybody to deal with SBA. I have read and understand SBA Form 159 which explains SBA policy on representatives and their fees.

(d) As consideration for any Management, Technical, and Business Development Assistance that may be provided, I waive all claims against SBA and its consultants.

If you make a statement that you know to be false or if you over value a security in order to help obtain a loan under the provisions of the Small Business Act, you can be fined up to $5,000 or be put in jail for up to two years, or both.

If Applicant is a proprietor or general partner, sign below.

By: *John A. Doe*   12/1/xx
                                                 Date

If Applicant is a Corporation, sign below:

Corporate Name and Seal   Date

By: _____
           Signature of President

Attested by: _____
                 Signature of Corporate Secretary

SBA Form 4 (1-93) Previous Edition is Obsolete

APPLICANT'S CERTIFICATION

By my signature I certify that I have read and received a copy of the "STATEMENTS REQUIRED BY LAW AND EXECUTIVE ORDER" which was attached to this application. My signature represents my agreement to comply with the approval of my loan request and to comply, whenever applicable, with the hazard insurance, lead-based paint, civil rights or other limitations in this notice.

Each Proprietor, each General Partner, each Limited Partner or Stockholder owning 20% or more, and each Guarantor must sign. Each person should sign only once.

Business Name Hamburger Delight

Date	Signature and Title
12/1/xx	By *John A. Doe*

SBA Form 4 (1-93) Previous Edition is Obsolete   • U.S. GOVERNMENT PRINTING OFFICE: 1993 O—347-226   Page 4

96 *The Insider's Guide to Small Business Loans*

U.S. SMALL BUSINESS ADMINISTRATION

OMB Approval No. 3245-0188

PERSONAL FINANCIAL STATEMENT

As of ___Dec. 1___, 19 XX

Complete this form for: (1) each proprietor, or (2) each limited partner who owns 20% or more interest and each general partner, or (3) each stockholder owning 20% or more of voting stock, or (4) any person or entity providing a guaranty on the loan.

Name	John A. & Mary Doe	Business Phone	(410) 555-1112
Residence Address	77 Howard Street	Residence Phone	(410) 111-1313
City, State, & Zip Code	Anytown, MD 00002		
Business Name of Applicant/Borrower	Hamburger Delight		

ASSETS	Omit Cents	LIABILITIES	Omit Cents
Cash on hands & in Banks	$ 2,480	Accounts Payable	$ 1,200
Savings Accounts	$ 44,000	Notes Payable to Banks and Others	$ N/A
IRA or Other Retirement Account	$ N/A	(Describe in Section 2)	
Accounts & Notes Receivable	$ N/A	Installment Account (Auto)	$ 19,774
Life Insurance–Cash Surrender Value Only	$ 16,000	Mo. Payments $	
(Complete Section 8)		Installment Account (other)	$ N/A
Stocks and Bonds	$ 18,000	Mo. Payments $	
(Describe in Section 3)		Loan on Life Insurance	$ N/A
Real Estate	$ 195,000	Mortgages on Real Estate	$ 50,000
(Describe in Section 4)		(Describe in Section 4)	
Automobile–Present Value	$ 28,000	Unpaid taxes	$ N/A
Other Personal Property	$ 15,500	(Describe in Section 6)	
(Describe in Section 5)		Other Liabilities	$ N/A
Other Assets	$	(Describe in Section 7)	
(Describe in Section 5)		Total Liabilities	$ 70,974
		Net Worth	$ 248,006
Total	$ 318,980	Total	$ 318,980

Section 1. Source of Income		Contingent Liabilities	
Salary	$ 45,000	As Endorser or Co-Maker	$ N/A
Net Investment Income	$ 1,800	Legal Claims & Judgments	$ N/A
Real Estate Income	$	Provision for Federal Income tax	$ N/A
Other Income (Describe below)*	$ 17,000	Other Special Debt	$ N/A

Description of Other Income in Section 1.

Wife's salary $17,000 per year

*Alimony or child support payments need not be disclosed in "Other Income" unless it is desired to have such payments counted toward total income.

Section 2. Notes Payable to Bank and Others. (Use attachments if necessary. Each attachment must be identified as part of this statement and signed.)

Name and Address of Noteholder(s)	Original Balance	Current Balance	Payment Amount	Frequency (monthly, etc.)	How Secured or Endorsed Type of Collateral
Anytown Bank, MD 00001	10,500	10,324	263	Monthly	19XX Buick
Anytown Bank, MD 00001	10,000	9,450	239	Monthly	19XX Toyota truck

SBA Form 413 (2-94) Use 5-91 Edition until stock is exhausted. Ref: SOP 50-10 - and 50-30

(tumble)

Section 3. Stocks and Bonds. (Use attachments if necessary. Each attachment must be identified as part of this statement and signed.)

Number of Shares	Name of Securities	Cost	Market Value Quotation/Exchange	Date of Quotation/Exchange	Total Value
80	BRC	3,400	127.50	12/1/XX	10,200
100	NNC Corp.	2,000	78.00	12/1/XX	7,800

Section 4. Real Estate Owned. (List each parcel separately. Use attachments if necessary. Each attachment must be identified as a part of this statement and signed.)

	Property A	Property B	Property C
Type of Property	Personal Home		
Address	John & Mary Doe 77 Howard Street Anytown, MD 00002		
Date Purchased	January 19XX		
Original Cost	$80,000		
Present Market Value	$195,000		
Name & Address of Mortgage Holder	Anytown S&L 14 West Street Anytown, MD 00001		
Mortgage Account Number	590750-8		
Mortgage Balance	$50,000		
Amount of Payment per Month/Year	$514		
Status of Mortgage	Current		

Section 5. Other Personal Property and Other Assets. (Describe, and if any is pledged as security, state name and address of lien holder, amount of lien, terms of payment, and if delinquent, describe delinquency.)

Household Furnishings, Personal Property & Jewelry

Section 6. Unpaid Taxes. (Describe in detail, as to type, to whom payable, when due, amount, and to what property, if any, a tax lien attaches.)

All Taxes are current

Section 7. Other Liabilities. (Describe in detail.)

Automobile notes described on SBA Form 4

Section 8. Life Insurance Held. (Give face amount and cash surrender value of policies – name of insurance company and beneficiaries.)

$100,000 Whole Life with present cash surrender value of $16,000.

I authorize SBA/Lender to make inquiries as necessary to verify the accuracy of the statements made and to determine my creditworthiness. I certify the above and the statements contained in the attachments are true and accurate as of the stated date(s). These statements are made for the purpose of either obtaining a loan or guaranteeing a loan. I understand FALSE statements may result in forfeiture of benefits and possible prosecution by the U.S. Attorney General (Reference 18 U.S.C. 1001).

| Signature | *John A. Doe* | Date: 12/1/XX | Social Security Number 400-11-0000 |
| Signature | *Mary Doe* | Date: 12/1/xx | Social Security Number 987-34-0000 |

PLEASE NOTE: The estimated average burden hours for the completion of this form is 1.5 hours per response. If you have questions or comments concerning this estimate or any other aspect of this information, please contact Chief, Administrative Branch, U.S. Small Business Administration, Washington, D.C. 20416, and Clearance Office, Paper Reduction Project (3245-0188), Office of Management and Budget, Washington, D.C. 20503.

Federal Recycling Program — Printed on Recycled Paper

United States of America
SMALL BUSINESS ADMINISTRATION
STATEMENT OF PERSONAL HISTORY

OMB Approval No.: 3245-0178
Expiration Date: 2-28-97

Return Executed Copies 1, 2, and 3 to SBA

Please Read Carefully — Print or Type
Each member of the small business concern or the development company requesting assistance must submit this form in TRIPLICATE for filing with the SBA application. This form must be filled out and submitted by:
1. If a sole proprietorship by the proprietor.
2. If a partnership by each partner.
3. If a corporation or a development company, by each officer, director, and additionally by each holder of 20% or more of the voting stock.
4. Any other person including a hired manager, who has authority to speak for and commit the borrower in the management of the business.

Name and Address of Applicant (Firm Name)(Street, City, State, and Zip Code)
John Alvin Doe dba Hamburger Delight
62 Highway #2, Anytown, MD 00001

SBA District/Disaster Area Office: Baltimore

Amount Applied for: $128,000

Loan Case No.:

1. Personal Statement of: [State name in full, if no middle name, state (NMN), or if initial only, indicate initial. List all former names used, and dates each name was used. Use separate sheet if necessary.

First	Middle	Last
John	Alvin	Doe

Name and Address of participating bank (when applicable)
Bank of Anytown
64 Main Street
Anytown, MD 00001

2. Date of Birth: (Month, day, and year) 7/22/xx

3. Place of Birth: (City & State or Foreign Country)

1. Give the percentage of ownership or stock owned or to be owned in the small business concern or the Development Company

Social Security No. 400-11-0000

U.S. Citizen? [X] YES [ ] NO
If no, give alien registration number:

5. Present residence Address:
From: 4/19xx To: Present Address: 77 Howard Street, Anytown, MD

Home Telephone No. (Include A/C): (410) 111-1313
Business Telephone No. (Include A/C): (410) 555-1112

Immediate past residence address:
From: 1/19xx To: 4/19xx Address: 42 Way Street, Norwalk, CT

BE SURE TO ANSWER THE NEXT 3 QUESTIONS CORRECTLY BECAUSE THEY ARE IMPORTANT.

THE FACT THAT YOU HAVE AN ARREST OR CONVICTION RECORD WILL NOT NECESSARILY DISQUALIFY YOU. BUT AN INCORRECT ANSWER WILL PROBABLY CAUSE YOUR APPLICATION TO BE TURNED DOWN.

IF YOU ANSWER "YES" TO 6, 7, OR 8, FURNISH DETAILS IN A SEPARATE EXHIBIT. INCLUDE DATES; LOCATION; FINES, SENTENCES, ETC.; WHETHER MISDEMEANOR OR FELONY; DATES OF PAROLE/PROBATION; UNPAID FINES OR PENALTIES; NAMES UNDER WHICH CHARGED; AND ANY OTHER PERTINENT INFORMATION.

6. Are you presently under indictment, on parole or probation?
[ ] Yes [X] No (If yes, indicate date parole or probation is to expire.)

7. Have you ever been charged with or arrested for any criminal offense other than a minor motor vehicle violation? Include offenses which have been dismissed, discharged, or nolle prosequi. (All arrests and charges must be disclosed and explained on an attached sheet.)
[ ] Yes [X] No

8. Have you ever been convicted, placed on pretrial diversion, or placed on any form of probation, including adjudication withheld pending probation, for any criminal offense other than a minor motor vehicle violation?
[ ] Yes [X] No

9. [ ] Fingerprints Waived Date ___ Approving Authority ___
   [ ] Fingerprints Required Date Sent to FBI ___ Date ___ Approving Authority ___

10. [ ] Cleared for Processing Date ___ Approving Authority ___
    [ ] Request a Character Evaluation Date ___ Approving Authority ___

The information on this form will be used in connection with an investigation of your character. Any information you wish to submit that you feel will expedite this investigation should be set forth.

See attached proposal. Letters of recommendation and personal resumé in Exhibits.

CAUTION: Knowingly making a false statement on this form is a violation of Federal law and could result in criminal prosecution, significant civil penalties, and a denial of your loan. A false statement is punishable under 18 USC 1001 by imprisonment of not more than five years and/or a fine of not more than $10,000; under 15 USC 645 by imprisonment of not more than two years and/or a fine of not more than $5,000; and, if submitted to a Federally insured institution, under 18 USC 1014 by imprisonment of not more than twenty years and/or a fine of not more than $1,000,000.

Signature: John Alvin Doe
Title: Applicant
Date: 12/1/xx

It is against SBA's policy to provide assistance to persons not of good character and therefore consideration is given to the qualities and personality traits of a person, favorable and unfavorable, relating thereto, including behavior, integrity, candor and disposition toward criminal actions. It is also against SBA's policy to provide assistance not in the best interests of the United States, for example, if there is reason to believe that the effect of such assistance will be to encourage or support, directly or indirectly, activities inimical to the Security of the United States. Anyone concerned with the collection of this information, as to its voluntariness, disclosure of routine uses may contact the FOIA Office, 409 3rd St. S.W., and a copy of 9 "Agency Collection of Information" from SOP 40 04 will be provided.

SBA Form 912 (12-93) SOP 9020 USE 5-87 EDITION UNTIL EXHAUSTED Copy 1- SAB File Copy

PLEASE NOTE: The estimated burden hours for the completion of this form is 15 minutes per response. If you have any questions or comments concerning this estimate or any other aspect of this information collection please contact, Chief Administrative Information Branch, U.S. Small Business Administration, 409 Third St. S.W. Washington, D.C. 20416 or Gary Waxman, Clearance Officer, Paperwork Reduction Project (3245-0201), Office of Management and Budget, Washington, D.C. 20503.

Federal Recycling Program — Printed on Recycled Paper

Exhibit A1

Hamburger Delight: Sources and Application of Funds

Sources

Term Loan	$128,000
*Owner's Investment	44,000
Total	$172,000

Application

Equipment	$ 40,000
Tables, Chairs, Booths	8,000
Leasehold Improvements	38,000
Decorations	10,000
Franchise Fee	24,000
Inventory	10,000
Deposits and Tax Permit	4,000
Working Capital	38,000
Total	$172,000

*Consists of $44,000 from savings

To Be Secured by
Assets of the Business
Signatures of the Principal and
SBA Guarantee

Signature _John A. Doe_   Date _12-1-xx_

Exhibit A2

Hamburger Delight: Application and Expected Effect of Loan

The $128,000 will be used as follows:

Equipment (see Exhibit G for details)	$ 40,000
Tables, Chairs, Booths	8,000
Leasehold Improvements	38,000
Decorations (antiques, rustic wall decorations)	10,000
Start-Up Inventory	10,000
Deposits and Tax Permit	4,000
Additional Working Capital	18,000
Total	$128,000

Signature _John A. Doe_ Date _12-1-xx_

Exhibit A3

Hamburger Delight: Collateral

Machinery and Equipment (see Exhibit G for details*)	$ 40,000
Tables, Chairs, Booths	8,000
Leasehold Improvements (see Exhibit T for details)	38,000
Decorations (includes antiques and other decorative items)	10,000
Inventory (start-up inventory required)	10,000
Automobile	8,226
Total	$114,226

Owner will make a cash investment to be used as follows:
    $24,000 will be used for the franchise fee
    $20,000 will be used as part of working capital

*Identification numbers for articles costing more than $500 may not be available at time application is presented to lender, but may be supplied later.

Signature _John A. Doe_ Date _12-1-xx_

Exhibit C1

Hamburger Delight: Balance Sheet (First Day of Operations)

Assets		**Liabilities**	
Cash	$ 38,000	Term Loan	$128,000
Inventory	10,000		
Decorative Items	10,000		
Tables, Chairs, Booths	8,000		
Automobile	28,000	Automobile Notes	19,774
Leasehold Improvements	38,000	Total Liabilities	147,774
Equipment	40,000	Net Worth	52,226
Deposits and Tax Permits	4,000		
Franchise Rights	24,000		
TOTAL ASSETS	$200,000	TOTAL LIABILITIES	$200,000

Signature _John A. Doe_ Date _12-1-XX_

Exhibit C2

Hamburger Delight: Debts of the Business

Hamburger Delight, when it is established, will have no outstanding business loans other than the loan that this application is for. Hamburger Delight will, however, assume the note for the car that the owner is putting into the business. Details concerning this note are as follows:

19XX Buick Century

Original Date	11/XX
Cost	15,000
Down Payment and Trade In	4,500
Present Balance Owed	10,324
Interest Rate	7%
Monthly Payment	263
Maturity Date	11/XX

19XX Toyota Truck

Original Date	8/XX
Cost	13,000
Down Payment and Trade In	3,000
Present Balance Owed	9,450
Interest Rate	7%
Monthly Payment	239
Maturity Date	8/XX

Signature _John A. Doe_   Date _12-1-XX_

Exhibit C3 (a)

Hamburger Delight: Pro Forma Profit & Loss

JOHN A. DOE – HAMBURGER DELIGHT
Income Projection – January through December 19XX

	January	February	March	April	May
TOTAL SALES	30,000	36,000	36,000	38,000	40,000
Cost of Sales	7,500	9,000	9,000	9,500	10,000
GROSS MARGIN	22,500	27,000	27,000	28,500	30,000
Operating Expenses					
Wages	2,000	2,600	2,600	2,800	3,000
Salaries	3,000	3,300	3,300	3,400	3,500
Payroll Taxes	400	472	472	496	520
Rent	2,000	2,000	2,000	2,000	2,000
Maintenance	480	480	480	480	480
Utilities (Budgeted)	1,600	1,600	1,600	1,600	1,600
Laundry	200	200	200	200	480
Car & Truck	900	900	900	900	900
Advertising	800	800	800	800	800
Insurance	500	500	500	500	500
Legal & Accounting	500	500	500	500	500
Licenses	25	25	25	25	25
Franchise Fee (5%)	1,500	1,800	1,800	1,900	2,000
Depreciation	8,000	8,000	8,000	8,000	8,000
Miscellaneous	500	500	500	500	500
Total Operating Expenses	22,405	23,677	23,677	24,101	24,805
Interest on $128,000 Loan at 8.5% for 7 Yrs.	907	907	907	907	907
TOTAL ALL EXPENSES	23,312	24,584	24,584	25,008	25,712
PROFIT BEFORE INCOME	(812)	2,416	2,416	3,492	4,288

SIGNATURE _John A. Doe_   DATE _12/1/xx_

June	July	August	September	October	November	December	Total
40,000	36,000	36,000	40,000	42,000	42,000	40,000	456,000
10,000	9,000	9,000	10,000	10,500	10,500	10,000	114,000
30,000	27,000	27,000	30,000	31,500	31,500	30,000	342,000
3,000	2,600	2,600	3,000	3,200	3,200	3,000	33,600
3,500	3,300	3,300	3,500	3,600	3,600	3,500	40,800
520	472	472	520	544	544	520	5,952
2,000	2,000	2,000	2,000	2,000	2,000	322	22,322
480	480	480	480	480	480	480	5,760
1,600	1,600	1,600	1,600	1,600	1,600	1,600	19,200
200	200	200	200	200	200	200	2,680
900	900	900	900	900	900	900	10,800
800	800	800	800	800	800	800	9,600
800	800	800	800	800	800	800	8,100
500	500	500	500	500	500	500	6,000
25	25	25	25	25	25	25	300
2,000	1,800	1,800	2,000	2,100	2,100	2,000	22,800
8,000	8,000	8,000	8,000	8,000	8,000	8,000	96,000
500	500	500	500	500	500	500	6,000
24,825	23,977	23,977	24,825	25,249	25,249	23,147	289,914
907	907	907	907	907	907	907	10,884
25,732	24,884	24,884	25,732	26,156	26,156	24,054	300,798
4,268	2,116	2,116	4,268	5,344	5,344	5,946	41,202

Exhibit C3 (b)

Hamburger Delight: Pro Forma Cash Flow

JOHN A. DOE – HAMBURGER DELIGHT
January through December 19XX

	January	February	March	April	May
Receipts from Sales	30,000	36,000	36,000	38,000	40,000
Cash Disbursements					
Cost of Sales	7,500	9,000	9,000	9,500	10,000
Operating Expenses					
Wages	2,000	2,600	2,600	2,800	3,000
Salaries	3,000	3,300	3,300	3,400	3,500
Payroll Taxes	400	472	472	496	520
Rent	2,000	2,000	2,000	2,000	2,000
Maintenance	480	480	480	480	480
Utilities	1,600	1,600	1,600	1,600	1,600
Laundry	200	200	200	200	480
Car & Truck	900	900	900	900	900
Advertising	800	800	800	800	800
Insurance	500	500	500	500	500
Legal & Accounting	500	500	500	500	500
Licenses	25	25	25	25	25
Franchise Fee (5%)	1,500	1,800	1,800	1,900	2,000
Miscellaneous	500	500	500	500	500
Total Operating Expenses	21,905	24,677	24,677	25,601	26,805
Loan Repayment					
$128,000 at 8.5% for 7 Yrs.	2,028	2,028	2,028	2,028	2,028
Total All Disbursements	23,933	26,705	26,705	27,629	28,833
Net Cash Flow	6,067	9,295	9,295	10,371	11,167

SIGNATURE *John A. Doe*   DATE 12/1/xx

June	July	August	September	October	November	December	Total
40,000	36,000	36,000	40,000	42,000	42,000	40,000	456,000
10,000	9,000	9,000	10,000	10,500	10,500	10,000	114,000
3,000	2,600	2,600	3,000	3,200	3,200	3,000	33,600
3,500	3,300	3,300	3,500	3,600	3,600	3,500	40,800
520	472	472	520	544	544	520	5,952
2,000	2,000	2,000	2,000	2,000	2,000	322	22,322
480	480	480	480	480	480	480	5,760
1,600	1,600	1,600	1,600	1,600	1,600	1,600	19,200
200	200	200	200	200	200	200	2,680
900	900	900	900	900	900	900	10,800
800	800	800	800	800	800	800	9,600
800	800	800	800	800	800	800	8,100
500	500	500	500	500	500	500	6,000
25	25	25	25	25	25	25	300
2,000	1,800	1,800	2,000	2,100	2,100	2,000	22,800
500	500	500	500	500	500	500	6,000
26,825	24,977	24,977	26,825	27,749	25,749	25,147	307,914
2,028	2,028	2,028	2,028	2,028	2,028	2,028	24,336
28,853	27,005	27,005	28,853	29,777	29,777	27,175	332,250
11,147	8,995	8,995	11,147	12,223	12,223	12,825	123,750

> **Exhibit C4**

Hamburger Delight: Explanation of Profit & Loss and Cash Flow Items

Receipts from Sales
Most of the business will be handled on a cash basis; however, financial statements and tax returns will be prepared on an accrual basis because we will have some inventories and we may also have some accounts payable. Sales figures are an extremely conservative estimate based on the actual first-year performance of the fast-food restaurant in Troy.

Cost of Goods Sold
Approximately 25% of total sales. Includes the cost of paper goods associated with sales.

Wages
Starting at $2,000, can be expected to increase with sales volume at a rate of about 10% of sales.

Salaries
Owner will take a base of $3,000 a month plus bonus of 5% of gross sales of more than $30,000.

Payroll Taxes
FICA, Medicare, and Unemployment.

Rent
Rent of structure in Anytown.

Maintenance
Based on actual operation of the restaurant in Troy.

Utilities
Gas, water, electricity, and telephone.

Laundry
Aprons, towels, miscellaneous.

Car and Truck Expense
Payment on car note, gas, insurance and maintenance.

Advertising
Local radio and newspaper spots and flyers.

Insurance
Workers' compensation, liability, and fire and extended coverage of building and equipment.

Legal and Accounting
Monthly profit and loss, quarterly reports, and annual audit.

Licenses
Required by state and municipality.

Franchise Fee
5% of total sales.

Depreciation
Equipment, car and truck

Miscellaneous
Operating expense too small to itemize.

Interest (Loan)
$128,000 at 8.5% for 7 years.

Signature _John A. Doe_   Date _12-1-XX_

Exhibit D (page 1)

Hamburger Delight: Description of the Business

Hamburger Delight, to be established in Anytown, MD, in the form of a sole proprietorship, will be a fast-food restaurant serving a variety of specialty and gourmet hamburgers. It will serve a full range of entrées, including six separate types of hamburgers, french fries, soft drinks, salads, and a variety of desserts. The cost per portion will be somewhat less than that of similar operations.

Hamburger Delight will operate with a unique concept in food merchandising — while the customer prepares his/her own salad and dessert, the restaurant employees will prepare the hamburgers and french fries. Patrons will dine in a nostalgic atmosphere reminiscent of the 1950s, with friendly decor.

Hamburger Delight will operate under a franchise agreement granted by the King Organization based in Westport, CT, and will be open six days a week from 10:30 AM to 8:00 PM — later if business justifies it. The noon lunch and evening meals will be the busiest times. The business will be located next to an industrial park and apartment complex on Highway #2. As a franchisee, the business will be able to draw upon the knowledge and experience of the King Organization's operations in Troy, where Mrs. Doe worked.

Similar operations in two Maryland cities — Annapolis and Columbia — have been observed and several articles on the subject are included as exhibits. We believe that the potential is excellent.

The Market

Hamburger Delight will provide a healthy and relatively low-priced meal to a potential market of 52,000 people. At the present time there are 1,300 employees working in the industrial park who either bring their lunch, drive three miles to town, or deal with lunch wagons. We plan to circulate our menu with our fax number and will offer delivery for orders of $20 or more. We also will have a drive-up window. Because of the uniqueness of the business, it can expect to draw customers from other areas in Montgomery County, with a population of 225,000. The food fare, consisting of gourmet hamburgers, french fries, salads, and desserts served with soft drinks, tea, and coffee will average approximately $7.25 per meal.

Exhibit D (page 2)

Hamburger Delight: Description of the Business

Management

I, John A. Doe, the franchisee, was born in Norwalk, CT, and moved to Anytown, MD, two years ago. After serving four years in the U.S. Navy, I worked as a specification writer on small electronic parts for a company under contract to the U.S. Department of Defense. I was responsible for contract negotiations and managed 55 people. During this time, I took courses in accounting, EDP, and management.

I left that position to open a direct sales organization in Norwalk, which I ran for four years. I then bought a franchise in the knowledge, communication, and management training business, and later became a partner in a security business. This business was sold at a profit two years later.

Other experience includes being a marketing manager who promoted franchises for the auto aftermarket. I was later a salesperson, district manager, and plant manager for an industrial laundry company in Troy. Most recently I served as National Development Director for Coalridge, Coalridge & Kane, based in Anytown, MD.

My wife, Mrs. Doe, will be active in the day-to-day operations and she will maintain the books; she has had experience in both accounting and restaurant work. Her experience includes working for Hamburger Delight as a manager in Troy. She has also had accounting responsibilities for a Best Foods franchise, as well as a management position for Taco Bell. Currently, she is a homemaker.

Resumés for the two of us are included in the Appendix Section.

Our salaries for the first year will be 10% of gross sales to enable the business to pay off start-up costs.

To augment our skills, we have enlisted the help of Mr. F. E. Smith, a CPA; Ms. K. B. Jones, a lawyer; and Mr. F. X. Brown of Brown Insurance Agency. Other potential resources have been located and consulted with, including the Small Business Development Program of the District and the SCORE Technical Assistance Program under the Small Business Administration.

The major markets will be those people seeking lunches and evening meals. Hamburger Delight's ideal location will make it a convenient lunch alternative for the large number of individuals working in the industrial park and in the nearby town as well as those living in the apartments. There are 300 units in the Anytown Apartments. Also, its position on Highway #2, which has high traffic volume, will make it accessible for the evening meal crowd.

Exhibit D (page 3)

Hamburger Delight: Description of the Business

Customers will be attracted by: (1) a local radio and newspaper advertising campaign; (2) word-of-mouth advertising from customers; (3) the visible location opposite the main gate to the Anytown Industrial Park, as well as the location on busy Highway #2; and (4) directly approaching employers and employees with our menu and fax number and offering delivery service.

Competition

Currently Hamburger Delight does not have major competition, with the exception of mobile lunch trucks. There are, of course, other eating establishments, but they are located three miles away. For the most part they are older businesses offering a standard menu and need refurbishing. This situation can be viewed as beneficial since it will draw individuals looking for meals to my location.

Location

Hamburger Delight will lease a building at 64 Highway #2 in Anytown, MD, for $2,000 per month with an option to buy. This one-story building with 1,500 sq. ft. will be renovated to fit the needs of a restaurant. It is situated on a 75' x 233' lot that will be adequate for parking 40 or more cars. The area is zoned for commercial use. We will undertake leasehold improvements, including new siding and redecorating the interior. The building is divided into: (1) three dining rooms plus a patio for outdoor dining — total seating is approximately 80; (2) a room to prepare the food; (3) a kitchen that will house the equipment listed in the Capital Equipment List, Exhibit G; (4) two bathrooms; and (5) adequate storage space. See diagram included in Exhibit V.

Mr. King, the franchisor, with many years of experience in the industry, will be providing ongoing management review, assisting in start-up and cash control, and consulting in the areas of promotion and food preparation. Other resources we will utilize include the Anytown Chamber of Commerce, and the National Restaurant Association.

Personnel

Hamburger Delight will initially require part-time personnel and include: (1) a cashier and drink server for the lunch and evening shifts; (2) a utility person to clean up and make deliveries during the lunch and evening shifts; and (3) additional part-time help as needed to provide backup for food preparation and kitchen help. The bulk of the food preparation will be handled by my wife and myself. Employees will be paid $5.00 an hour, and we don't anticipate fringe benefits or overtime.

Signature _John A. Doe_ Date _12-1-xx_

Exhibit D (page 4)

Hamburger Delight: Description of the Business

Application and Expected Effect of Loan

The $128,000 will be used as follows:

Equipment (see Exhibit G for details)	$ 40,000
Table, Chairs, Booths	8,000
Leasehold Improvements	38,000
Decorations (antiques, rustic wall decorations)	10,000
Start-up Inventory	10,000
Deposits and Tax Permit	4,000
Part of Working Capital	18,000
Total	$128,000

Summary

Hamburger Delight will be a fast-food restaurant serving gourmet hamburgers, french fries, salads, and desserts to the community and surrounding areas. I am seeking a $128,000 loan to purchase equipment, perform necessary renovations, maintain cash reserves, and to help provide adequate working capital. This amount will be sufficient to finance transition through the start-up phase so that the business can establish itself as a profitable enterprise.

Careful analysis of the potential market indicates a high concentration of the kinds of individuals who will be patrons of this fast-food restaurant and an unfulfilled need for this kind of operation. My managerial experience ensures that the entire operation will be carefully controlled. My wife's experience in accounting and in running a Hamburger Delight, as well as other fast-food restaurants, along with the assistance offered by Mr. King, the franchisor, will be invaluable to successful day-to-day operations and effective cash control. It should be noted that the Hamburger Delight Franchise is ranked 20th for success by the Franchise Institute of America.

The funds sought will enable my wife and I to establish a Hamburger Delight in Anytown, MD.

Signature _John A. Doe_ Date _12-1-XX_

My wife, Mary Doe, is willing to sign any necessary loan documents.

Signature _Mary Doe_ Date _12/1/XX_

Chapter 5: The Application Case Histories **113**

Exhibit E (page 1)

Hamburger Delight: Resumés of Management

John A. Doe
77 Howard Street
Anytown, MD 00002
(410) 111-1313

PERSONAL: Height 5' 10"; Weight 189

MARITAL STATUS: Married, Two Children

MILITARY: U.S. Navy, Honorable Discharge

SUMMARY: Eighteen months' experience as District Manager. Nine years' experience in marketing, sales, training, supervising, and motivating sales organizations. Five years' experience in a diversified field of engineering and standardization activities encompassing various phases of research, test, and system analysis.

EXPERIENCE: **Coalridge, Coalridge & Kane**
Anytown, MD
January 19XX – present

National Development Director – Responsibilities included contracting and evaluating prospective franchisees of the management and development programs, presenting and explaining the plan to qualifying individuals, and providing aid to those individuals seeking funds to start their new businesses.

February 19XX – December 19XX

District Manager – Responsibilities were to assist in the planning of volume and expense forecast for the fiscal year operating budget, fill workforce requirements and implement training programs. Hire, manage and discharge personnel as required in the operation of the district.

December 19XX – February 19XX

Marketing Manager – Major responsibilities were to locate suitable trade areas and sell the associate jobber program to as many good prospects as possible. This was accomplished by selling the program to new stores or existing store owners. Duties of the associate jobber included explaining and showing the needs of a good inventory control and classification system, keeping expenses in line with sales, and assisting a new store owner in obtaining financial assistance by detailing a budget and projecting a twelve-month profit and loss, then presenting it to his or her banker.

March 19XX – December 19XX

Vice President and Part Owner – Supervising and training of salespeople and installation crews, maintaining inventory and associated activities. Public relations work with local fire and police chiefs.

January 19XX March 19XX

President and Owner – Merchandising. Leadership and motivation programs to individuals and companies. Received six personal sales awards.

January 19XX – March 19XX

President and Owner – Merchandising of home appliances. This distributorship encompassed Columbus and the seven surrounding counties. During this time, my main objective was building a top sales organization utilizing motivation and goal setting.

November 19XX – June 19XX

Project Director and Engineer – Contract with the Air Force and the Defense Electronic Supply Center. Contract was in association with the Federal Standardization Program of electronic components. Duties included supervision, specifications writing, EDP, research, and system analysis.

PERSONAL REFERENCES:

Mr. Peter Williams	Mr. John Roff	Mr. John Hayes
5100 North Street	9506 West Avenue	Old Mill Street
Anytown, MD	Anytown, CT	Anytown, MD

Signature _John A. Doe_   Date _12-1-XX_

Exhibit E (page 2)

Hamburger Delight: Resumés of Management

        Mary Doe
        77 Howard Street
        Anytown, MD 00002
        (410) 111-1313

PERSONAL: Height 5' 5"; Weight 120

MARITAL STATUS: Married, Two Children

SUMMARY: Over the years, my responsibilities have included working with receivables and working on a computer. I have worked with payroll and have handled company cash. I am familiar with word processing and spreadsheet applications. I have a background in fast-food management.

EXPERIENCE: **Hamburger Delight**
Troy
19XX – 19XX
Manager, Hamburger Delight – Responsibilities included hiring, payroll, and inventory control. Attended the Hamburger Delight School of Gourmet Cooking and Management at its national headquarters.

19XX – 19XX
Assistant Manager at Taco Bell in Troy. I also worked for Best Foods as a food preparer.

Signature _Mary Doe_ Date _12/1/xx_

Exhibit G

Hamburger Delight: Capital Equipment List

Major Equipment and Normal Accessories

	Model	List Price
Montague Convection Oven, gas	#115A	$8,000
Montague 6 Burner Range with Oven, gas	#R26-6	2,900
Univex Slicer	#7512	2,000
Univex Power Base with VS9H Shredder	#PB1	1,800
6' s/s Work Table w/Galv. Undershelf and Drawer, 2 @ $600		1,200
4' Work Table w/Galv. Undershelf		600
Sharp Microwave Oven, 650 Watt	#2110	2,000
Continental Double Door Refrigerator 2 @ $3,375	#45-CRA-25	6,750
3 Complete s/s Sink with 2 only 18" x 24" Drainboards		1,000
Duke 6' Refrigerated Salad Bar w/Sneeze Guard, Lights, and Tray Slides	#85CM	5,000
G.E. 3 Drawer Bun Warmer	#CF-031	1,500
Duke 3 Complete Drop-In Steam Table Alum. Spillage Pans for Above, 3 @ $50	#576	150
Wear-Ever Alum. Holding Cart		600
G.E. Hi/Lo Griddle (Sandwiches)	#HG-5	2,000
Table Bases for 30" Tables, 20 @ $100		2,000
24" x 6' Storage Shelves, 5 Tier @ $200		1,000
Capital Equipment Total		$40,000

Note: Before loan application is approved, borrower must submit at least one bid for above items.

Signature _John A. Doe_ Date _12-1-xx_

Exhibits M, T, V, W, & Y

Hamburger Delight: Summary of Other Exhibits

Exhibit M

Franchise Agreement and Copy of FTC Disclosure Statement
(if appropriate)
Must be submitted with application

Exhibit T

Cost of Leasehold Improvements
(break this down)
Must be submitted with application

Exhibit V

Preliminary Construction Plans
(if available)

Exhibit W

Preliminary Copy of Lease

Exhibit Y

Income Tax Returns

1. If you already have an established business, include signed and dated photocopies of the business income tax returns for the last three years. Sign and date the photocopies in ink.
2. If you are delinquent in your taxes, the SBA will not consider the loan.
3. If you are just starting your business, include photocopies of your personal income tax returns for the last three years.
4. **In all cases, remember to sign and date the photocopies of the tax returns.**
5. Existing businesses will have their tax returns checked against the IRS records. Check with your local SBA office for the necessary forms you will need to sign.

Exhibit Z (front)

OMB Approval No 3245-0201

SBA LOAN NUMBER

COMPENSATION AGREEMENT FOR SERVICES IN CONNECTION WITH APPLICATION AND LOAN FROM (OR IN PARTICIPATION WITH) SMALL BUSINESS ADMINISTRATION

The undersigned representative (attorney, accountant, engineer, appraiser, etc.) hereby agrees that the undersigned has not and will not, directly or indirectly, charge or receive any payment in connection with the application for or the making of the loan except for services actually performed on behalf of the Applicant. The undersigned further agrees that the amount of payment for such services shall not exceed an amount deemed reasonable by the SBA (and, if it is a participation loan, by the participating lending institution), and to refund any amount in excess of that deemed reasonable by SBA (and the participating institution). This agreement shall supersede any other agreement covering payment for such services.

A general description of the services performed, or to be performed, by the undersigned and the compensation paid or to be paid are set forth below. <u>If the total compensation in any case exceeds $1,000 (or $300 for: (1) regular business loans of $15,000 or less; or (2) all disaster home loans) or if SBA should otherwise require, the services must be itemized on a schedule attached showing each date services were performed, time spent each day, and description of service rendered on each day listed.</u>

The undersigned Applicant and representative hereby certify that no other fees have been charged or will be charged by the representative in connection with this loan, unless provided for in the loan authorization specifically approved by SBA.

GENERAL DESCRIPTION OF SERVICES

Paid Previously	$	1,800
Additional Amount to be Paid	$	-0-
Total Compensation	$	1,800

(Section 13 of the Small Business Act (15 USC 642) requires disclosures concerning fees. Parts 103, 108 and 120 of Title 13 of the Code of Federal Regulations contain provisions covering appearances and compensation of persons representing SBA applicants. Section 103.13-5 authorizes the suspension or revocation of the privilege of any such person to appear before SBA for charging a fee deemed unreasonable by SBA for services actually performed, charging of unreasonable expenses, or violation of this agreement. Whoever commits any fraud, by false or misleading statement or representation, or by conspiracy, shall be subject to the penalty of any applicable Federal or State statute.)

Dated 11/1, 19 XX

Richard Roe, CPA
(Representative)

By *Richard Roe*

The Applicant hereby certifies to SBA that the above representations, description of services and amounts are correct and satisfactory to Applicant.

Dated 11/2, 19 XX

John A. Doe
(Applicant)

By *John A. Doe*

The participating lending institution hereby certifies that the above representations of service rendered and amounts charged are reasonable and satisfactory to it.

Dated 11/5, 19 XX

Anytown Bank
(Lender)

By *Barbara Brown, Assist. V.P.*

NOTE: Foregoing certification must be executed, if by a corporation, in corporate name by duly authorized officer and duly attested; if by a partnership, in the firm name together with signature of general partner.

PLEASE NOTE: The estimated burden hours for the completion of SBA Form 147, 148, 159, 160, 160A, 529B, 928 and 1059 is 6 hrs. per response. If you have any questions or comments concerning this estimate or any other aspect of this information collection please contact, Chief Administrative Information Branch, U.S. Small Business Administration, 409 3rd St. S.W. Washington, D.C. 20416 and Gary Waxman, Clearance Officer, Paperwork Reduction Project (3245-0201), Office of Management and Budget, Washington, D.C. 20503.

SBA FORM 159 (2-93) REF SOP 70 50 Use 7-89 Edition Until Exhausted

Exhibit Z (back)

SMALL BUSINESS ADMINISTRATION

POLICY AND REGULATIONS CONCERNING REPRESENTATIVES AND THEIR FEES

An applicant for a loan from SBA may obtain the assistance of any attorney, accountant, engineer, appraiser or other representative to aid him in the preparation and presentation of his application to SBA; however, such representation is not mandatory. In the event a loan is approved, the services of an attorney may be necessary to assist in the preparation of closing documents, title abstracts, etc. SBA will allow the payment of reasonable fees or other compensation for services performed by such representatives on behalf of the applicant.

There are no "authorized representatives" of SBA, other than our regular salaried employees. Payment of any fee or gratuity to SBA employees is illegal and will subject the parties to such a transaction to prosecution.

SBA Regulations [Part 103, Sec. 103.13-5(c)] prohibit representatives from charging or proposing to charge any contingent fee for any services performed in connection with an SBA loan unless the amount of such fee bears a necessary and reasonable relationship to the services actually performed; or to charge for any expenses which are not deemed by SBA to have been necessary in connection with the application. The Regulations (Part 120, Sec. 120.104-2) also prohibit the payment of any bonus, brokerage fee or commission in connection with SBA loans.

In line with these Regulations SBA will not approve placement or finder's fees for the use or attempted use of influence in obtaining or trying to obtain an SBA loan, or fees based solely upon a percentage of the approved loan or any part thereof.

Fees which will be approved will be limited to reasonable sums of services actually rendered in connection with the application or the closing, based upon the time and effort required, the qualifications of the representative and the nature and extent of the services rendered by such representatives. Representatives of loan applicants will be required to execute an agreement as to their compensation for services rendered in connection with said loan.

It is the responsibility of the applicant to set forth in the appropriate section of the application the names of all persons or firms engaged by or on behalf of the applicant. Applicants are required to advise the Regional Office in writing the names and fees of any representatives engaged by the applicant subsequent to the filing of the application. This reporting requirement is approved under OMB Approval Number 3245-0016.

Any loan applicant having any questions concerning the payments of fees, or the reasonableness of fees, should communicate with the Field Office where the application is filed.

U.S. GOVERNMENT PRINTING OFFICE : 1993 - 348-097

Appendix F

Hamburger Delight: Letters of Recommendation

Date: 11-7-XX

To Whom It May Concern:

I have known John Doe personally since February 1970. In working with and for him I have found him to be an excellent businessperson. He is self-motivated and goal directed — a highly ethical businessperson, excellent money manager, problem solver, and people manager.

I feel honored to have John Doe not only as a business associate but as a friend. I can highly recommend him for any business endeavor, knowing that he will be successful at whatever he does.

The biggest need in America today is strong leadership. John Doe is a man other people can look to for that leadership.

If more information is desired, please don't hesitate to call me.

B. Ready
B. Ready
Vice President of Development

Date: 9-28-XX

To Whom it May Concern:

During the time that John Doe was employed here, he was conscientious, dependable and honest. He was committed to his goals within the company and could be counted on to come through for us. He was an asset to our company and a fine representative of ours in the state of Connecticut.

Sincerely,

Robert Wilson
Robert Wilson
National Director of Sales
YYC Company
Anytown, MD 00003

Acme Sheet Metal: Financing Proposal

Financing Proposal for Acme Sheet Metal

Statement of Purpose

We, Timothy G. Wilson and John B. Smith, a partnership*, are seeking a loan of $400,000 for ten-and-a-half years for the following purpose:

1. $40,000 for land acquisition,
2. $160,000 for construction,
3. $100,000 for machinery and equipment,
4. $80,000 for working capital, and
5. $20,000 other.

These sums will be sufficient to finance the continued growth of Acme Sheet Metal for the foreseeable future.

Signature _Timothy G. Wilson_   Date _3-10-xx_

*Note: Both partners need to sign the SBA forms. However, only the partner having signatory authority needs to sign the exhibits. In this application, Timothy G. Wilson is that official. Keep in mind, the primary reasons for loan processing delays are missing documentation and failure to sign and date each exhibit.

Acme Sheet Metal: Table of Contents

		Page
Financing Proposal for Acme Sheet Metal — Statement of Purpose		xx

SBA DOCUMENTS
Application for Business Loan (SBA Form 4) xx
Personal Financial Statements (SBA Form 413) xx
Personal History Statements (SBA Form 912) xx

EXHIBITS
Exhibit A1:	Description of Existing Machinery and Equipment	xx
Exhibit C1:	Balance Sheets	xx
Exhibit C2:	Net Worth Reconciliation	xx
Exhibit C3:	Profit & Loss Statement	xx
Exhibit C4:	Aging of Accounts Receivable and Payable	xx
Exhibit C5:	Income Projection for Year 19XX	xx
Exhibit D:	Description of the Business	xx
Exhibit E:	Resumés of Management	xx
Exhibit F:	Consent of Spouses to Sign Loan Agreement	xx
Exhibit G:	Equipment List	xx
Exhibit I:	Applicant's Agreement of Compliance	xx
Exhibit T:	Cost of Construction	xx
Exhibit V:	Preliminary Construction Plans	xx
Exhibit W:	Copy of Lease	xx
Exhibit Z:	Compensation Agreement	xx

Signature _Timothy G. Wilson_   Date _3-10-xx_

Note: When you prepare your loan application package, it is wise to identify page numbers for the documents and exhibits you have included. This sample table of contents gives you an idea of how to properly structure and present your material.

U.S. Small Business Administration
APPLICATION FOR BUSINESS LOAN

OMB Approval No. 3245-0016
Expiration Date: 6-30-94

Individual Timothy G. Wilson & John B. Smith	**Full Address** 2000 Knoll Road, Anytown, NY 00000 / 620 Ridge Street, Anytown, NY 00000	
Name of Applicant Business Acme Sheet Metal	**Tax I.D. No. or SSN** 00-0000	
Full Street Address of Business 123 Main Street	**Tel. No. (inc. A/C)** (914) 234-2121	

City	County	State	Zip	Number of Employees (Including subsidiaries and affiliates)
Anytown	Any	NY	00000	

Type of Business	Date Business Established	
Sheet Metal Work	9/22/XX	At Time of Application **7**

Bank of Business Account and Address
Bank of First State
23 Main Street
Anytown, MD 00000

If Loan is Approved **8**

Subsidiaries or Affiliates (Separate from above) **0**

Use of Proceeds: (Enter Gross Dollar Amounts Rounded to the Nearest Hundreds)	Loan Requested		Loan Requested
Land Acquisition	40,000	Payoff SBA Loan	N/A
New Construction/ Expansion Repair	160,000	Payoff Bank Loan (Non SBA Associated)	N/A
Acquisition and/or repair of Machinery and Equipment	100,000	Other Debt Payment (Non SBA Associated)	20,000
Inventory Purchase	N/A	All Other	N/A
Working Capital (Including Accounts Payable)	80,000	Total Loan Requested	400,000
Acquisition of Existing Business	N/A	Term of Loan – (Requested Mat.)	10-1/2 Yrs.

PREVIOUS SBA OR OTHER FEDERAL GOVERNMENT DEBT: If you or any principals or affiliates have 1) ever requested Government financing or 2) are delinquent on the repayment of any Federal Debt complete the following:

Name of Agency	Original Amount of Loan	Date of Request	Approved or Declined	Balance	Current or Past Due
SBA	$ 60,000	19XX	Approved	$ -0-	Paid 19XX
	$			$	

ASSISTANCE List the name(s) and occupations of any who assisted in the preparation of this form, other than applicant.

Name and Occupation	Address	Total Fees Paid	Fees Due
Clark & Brown, CPAs,	1 State Street, Anytown, NY	$6,000	$6,000
Name and Occupation	Address	Total Fees Paid	Fees Due

PLEASE NOTE: The estimated burden hours for the completion of the form is 19.8 hours per response. If you have any questions or comments concerning this estimate or any other aspect of this information collection please contact Chief Administrative Information Branch, U.S. Small Business Administration, Washington, D.C. 20416 and Gary Waxman, Clearance Officer, Paperwork Reduction Project (3245-0016), Office of Management and Budget, Washington, D.C. 20503.

SBA Form 4 (1-93) Previous Edition is Obsolete

ALL EXHIBITS MUST BE SIGNED AND DATED BY PERSON SIGNING THIS FORM

BUSINESS INDEBTEDNESS: Furnish the following information on all installment debts, contracts, notes, and mortgages payable. Indicate by an asterisk (*) items to be paid by loan proceeds and reason for paying same (present balance should agree with the latest balance sheet submitted).

To Whom Payable	Original Amount	Original Date	Present Balance	Rate of Interest	Maturity Date	Monthly Payment	Security	Current or Past Due
Bank of First St. Acct. # 1309-98*	$28,000	19XX	$20,000	9%	11/1/XX	$355	Lathe	Current
* To be paid to provide a blanket first lien on all M/E. Acct. #	$		$			$		
Acct. #	$		$			$		
Acct. #	$		$			$		

MANAGEMENT (Proprietor, partners, officers, directors all holders of outstanding stock – <u>100% of ownership must be shown.</u>) Use separate sheet if necessary.

Name and Social Security Number and Position Title	Complete Address	% Owned	*Military Service From	*Military Service To	*Race	*Sex
Timothy G. Wilson 411-32-0458	2000 Knoll Road Anytown, NY 00000	50	10/XX	9/XX	W	M
John B. Smith 620-41-2181	620 Ridge Street Anytown, NY 00000	50	3/XX	3/XX	W	M

*This data is collected for statistical purpose only. It has no bearing on the credit decision to approve or decline this application.

THE FOLLOWING EXHIBITS MUST BE COMPLETED WHERE APPLICABLE. ALL QUESTIONS ANSWERED ARE MADE A PART OF THE APPLICATION.

For Guaranty Loans please provide an original and one copy (Photocopy is Acceptable) of the Application Form, and all Exhibits to the participating lender. For Direct Loans submit one original copy of the application and Exhibits to SBA.

1. Submit SBA Form 912 (Personal History Statement) for each person, e.g., owners, partners, officers, directors, major stockholders, etc.; the instructions are on SBA Form 912.

2. If your collateral consists of (A) Land and Building, (B) Machinery and Equipment, (C) Furniture and Fixtures, (D) Accounts Receivable, (E) Inventory, (F) Other, please provide an itemized list (labeled Exhibit A) that contains serial and identification numbers for all articles that had an original value greater than $500. Include a legal description of Real Estate offered as collateral.

3. Furnish a signed current personal balance sheet (SBA Form 413 may be used for this purpose) for each stockholder (with 20% or greater ownership), partner, officer, and owner. Social Security number should be included on personal financial statement. It should be as of the same date as the most recent business financial statements. Label this Exhibit B.

4. Include the statements listed below: 1,2,3 for the last three years; also 1,2,3,4 as of the same date, which are current within 90 days of filing the application; and statement 5, if applicable. This is Exhibit C (SBA has Management Aids that help in the preparation of financial statements). All information must be **signed and dated**.

1. Balance Sheet   2. Profit and Loss Statement
3. Reconciliation of Net Worth
4. Aging of Accounts Receivable and Payable
5. Earnings projects for at least one year where financial statements for the last three years are unavailable or where requested by District Office.
    (If Profit and Loss Statement is not available, explain why and substitute Federal Income Tax Forms.)

5. Provide a brief history of your company and a paragraph describing the expected benefits it will receive from the loan. Label it Exhibit D.

6. Provide a brief description similar to a resume of the education, technical and business background for all the people listed under Management. Please mark it Exhibit E.

SBA Form 4 (1-93) Previous Edition is Obsolete

ALL EXHIBITS MUST BE SIGNED AND DATED BY PERSON SIGNING THIS FORM

7. Do you have any co-signers and/or guarantors for this loan? If so, please submit their names, addresses, tax Id Numbers, and current personal balance sheet(s) as Exhibit F.

8. Are you buying machinery or equipment with your loan money? If so, you must include a list of equipment and cost as quoted by the seller and his name and address. This is Exhibit G.

9. Have you or any officer of your company ever been involved in bankruptcy or insolvency proceedings? If so, please provide the details as Exhibit H. If none, check here: [ ] Yes [x] No

10. Are you or your business involved in any pending lawsuits? If yes, provide the details as Exhibit I. If none, check here: [ ] Yes [x] No

11. Do you or your spouse or any member of your household, or anyone who owns, manages, or directs your business or their spouses or members of their households work for the Small Business Administration, Small Business Advisory Council, SCORE or ACE, any Federal Agency, or the participating lender? If so, please provide the name and address of the person and the office where employed. Label this Exhibit J. If none, check here: [ ] Yes [x] No

12. Does your business, its owners or majority stockholders own or have a controlling interest in other businesses? If yes, please provide their names and the relationship with your company along with a current balance sheet and operating statement for each. This should be Exhibit K.

13. Do you buy from, sell to, or use the services of any concern in which someone in your company has a significant financial interest? If yes, provide details on a separate sheet of paper labeled Exhibit L.

14. If your business is a franchise, include a copy of the franchise agreement and a copy of the FTC disclosure statement supplied to you by the Franchisor. Please include it as Exhibit M.

CONSTRUCTION LOANS ONLY

15. Include a separate exhibit (Exhibit N) the estimated cost of the project and a statement of the source of any additional funds.

16. Provide copies of preliminary construction plans and specifications. Include them as Exhibit O. Final plans will be required prior to disbursement.

DIRECT LOANS ONLY

17. Include two bank declination letters with your application. (In cities with 200,000 people or less, one letter will be sufficient.) These letters should include the name and telephone number of the persons contacted at the banks, the amount and terms of the loan, the reason for decline and whether or not the bank will participate with SBA.

EXPORT LOANS

18. Does your business presently engage in Export Trade? Check here: [ ] Yes [x] No

19. Do you have plans to begin exporting as a result of this loan? Check here: [ ] Yes [x] No

20. Would you like information on Exporting? Check here: [ ] Yes [x] No

AGREEMENTS AND CERTIFICATIONS

Agreements of non-employment SBA Personnel: I agree that if SBA approves this loan application I will not, for at least two years, hire as an employee or consultant anyone that was employed by the SBA during the one year period prior to the disbursement of the loan.

Certification: I certify: (a) I have not paid anyone connected with the Federal Government for help in getting this loan. I also agree to report to the SBA office of the Inspector General, Washington, D.C. 20416 any Federal Government employee who offers, in return for any type of compensation, to help get this loan approved.

(b) All information in this application and the Exhibits are true and complete to the best of my knowledge and are submitted to SBA so SBA can decide whether to grant a loan or participate with a lending institution in a loan to me. I agree to pay for or reimburse SBA for the cost of any surveys, title or mortgage examinations, appraisals, credit reports, etc., performed by non-SBA personnel provided I have given my consent.

(c) I understand that I need not pay anybody to deal with SBA. I have read and understand SBA Form 159 which explains SBA policy on representatives and their fees.

(d) As consideration for any Management, Technical, and Business Development Assistance that may be provided, I waive all claims against SBA and its consultants.

If you make a statement that you know to be false or if you over value a security in order to help obtain a loan under the provisions of the Small Business Act, you can be fined up to $5,000 or be put in jail for up to two years, or both.

If Applicant is a proprietor or general partner, sign below.

By: *Timothy G. Wilson* 3/10/xx
Date

If Applicant is a Corporation, sign below:

Corporate Name and Seal   Date

By: _____
Signature of President

Attested by: _____
Signature of Corporate Secretary

SBA Form 4 (1-93) Previous Edition is Obsolete

APPLICANT'S CERTIFICATION

By my signature I certify that I have read and received a copy of the "STATEMENTS REQUIRED BY LAW AND EXECUTIVE ORDER" which was attached to this application. My signature represents my agreement to comply with the approval of my loan request and to comply, whenever applicable, with the hazard insurance, lead-based paint, civil rights or other limitations in this notice.

Each Proprietor, each General Partner, each Limited Partner or Stockholder owning 20% or more, and each Guarantor must sign. Each person should sign only once.

Business Name: Acme Sheet Metal

Date: 3/10/xx
By: *Timothy G. Wilson, Partner*
Signature and Title

Date: 3/10/xx
John B. Smith, Partner
Signature and Title

Date
Signature and Title

Date
Signature and Title

Date
Signature and Title

SBA Form 4 (1-93) Previous Edition is Obsolete

126 *The Insider's Guide to Small Business Loans*

OMB Approval No. 3245-0188

PERSONAL FINANCIAL STATEMENT

U.S. SMALL BUSINESS ADMINISTRATION

As of __March 1__, 19 __XX__

Complete this form for: (1) each proprietor, or (2) each limited partner who owns 20% or more interest and each general partner, or (3) each stockholder owning 20% or more of voting stock, or (4) any person or entity providing a guaranty on the loan.

Name Timothy & Marilyn Wilson	**Business Phone** (914) 234-2121
Residence Address 2000 Knoll Road	**Residence Phone** (914) 222-2324
City, State, & Zip Code Anytown, NY 00000	
Business Name of Applicant/Borrower Acme Sheet Metal	

ASSETS (Omit Cents)

Cash on hands & in Banks	$ 2,400
Savings Accounts	$ 18,000
IRA or Other Retirement Account	$ None
Accounts & Notes Receivable	$ None
Life Insurance–Cash Surrender Value Only (Complete Section 8)	$ 8,400
Stocks and Bonds (Describe in Section 3)	$ 40,800
Real Estate (Describe in Section 4)	$ 260,000
Automobile–Present Value	$ 14,800
Other Personal Property (Describe in Section 5)	$ 30,000
Other Assets (Describe in Section 5)	$ 80,120
Total	**$ 454,520**

LIABILITIES (Omit Cents)

Accounts Payable	$ 1,400
Notes Payable to Banks and Others (Describe in Section 2)	$ 4,800
Installment Account (Auto)	$ 5,868
Mo. Payments $ _____	
Installment Account (other)	$ -0-
Mo. Payments $ _____	
Loan on Life Insurance	$ -0-
Mortgages on Real Estate (Describe in Section 4)	$ 168,680
Unpaid taxes (Describe in Section 6)	$ Current
Other Liabilities (Describe in Section 7)	$ -0-
Total Liabilities	$ 180,748
Net Worth	$ 273,772
Total	**$ 454,520**

Section 1. Source of Income

Salary	$ 68,000
Net Investment Income	$ 2,940
Real Estate Income	$ -0-
Other Income (Describe below)*	$ 37,600

Contingent Liabilities

As Endorser or Co-Maker	$ -0-
Legal Claims & Judgments	$ -0-
Provision for Federal Income tax	$ Current
Other Special Debt	$ -0-

Description of Other Income in Section 1.

All Items are stated on an Annual Basis

Military disability of $800 per month

Wife's salary of $28,000 per year

*Alimony or child support payments need not be disclosed in "Other Income" unless it is desired to have such payments counted toward total income.

Section 2. Notes Payable to Bank and Others.

(Use attachments if necessary. Each attachment must be identified as part of this statement and signed.)

Name and Address of Noteholder(s)	Original Balance	Current Balance	Payment Amount	Frequency (monthly, etc.)	How Secured or Endorsed Type of Collateral
Bank of First Nat'l State	8,000	4,800	400	Monthly	Unsecured
Crack Finance	19,000	5,868	521	Monthly	19XX Buick

SBA Form 413 (2-94) Use 5-91 Edition until stock is exhausted. Ref: SOP 50-10 - and 50-30   (tumble)

Section 3. Stocks and Bonds.
(Use attachments if necessary. Each attachment must be identified as part of this statement and signed.)

Number of Shares	Name of Securities	Cost	Market Value Quotation/Exchange	Date of Quotation/Exchange	Total Value
160	ABM Ltd.	6,800	130	3/29/XX	20,800
200	NNN Corp.	12,000	100	3/29/XX	20,000

Section 4. Real Estate Owned.
(List each parcel separately. Use attachments if necessary. Each attachment must be identified as a part of this statement and signed.)

	Property A	Property B	Property C
Type of Property	Personal Home		
Address	Timothy & Marilyn Wilson 2000 Knoll Road Anytown, NY 00000		
Date Purchased	August 19XX		
Original Cost	$220,000		
Present Market Value	$260,000		
Name & Address of Mortgage Holder	Bruce Savings & Loan 220 Echo Avenue Anytown, NY 00000		
Mortgage Account Number	98765-07		
Mortgage Balance	$168,680		
Amount of Payment per Month/Year	$1,259		
Status of Mortgage	Current		

Section 5. Other Personal Property and Other Assets.
(Describe, and if any is pledged as security, state name and address of lien holder, amount of lien, terms of payment, and if delinquent, describe delinquency.)

Acme Sheet Metal Partnership interest - $80,120

Household furnishing - Personal Property - Jewelry $30,000

Section 6. Unpaid Taxes.
(Describe in detail, as to type, to whom payable, when due, amount, and to what property, if any, a tax lien attaches.)

All Taxes are current

Section 7. Other Liabilities. (Describe in detail.)

No other Liabilities

Section 8. Life Insurance Held.
(Give face amount and cash surrender value of policies – name of insurance company and beneficiaries.)

$100,000 Amer. Life - Marilyn Wilson is Beneficiary
$100,000 National Life - Marilyn Wilson is Beneficiary

I authorize SBA/Lender to make inquiries as necessary to verify the accuracy of the statements made and to determine my creditworthiness. I certify the above and the statements contained in the attachments are true and accurate as of the stated date(s). These statements are made for the purpose of either obtaining a loan or guaranteeing a loan. I understand FALSE statements may result in forfeiture of benefits and possible prosecution by the U.S. Attorney General (Reference 18 U.S.C. 1001).

| Signature | *Timothy G. Wilson* | Date: 3/8/xx | Social Security Number 411-32-0458 |
| Signature | *Marilyn Wilson* | Date: 3/8/xx | Social Security Number 611-21-0102 |

PLEASE NOTE: The estimated average burden hours for the completion of this form is 1.5 hours per response. If you have questions or comments concerning this estimate or any other aspect of this information, please contact Chief, Administrative Branch, U.S. Small Business Administration, Washington, D.C. 20416, and Clearance Office, Paper Reduction Project (3245-0188), Office of Management and Budget, Washington, D.C. 20503.

Federal Recycling Program   Printed on Recycled Paper

PERSONAL FINANCIAL STATEMENT

OMB Approval No. 3245-0188

U.S. SMALL BUSINESS ADMINISTRATION

As of __March 1__, 19 XX

Complete this form for: (1) each proprietor, or (2) each limited partner who owns 20% or more interest and each general partner, or (3) each stockholder owning 20% or more of voting stock, or (4) any person or entity providing a guaranty on the loan.

Name	John B. & Nancy Smith
Business Phone	(914) 234-2121
Residence Address	620 Ridge Street
Residence Phone	(914) 999-6543
City, State, & Zip Code	Anytown, NY 00000
Business Name of Applicant/Borrower	Acme Sheet Metal

ASSETS	Omit Cents	LIABILITIES	Omit Cents
Cash on hands & in Banks	$ 4,080	Accounts Payable	$ 1,680
Savings Accounts	$ 10,000	Notes Payable to Banks and Others	$ 4,000
IRA or Other Retirement Account	$ 16,000	(Describe in Section 2)	
Accounts & Notes Receivable	$ -0-	Installment Account (Auto)	$ -0-
Life Insurance–Cash Surrender Value Only	$ 8,800	Mo. Payments $	
(Complete Section 8)		Installment Account (other)	$ -0-
Stocks and Bonds	$ -0-	Mo. Payments $	
(Describe in Section 3)		Loan on Life Insurance	$ -0-
Real Estate	$ 220,000	Mortgages on Real Estate	$ 80,720
(Describe in Section 4)		(Describe in Section 4)	
Automobile–Present Value	$ 8,200	Unpaid taxes	$ None
Other Personal Property	$ 40,000	(Describe in Section 6)	
(Describe in Section 5)		Other Liabilities	$ None
Other Assets	$ 86,120	(Describe in Section 7)	
(Describe in Section 5)		Total Liabilities	$ 86,400
		Net Worth	$ 306,800
Total	$ 393,200	Total	$ 393,200

Section 1. Source of Income

		Contingent Liabilities	
Salary	$ 60,000	As Endorser or Co-Maker	$ 4,800
Net Investment Income	$ 1,440	Legal Claims & Judgments	$ -0-
Real Estate Income	$ -0-	Provision for Federal Income tax	$ -0-
Other Income (Describe below)*	$ 20,000	Other Special Debt	$ -0-

Description of Other Income in Section 1.

    * Wife is a substitute teacher for Anytown school system.

    ** Cosigner for son's boat loan.

*Alimony or child support payments need not be disclosed in "Other Income" unless it is desired to have such payments counted toward total income.

Section 2. Notes Payable to Bank and Others. (Use attachments if necessary. Each attachment must be identified as part of this statement and signed.)

Name and Address of Noteholder(s)	Original Balance	Current Balance	Payment Amount	Frequency (monthly, etc.)	How Secured or Endorsed Type of Collateral
Bank of First Nat'l State	4,000	4,000	Var. Min= $80/Mo	Monthly	Signature

SBA Form 413 (2-94) Use 5-91 Edition until stock is exhausted. Ref: SOP 50-10 - and 50-30   (tumble)

Section 3. Stocks and Bonds. (Use attachments if necessary. Each attachment must be identified as part of this statement and signed.)

Number of Shares	Name of Securities	Cost	Market Value Quotation/Exchange	Date of Quotation/Exchange	Total Value

Section 4. Real Estate Owned. (List each parcel separately. Use attachments if necessary. Each attachment must be identified as a part of this statement and signed.)

	Property A	Property B	Property C
Type of Property	Personal Home		
Address	John B. & Nancy Smith 620 Ridge Street Anytown, NY 00000		
Date Purchased	June 19XX		
Original Cost	$124,000		
Present Market Value	$220,000		
Name & Address of Mortgage Holder	Bank of Anytown 340 Main Street Anytown, NY 00000		
Mortgage Account Number	98710-56		
Mortgage Balance	$80,720		
Amount of Payment per Month/Year	$834		
Status of Mortgage	Current		

Section 5. Other Personal Property and Other Assets. (Describe, and if any is pledged as security, state name and address of lien holder, amount of lien, terms of payment, and if delinquent, describe delinquency.)

Acme Sheet Metal partnership interest - $80,120
Gun Collection - $6,000

Section 6. Unpaid Taxes. (Describe in detail, as to type, to whom payable, when due, amount, and to what property, if any, a tax lien attaches.)

None

Section 7. Other Liabilities. (Describe in detail.)

None

Section 8. Life Insurance Held. (Give face amount and cash surrender value of policies – name of insurance company and beneficiaries.)

$50,000 American Life - Nancy Smith is the beneficiary

I authorize SBA/Lender to make inquiries as necessary to verify the accuracy of the statements made and to determine my creditworthiness. I certify the above and the statements contained in the attachments are true and accurate as of the stated date(s). These statements are made for the purpose of either obtaining a loan or guaranteeing a loan. I understand FALSE statements may result in forfeiture of benefits and possible prosecution by the U.S. Attorney General (Reference 18 U.S.C. 1001).

Signature *John B. Smith* Date: 3/5/xx Social Security Number 620-41-2181
Signature *Nancy Smith* Date: 3/5/xx Social Security Number 161-41-2181

PLEASE NOTE: The estimated average burden hours for the completion of this form is 1.5 hours per response. If you have questions or comments concerning this estimate or any other aspect of this information, please contact Chief, Administrative Branch, U.S. Small Business Administration, Washington, D.C. 20416, and Clearance Office, Paper Reduction Project (3245-0188), Office of Management and Budget, Washington, D.C. 20503.

Federal Recycling Program   Printed on Recycled Paper

OMB Approval No.: 3245-0178
Expiration Date: 2-28-97

Return Executed Copies 1, 2, and 3 to SBA

United States of America
SMALL BUSINESS ADMINISTRATION
STATEMENT OF PERSONAL HISTORY

Please Read Carefully – Print or Type
Each member of the small business concern or the development company requesting assistance must submit this form in TRIPLICATE for filing with the SBA application. This form must be filled out and submitted by:
1. If a sole proprietorship by the proprietor.
2. If a partnership by each partner.
3. If a corporation or a development company, by each officer, director, and additionally by each holder of 20% or more of the voting stock.
4. Any other person including a hired manager, who has authority to speak for and commit the borrower in the management of the business.

Name and Address of Applicant (Firm Name)(Street, City, State, and Zip Code)

Acme Sheet Metal
123 Main Street, Anytown, NY 00000

SBA District/Disaster Area Office: Anytown

Amount Applied for: $400,000
Loan Case No.

1. Personal Statement of: [State name in full, if no middle name, state (NMN), or if initial only, indicate initial]. List all former names used, and dates each name was used. Use separate sheet if necessary.

First: Timothy   Middle: George   Last: Wilson

Name and Address of participating bank (when applicable)
Bank of First National State
23 Main Street
Anytown, NY 00000

2. Date of Birth: (Month, day, and year) 9/19/XX
3. Place of Birth: (City & State or Foreign Country)

1. Give the percentage of ownership or stock owned or to be owned in the small business concern or the Development Company: 50%
Social Security No.: 411-32-0458
U.S. Citizen? [X] YES [ ] NO
If no, give alien registration number: _____

5. Present residence Address:
From: 1/6/XX To: Present Address: 2000 Knoll Road, Anytown State: NY

Home Telephone No. (Include A/C): (914) 222-2324
Business Telephone No. (Include A/C): (914) 234-2121

Immediate past residence address:
From: 4/6/XX To: 1/6/XX Address: 473 Martin Street, Anytown NY

BE SURE TO ANSWER THE NEXT 3 QUESTIONS CORRECTLY BECAUSE THEY ARE IMPORTANT.

THE FACT THAT YOU HAVE AN ARREST OR CONVICTION RECORD WILL NOT NECESSARILY DISQUALIFY YOU. BUT AN INCORRECT ANSWER WILL PROBABLY CAUSE YOUR APPLICATION TO BE TURNED DOWN.

IF YOU ANSWER "YES" TO 6, 7, OR 8, FURNISH DETAILS IN A SEPARATE EXHIBIT. INCLUDE DATES; LOCATION; FINES, SENTENCES, ETC.; WHETHER MISDEMEANOR OR FELONY; DATES OF PAROLE/PROBATION; UNPAID FINES OR PENALTIES; NAMES UNDER WHICH CHARGED; AND ANY OTHER PERTINENT INFORMATION.

6. Are you presently under indictment, on parole or probation?
[ ] Yes [X] No   (If yes, indicate date parole or probation is to expire.)

7. Have you ever been charged with or arrested for any criminal offense other than a minor motor vehicle violation? Include offenses which have been dismissed, discharged, or nolle prosequi. (All arrests and charges must be disclosed and explained on an attached sheet.)
[ ] Yes [X] No

8. Have you ever been convicted, placed on pretrial diversion, or placed on any form of probation, including adjudication withheld pending probation, for any criminal offense other than a minor motor vehicle violation?
[ ] Yes [X] No

9. [ ] Fingerprints Waived   Date ____ Approving Authority ____
   [ ] Fingerprints Required
       Date Sent to FBI ____ Date ____ Approving Authority ____

10. [ ] Cleared for Processing   Date ____ Approving Authority ____
    [ ] Request a Character Evaluation   Date ____ Approving Authority ____

The information on this form will be used in connection with an investigation of your character. Any information you wish to submit that you feel will expedite this investigation should be set forth.

I am a lifelong citizen of Anytown, NY, aside from two years of Army service during the Vietnam war.

CAUTION: Knowingly making a false statement on this form is a violation of Federal law and could result in criminal prosecution, significant civil penalties, and a denial of your loan. A false statement is punishable under 18 USC 1001 by imprisonment of not more than five years and/or a fine of not more than $10,000; under 15 USC 645 by imprisonment of not more than two years and/or a fine of not more than $5,000; and, if submitted to a Federally insured institution, under 18 USC 1014 by imprisonment of not more than twenty years and/or a fine of not more than $1,000,000.

Signature: *Timothy George Wilson*   Title: Partner   Date: 3/10/xx

It is against SBA's policy to provide assistance to persons not of good character and therefore consideration is given to the qualities and personality traits of a person, favorable and unfavorable, relating thereto, including behavior, integrity, candor and disposition toward criminal actions. It is also against SBA's policy to provide assistance not in the best interests of the United States, for example, if there is reason to believe that the effect of such assistance will be to encourage or support, directly or indirectly, activities inimical to the Security of the United States. Anyone concerned with the collection of this information, as to its voluntariness, disclosure of routine uses may contact the FOIA Office, 409 3rd St. S.W., and a copy of 9 "Agency Collection of Information" from SOP 40 04 will be provided.

SBA Form 912 (12-93) SOP 9020 USE 5-87 EDITION UNTIL EXHAUSTED   Copy 1- SAB File Copy

PLEASE NOTE: The estimated burden hours for the completion of this form is 15 minutes per response. If you have any questions or comments concerning this estimate or any other aspect of this information collection please contact, Chief Administrative Information Branch, U.S. Small Business Administration, 409 Third St. S.W. Washington, D.C. 20416 or Gary Waxman, Clearance Officer, Paperwork Reduction Project (3245-0201), Office of Management and Budget, Washington, D.C. 20503.

Federal Recycling Program   Printed on Recycled Paper

OMB Approval No.: 3245-0178
Expiration Date: 2-28-97

Return Executed Copies 1, 2, and 3 to SBA

United States of America
SMALL BUSINESS ADMINISTRATION
STATEMENT OF PERSONAL HISTORY

Please Read Carefully – Print or Type
Each member of the small business concern or the development company requesting assistance must submit this form in TRIPLICATE for filing with the SBA application. This form must be filled out and submitted by:

1. If a sole proprietorship by the proprietor.
2. If a partnership by each partner.
3. If a corporation or a development company, by each officer, director, and additionally by each holder of 20% or more of the voting stock.
4. Any other person including a hired manager, who has authority to speak for and commit the borrower in the management of the business.

Name and Address of Applicant (Firm Name)(Street, City, State, and Zip Code)

Acme Sheet Metal
123 Main Street, Anytown, NY 00000

SBA District/Disaster Area Office: Anytown

Amount Applied for: $400,000

Loan Case No.

1. Personal Statement of: [State name in full, if no middle name, state (NMN), or if initial only, indicate initial]. List all former names used, and dates each name was used. Use separate sheet if necessary.

First	Middle	Last
John	Berry	Smith

Name and Address of participating bank (when applicable)

Bank of First National State
23 Main Street
Anytown, NY 00000

2. Date of Birth: (Month, day, and year) 11/5/XX

3. Place of Birth: (City & State or Foreign Country)

1. Give the percentage of ownership or stock owned or to be owned in the small business concern or the Development Company: 50%

Social Security No.: 620-41-2181

U.S. Citizen? [X] YES [ ] NO
If no, give alien registration number: _____

5. Present residence Address:
From: 6/1/XX To: Present Address: 620 Ridge Street, Anytown State: NY

Home Telephone No. (Include A/C): (914) 999-6543
Business Telephone No. (Include A/C): (914) 234-2121

Immediate past residence address:
From: 7/1/XX To: 6/1/XX Address: 51 Ridgewood Parkway, Anytown NY

BE SURE TO ANSWER THE NEXT 3 QUESTIONS CORRECTLY BECAUSE THEY ARE IMPORTANT.

THE FACT THAT YOU HAVE AN ARREST OR CONVICTION RECORD WILL NOT NECESSARILY DISQUALIFY YOU. BUT AN INCORRECT ANSWER WILL PROBABLY CAUSE YOUR APPLICATION TO BE TURNED DOWN.

IF YOU ANSWER "YES" TO 6, 7, OR 8, FURNISH DETAILS IN A SEPARATE EXHIBIT. INCLUDE DATES; LOCATION; FINES, SENTENCES, ETC.; WHETHER MISDEMEANOR OR FELONY; DATES OF PAROLE/PROBATION; UNPAID FINES OR PENALTIES; NAMES UNDER WHICH CHARGED; AND ANY OTHER PERTINENT INFORMATION.

6. Are you presently under indictment, on parole or probation?
[ ] Yes [X] No (If yes, indicate date parole or probation is to expire.)

7. Have you ever been charged with or arrested for any criminal offense other than a minor motor vehicle violation? Include offenses which have been dismissed, discharged, or nolle prosequi. (All arrests and charges must be disclosed and explained on an attached sheet.)
[ ] Yes [X] No

8. Have you ever been convicted, placed on pretrial diversion, or placed on any form of probation, including adjudication withheld pending probation, for any criminal offense other than a minor motor vehicle violation?
[ ] Yes [X] No

9. [ ] Fingerprints Waived _____ Date _____ Approving Authority
   [ ] Fingerprints Required _____ Date _____ Approving Authority
   Date Sent to FBI

10. [ ] Cleared for Processing _____ Date _____ Approving Authority
    [ ] Request a Character Evaluation _____ Date _____ Approving Authority

The information on this form will be used in connection with an investigation of your character. Any information you wish to submit that you feel will expedite this investigation should be set forth.

I am a lifelong resident of Anytown, NY. I was in the Army for three years.

CAUTION: Knowingly making a false statement on this form is a violation of Federal law and could result in criminal prosecution, significant civil penalties, and a denial of your loan. A false statement is punishable under 18 USC 1001 by imprisonment of not more than five years and/or a fine of not more than $10,000; under 15 USC 645 by imprisonment of not more than two years and/or a fine of not more than $5,000; and, if submitted to a Federally insured institution, under 18 USC 1014 by imprisonment of not more than twenty years and /or a fine of not more than $1,000,000.

Signature: *John Berry Smith* Title: Partner Date: 3/10/xx

It is against SBA's policy to provide assistance to persons not of good character and therefore consideration is given to the qualities and personality traits of a person, favorable and unfavorable, relating thereto, including behavior, integrity, candor and disposition toward criminal actions. It is also against SBA's policy to provide assistance not in the best interests of the United States, for example, if there is reason to believe that the effect of such assistance will be to encourage or support, directly or indirectly, activities inimical to the Security of the United States. Anyone concerned with the collection of this information, as to its voluntariness, disclosure of routine uses may contact the FOIA Office, 409 3rd St. S.W., and a copy of 9 "Agency Collection of Information" from SOP 40 04 will be provided.

SBA Form 912 (12-93) SOP 9020 USE 5-87 EDITION UNTIL EXHAUSTED Copy 1- SAB File Copy

PLEASE NOTE: The estimated burden hours for the completion of this form is 15 minutes per response. If you have any questions or comments concerning this estimate or any other aspect of this information collection please contact, Chief Administrative Information Branch, U.S. Small Business Administration, 409 Third St. S.W. Washington, D.C. 20416 or Gary Waxman, Clearance Officer, Paperwork Reduction Project (3245-0201), Office of Management and Budget, Washington, D.C. 20503.

Federal Recycling Program Printed on Recycled Paper

Exhibit A1

Acme Sheet Metal: Description of Existing Machinery and Equipment

**Description of Existing Machinery and Equipment,
Plus Furniture, Offered as Collateral***

ITEM	MODEL	SERIAL NUMBER
ACME Star Lathe	B-10	9-476
Teton Lathe	200	H-199
Wilson Lathe	H-40	19416
ACME Stamping Machine	B-80	2-612
ACME Stamping Machine	B-80	2-140
Rabu Grinder	R-100	922
Tandy Mfg. Co. Shaper	S-240	none
Tandy Mfg. Co. Shaper	S-240	none
ABC Forging Co. Press	60-T	114210
Teton Press	700	H-630
ABM Typewriter	1000	731
ABM Typewriter	1000	604
AT&T Computer	360TPC	15-2944
ACR Adding Machine	400	278
Munri Calculator	M-20	716249

Signature _Timothy G. Wilson_   Date _3-10-xx_

*Note: You can also include *SBA Form 4 Schedule A, Schedule of Collateral*. You can find a sample of this schedule at the end of Chapter 3.

Exhibits C1 and C2

Acme Sheet Metal: Balance Sheets

ACME SHEET METAL
BALANCE SHEETS as of DECEMBER 31, 19XX

	1991	1992	1993	1994 (3 mos.)
ASSETS				
Current Assets:				
Cash	2,808	9,520	31,316	33,252
Accounts Receivable	77,880	85,904	94,584	99,652
Inventory	75,652	78,064	80,960	84,468
Work in Process	30,276	31,276	32,624	33,784
Prepayments & Deposits	5,800	4,280	6,580	5,960
Total Current Assets	192,416	209,044	246,064	257,116
Fixed assets:				
Machinery & Equipment	76,480	94,880	148,720	148,720
Furniture & Fixtures	11,080	14,480	20,480	20,480
Autos & Trucks	35,780	51,060	51,060	51,060
Less depreciation	(32,400)	(47,680)	(61,480)	(64,880)
Other Assets		2,000	2,880	1,720
TOTAL ASSETS	283,356	323,784	407,724	414,216
LIABILITIES				
Current Liabilities:				
Accounts Payable	69,076	83,724	51,264	62,552
Notes Payable	48,200	33,600	18,800	8,400
Taxes Payable	1,840	5,160	480	5,640
Accruals	7,700	9,880	2,816	5,140
Total Current Liabilities	126,816	132,364	73,360	81,732
Long-term Liabilities				
Notes Payable	42,000	60,764	24,400	9,332
TOTAL LIABILITIES	168,816	193,128	97,760	91,064
NET WORTH	114,540	130,656	309,964	323,152
TOTAL LIABILITIES AND NET WORTH	283,356	323,784	407,724	414,216

This statement was prepared by the applicants and does not reflect the allocation of certain expenses to cost of goods sold.

Net Worth at beginning of year	72,284	114,540	130,656	309,964
Undistributed profits for the year	42,256	16,116	58,308	13,188
Infusion of cash by partners			121,000	
Net worth at end of year/period	114,540	130,656	309,964	323,152

Signature *Timothy G. Wilson* Date 3-10-xx

> **Exhibit C3**

Acme Sheet Metal: Profit & Loss Statement

ACME SHEET METAL
PROFIT AND LOSS FOR YEARS ENDING DECEMBER 31, 19XX

	1991	1992	1993	1994 (3 mos.)
NET SALES	714,364	703,516	797,158	210,334
COST OF GOODS SOLD				
Inventory - Beginning	79,404	75,652	78,064	80,960
Raw Material Purchases	96,448	100,064	104,872	28,484
Factory Supplies	18,680	19,400	20,160	5,800
Direct Labor	263,104	277,648	289,520	76,380
Inventory - End	(75,652)	(78,064)	(80,960)	(84,468)
Cost of Sales	381,984	394,700	411,656	107,156
GROSS PROFIT	332,380	308,816	385,502	103,178
EXPENSES				
Rent	36,000	39,200	41,600	11,760
Office Salaries	27,200	33,600	41,600	12,000
Depreciation	16,200	15,280	13,800	3,400
Vehicle Expenses	21,696	19,600	20,400	5,640
Utilities	14,120	15,000	16,720	4,504
Insurance	9,280	9,960	10,700	3,300
Advertising	2,000	1,400	2,000	1,000
Payroll Taxes	23,224	24,900	26,490	7,070
Other Taxes	6,064	6,440	6,820	1,888
Telephone	3,248	2,960	3,588	540
Legal and Accounting	3,600	2,880	2,200	1,320
Office Supplies	3,480	3,640	3,712	1,060
Maintenance and Repairs	18,528	11,360	14,096	2,080
Bad Debts	848	1,400	600	
Interest	2,100	4,200	5,120	1,200
Miscellaneous	4,536	2,880	3,748	1,228
TOTAL EXPENSES	192,124	194,700	213,194	57,990
NET PROFIT	140,256	114,116	172,308	45,188
PARTNERS' DRAWINGS	98,000	98,000	114,000	32,000
PROFITS LEFT IN THE BUSINESS	42,256	16,116	58,308	13,188

This statement was prepared by the applicants and does not reflect a proper allocation of certain expenses to cost of goods sold.

Signature *Timothy G. Wilson*   Date 3-10-xx

> Exhibit C4

Acme Sheet Metal: Aging of Accounts Receivable and Payable

AGING OF ACCOUNTS RECEIVABLE AND PAYABLE AS OF MARCH 31, 1990

	Receivables	Payables
Under 30 days	52,476	52,664
30-59 days	27,244	9,088
60-89 days	12,384	800*
90-119 days	4,736	
120 days or more	2,812	
Uncollectible	0	
Total	99,654	62,552

*Disputed bill

Signature _Timothy G. Wilson_ Date _3-10-xx_

Exhibit C5

Acme Sheet Metal: Income Projection for Year 19XX

Projected Income for the Full Year 19XX

SALES		1,265,200
Beginning inventory	80,960	
Materials Purchased & Factory	628,160	
Factory Supplies	28,800	
Less ending inventory	(100,000)	
COST OF GOODS SOLD		637,920
GROSS PROFIT		627,280
EXPENSES		
Rent	41,600	
Office salaries	57,600	
Depreciation	30,000	
Vehicle expenses	24,000	
Utilities	24,000	
Insurance	14,400	
Advertising	3,200	
Payroll taxes	43,000	
Other taxes	36,000	
Telephone	4,800	
Legal & Accounting	4,080	
Office supplies	16,000	
Maintenance & Repairs	96,000	
Bad debts	800	
Interest	37,500	
Miscellaneous	7,200	
TOTAL EXPENSES		440,180
NET PROFIT		187,100
PARTNERS' DRAWINGS		128,000
PROFITS LEFT IN BUSINESS		59,100

This statement was prepared by the applicants and does not reflect the allocation of certain expenses to cost of goods sold.

Signature _Timothy G. Wilson_ Date _3-10-xx_

Chapter 5: The Application Case Histories **137**

Exhibit D

Acme Sheet Metal: Description of the Business

Brief History of Acme Sheet Metal

The establishment of Acme Sheet Metal goes back to September 22, 19XX, although the idea of forming such a business was conceived at least five years earlier. We discussed this idea while we were both employed at Tyler Machine Shop, a similar type of business. We gained the necessary experience considered vital to an eventual entry into self-employment. We also gained a great deal of experience at Valley Manufacturing and O'Toole Manufacturing.

The business was started with an SBA loan and capital of $60,000. (Each 50% owner contributed $30,000 from savings set aside over the years for this specific purpose.) The first two years were the most difficult because sales were hard to develop in spite of the reputation we felt we had as good technicians. We also made a mistake in paying off our SBA loan ahead of schedule. The year 19XX saw our first satisfactory results. We were disappointed in 19XX when sales and earnings dropped as the result of a fire in our leased facility.

We rebounded strongly from that fire as reflected by our subsequent results. We are confident that added solid growth will occur in the future.

Benefits to Acme Sheet Metal from the Proposed Loan

We have been leasing our facility for some time and we now have the opportunity to buy a vacant lot that adjoins our present business site. We will construct a steel building on the new site. We have bids from three reliable contractors to construct the building and will use the low bidder who came in at $159,950. (See bids attached as Exhibit T.)

The new machinery and equipment we wish to purchase should increase productivity substantially because it uses computer-controlled devices. The requested working capital will help us handle the larger sales levels now possible and achievable. (Letters of Interest are available if you need them.) We also enclose preliminary plans and specs for the new building. (See Exhibit V.)

We will continue to lease our present facility for the next several years. However, our lease provides for a purchase option beginning four years from now. It is our hope that we are able to exercise that option when the time comes. (A copy of our lease is attached as Exhibit W.)

Signature _Timothy G. Wilson_ Date _3-10-xx_

Note: This is a very short business plan; however, the applicants have already paid off one SBA loan and have a close working relationship with their bank. In paragraph five they refer to "Letters of Interest." These letters indicate that someone is prepared to give them additional work for their new machines. They would be wise to include them in their application. Depending on your personal situation, you may wish to expand your business plan.

Exhibit E (page 1)

Acme Sheet Metal: Resumés of Management

>> Timothy G. Wilson
>> 2000 Knoll Road
>> Anytown, NY 00000
>> (914) 222-2324

BIRTH DATE: September 1, 19XX

PLACE OF BIRTH: Anytown, NY

EDUCATION: Attended schools in Anytown, NY through high school level. I also attended Valley Junior College in Anytown for two years. Following that I graduated from the University of NY.

WORK EXPERIENCE: U.S. Army – 19XX–19XX; Intervalley Trucking – 19XX–19XX; Bil's Donuts – 19XX–19XX; Valley Manufacturing 19XX–19XX; Tyler Machine Shop 19XX–19XX; Self Employed – 1980–to Present.

I have had a lifelong interest in working with my hands in a more efficient way. I learned to maintain my truck while working as a trucker. I devised ways of making donuts in a more efficient manner while working for Bill's Donuts. I became an expert machinist later and also a foreman at Valley Manufacturing. At Tyler Machine Shop I did job estimating and was later a foreman. I was offered an ownership position in the business when Mr. Tyler learned of my decision to leave his company to start my own business.

Signature _Timothy G. Wilson_   Date _3-10-xx_

> Exhibit E (page 2)

Acme Sheet Metal: Resumés of Management

John B. Smith
620 Ridge Street
Anytown, NY 00000
(914) 999-6543

BIRTH DATE: June 15, 19XX

PLACE OF BIRTH: Anytown, NY

EDUCATION: Graduated from Anytown High School. I attended Valley Junior College for two years.

WORK EXPERIENCE: U.S. Army – 19XX–19XX; Blaine Construction – 19XX–19XX; O'Toole Manufacturing – 19XX–19XX; Tyler Machine Shop – 19XX–19XX; Self employed – 19XX–Present.

During these years I acquired a good knowledge of the machine shop business. I worked as a journeyman machinist, a floor leadman and also became involved in estimating new jobs. I have also taken night school courses in accounting and business administration to further my knowledge.

Signature _John B. Smith_   Date _3-5-xx_

Exhibit F

Acme Sheet Metal: Consent of Spouses to Sign Loan Agreement

Our wives, Marilyn Wilson and Nancy Smith, are willing to sign any necessary loan documents.

Signatures *Marilyn Wilson*   *Nancy Smith*

Date *3/31/xx*

> **Exhibit G**

Acme Sheet Metal: Equipment List

List of all equipment and fixtures to be purchased with this loan.

ITEM	MODEL	Serial Number	COST
ACE Numerically Controlled Machine	A-450	#741134	$80,000
ACE Numerically Controlled Accessory Package	A-451	none	$20,000

Signature _Timothy G. Wilson_ Date _3-10-xx_

Exhibit I (front)

Applicant's Agreement of Compliance

U.S. Small Business Administration

AGREEMENT OF COMPLIANCE

In compliance with Executive Order 11246, as amended (Executive Order 11246, as amended prohibits discrimination because of race, color, religion, sex, or national origin, and requires affirmative action to ensure equality of opportunity in all aspects of employment by all contractors and subcontractors, performing work under a Federally assisted construction contract in excess of $10,000, regardless of the number of employees), the applicant/recipient, contractor or subcontractor agrees that in consideration of the approval and as a condition of the disbursement of all or any part of a loan by the Small Business Administration (SBA) that it will incorporate or cause to be incorporated into any contract or subcontract in excess of $10,000 for construction work, or modification thereof, as defined in the regulations of the Secretary of Labor, at 41 CFR Chapter 60, which is paid for in whole or in part with funds obtained from the Federal Government or borrowed on the credit of the Federal Government pursuant to a grant, contract, loan, insurance or guarantee, or undertaken pursuant to any Federal program involving such grant, contract, loan, insurance or guarantee, the following equal opportunity clause:

During the performance of this contract, the contractor agrees as follows:

(1) The contractor will not discriminate against any employee or applicant for employment because of race, color, religion, sex or national origin. The contractor will take affirmative action to insure that applicants are employed, and that employees are treated during employment without regard to their race, color, religion, sex or national origin. Such action shall include, but not be limited to the following: employment, upgrading, demotion or transfer, recruitment or advertising; layoff or termination; rates of pay or other forms of compensation; and selection for training, including apprenticeship. The contractor agrees to post in conspicuous places, available to employees and applicants for employment, notices to be provided setting forth the provisions of this nondiscrimination clause.

(2) The contractor will, in all solicitations or advertisements for employees placed by or on behalf of the contractor, state that all qualified applicants will receive consideration for employment without regard to race, color, religion, sex or national origin.

(3) The contractor will send to each labor union or representative of workers with which he has a collective bargaining agreement or other contract or understanding, a notice to be provided advising the said labor union or workers' representative of the contractor's commitments under Executive Order 11246, as amended, and shall post copies of the notice in conspicuous places available to employees and applicants for employment.

(4) The contractor will comply with all provisions of Executive Order 11246, as amended, and the rules and relevant orders of the Secretary of Labor created thereby.

(5) The contractor will furnish all information and reports required by Executive Order 11246, as amended, and by the rules, regulations and orders of the Secretary of Labor, or pursuant thereto, and will permit access to books, records and accounts by SBA (See SBA Form 793) and the Secretary of Labor for purposes of investigation to ascertain compliance with such rules, regulations and orders. (The information collection requirements contained in Executive Order 11246, as amended, are approved under OMB No. 1215-0072.)

(6) In the event of the contractor's noncompliance with the nondiscrimination clause or with any of the said rules, regulations or orders, this contract may be canceled, terminated or suspended in whole or in part and the contractor may be declared ineligible for further Government contracts or federally assisted construction contracts in accordance with procedures authorized in Executive Order 11246, as amended, and such other sanctions may be imposed and remedies invoked as provided in the said Executive Order or by rule, regulation or order of the Secretary of Labor, or as otherwise provided by law.

The contractor will include the portion of the sentence immediately preceding paragraph (1) and the provisions of paragraphs (1) through (6) in every subcontract or purchase order unless exempted by rules, regulations or orders of the Secretary of Labor issued pursuant to Executive Order 11246, as amended, so that such provisions will be binding upon each subcontractor or vendor. The contractor will take such action with respect to any subcontract or purchase order as SBA may direct as a means of enforcing such provisions, including sanctions for noncompliance. Provided, however, that in the event a contractor becomes involved in or is threatened with litigation with a subcontractor or vendor as a result of such direction by SBA, the contractor may request the United States to enter into such litigation to protect the interest of the United States.

Note: This form must be completed only when a contract in excess of $10,000 is involved, and is signed by the contractor.

Exhibit I (back)

U.S. Small Business Administration

The Applicant further agrees that it will be bound by the above equal opportunity clause with respect to its own employment practices when it participates in federally assisted construction work.

The Applicant agrees that it will assist and cooperate actively with SBA and the Secretary of Labor in obtaining the compliance of contractors and subcontractors with the equal opportunity clause and the rules, regulations and relevant orders of the Secretary of Labor, that it will furnish SBA and the Secretary of Labor such information as they may require for the supervision of such compliance, and that it will otherwise assist SBA in the discharge of the Agency's primary responsibility for securing compliance. The Applicant further agrees that it will refrain from entering into any contract or contract modification subject to Executive Order 11246, as amended, and will carry out such sanctions and penalties for violation of the equal opportunity clause as may be imposed upon contractors and subcontractors by SBA or the Secretary of Labor or such other sanctions and penalties for violation thereof as may, in the opinion of the Administrator, be necessary and appropriate.

In addition, the Applicant agrees that if it fails or refuses to comply with these undertakings SBA may take any or all of the following actions: cancel, terminate or suspend in whole or in part the loan; refrain from extending any further assistance to the applicant under the programs with respect to which the failure or refusal occurred until satisfactory assurance of future compliance has been received from such applicant; and refer the case to the Department of Justice for appropriate legal proceedings.

In consideration of the approval by the Small Business Administration of a loan to __Acme Sheet Metal__ Applicant, said Applicant and __Weaver Construction Company__ the general contractor, mutually promise and agree that the(y) will comply with all nondiscrimination provisions and requirements of Executive Order 11246, as amended.

Executed the __15th__ day of __March__ 19 __XX__

__Acme Sheet Metal__
Name, Address, & Phone No. of Applicant

By __Timothy G. Wilson__
Typed Name & Title of Authorized Official

Timothy G. Wilson
Signature of Authorized Official

Corporate Seal

__Weaver Construction Company__
Name, Address, & Phone No. of Subrecipient

By __Robert Weaver__
Typed Name & Title of Authorized Official

Robert Weaver, President
Signature of Authorized Official

Corporate Seal

SBA Form 601 (10-85) REF: SOP 9030 Previous editions are Obsolete

* U.S. GOVERNMENT PRINTING OFFICE: 1991 — 312-624/51731

> **Exhibits T, V, & W**

Acme Sheet Metal: Summary of Other Exhibits

Exhibit T

    Cost of Construction
    (Including bids)
    _____

Exhibit V

    Preliminary Construction Plans
    _____

Exhibit W

    Copy of Lease
    _____

Copies of Partnership Tax Returns

Remember, all exhibits must be signed and dated.

Note: The foregoing sample is a typical SBA loan guaranty request. Many actual cases would be simpler than Acme Sheet Metal. Others are more complex. If you are applying for a loan to purchase an existing business, the SBA will require you to submit:

- The reason the present owner is selling the business;
- A copy of the proposed Buy/Sell Agreement;
- The seller's income tax returns for the past three years;
- A balance sheet for the business being sold, dated within the last 90 days. (If the income tax returns are more than 90 days old, you must submit a current interim operating statement for the seller, dated within 90 days of application submission.); and
- Independent appraisal(s) of assets changing hands, if value cannot be readily determined from the other material submitted.

Exhibit Z (front)

OMB Approval No 3245-0201

SBA LOAN NUMBER

COMPENSATION AGREEMENT FOR SERVICES IN CONNECTION WITH APPLICATION AND LOAN FROM (OR IN PARTICIPATION WITH) SMALL BUSINESS ADMINISTRATION

The undersigned representative (attorney, accountant, engineer, appraiser, etc.) hereby agrees that the undersigned has not and will not, directly or indirectly, charge or receive any payment in connection with the application for or the making of the loan except for services actually performed on behalf of the Applicant. The undersigned further agrees that the amount of payment for such services shall not exceed an amount deemed reasonable by the SBA (and, if it is a participation loan, by the participating lending institution), and to refund any amount in excess of that deemed reasonable by SBA (and the participating institution). This agreement shall supersede any other agreement covering payment for such services.

A general description of the services performed, or to be performed, by the undersigned and the compensation paid or to be paid are set forth below. <u>If the total compensation in any case exceeds $1,000 (or $300 for: (1) regular business loans of $15,000 or less; or (2) all disaster home loans) or if SBA should otherwise require, the services must be itemized on a schedule attached showing each date services were performed, time spent each day, and description of service rendered on each day listed.</u>

The undersigned Applicant and representative hereby certify that no other fees have been charged or will be charged by the representative in connection with this loan, unless provided for in the loan authorization specifically approved by SBA.

GENERAL DESCRIPTION OF SERVICES

Paid Previously	$	-0-
Additional Amount to be Paid	$	6,000
Total Compensation	$	6,000

(Section 13 of the Small Business Act (15 USC 642) requires disclosures concerning fees. Parts 103, 108 and 120 of Title 13 of the Code of Federal Regulations contain provisions covering appearances and compensation of persons representing SBA applicants. Section 103.13-5 authorizes the suspension or revocation of the privilege of any such person to appear before SBA for charging a fee deemed unreasonable by SBA for services actually performed, charging of unreasonable expenses, or violation of this agreement. Whoever commits any fraud, by false or misleading statement or representation, or by conspiracy, shall be subject to the penalty of any applicable Federal or State statute.)

Dated _____3/10_____, 19 XX

_____Clark & Brown, CPAs_____
(Representative)

By _____*Carol Brown*_____

The Applicant hereby certifies to SBA that the above representations, description of services and amounts are correct and satisfactory to Applicant.

Dated _____3/11_____, 19 XX

_____Acme Sheet Metal_____
(Applicant)

By _____*Timothy G. Wilson*_____

The participating lending institution hereby certifies that the above representations of service rendered and amounts charged are reasonable and satisfactory to it.

Dated _____3/15_____, 19 XX

_____Bank of First National State_____
(Lender)

By _____*John J. Lynch, Assist. V.P.*_____

NOTE: Foregoing certification must be executed, if by a corporation, in corporate name by duly authorized officer and duly attested; if by a partnership, in the firm name together with signature of general partner.

PLEASE NOTE: The estimated burden hours for the completion of SBA Form 147, 148, 159, 160, 160A, 529B, 928 and 1059 is 6 hrs. per response. If you have any questions or comments concerning this estimate or any other aspect of this information collection please contact, Chief Administrative Information Branch, U.S. Small Business Administration, 409 3rd St. S.W. Washington, D.C. 20416 and Gary Waxman, Clearance Officer, Paperwork Reduction Project (3245-0201), Office of Management and Budget, Washington, D.C. 20503.

SBA FORM 159 (2-93) REF SOP 70 50 Use 7-89 Edition Until Exhausted

Exhibit Z (back)

SMALL BUSINESS ADMINISTRATION

POLICY AND REGULATIONS CONCERNING REPRESENTATIVES AND THEIR FEES

An applicant for a loan from SBA may obtain the assistance of any attorney, accountant, engineer, appraiser or other representative to aid him in the preparation and presentation of his application to SBA; however, such representation is not mandatory. In the event a loan is approved, the services of an attorney may be necessary to assist in the preparation of closing documents, title abstracts, etc. SBA will allow the payment of reasonable fees or other compensation for services performed by such representatives on behalf of the applicant.

There are no "authorized representatives" of SBA, other than our regular salaried employees. Payment of any fee or gratuity to SBA employees is illegal and will subject the parties to such a transaction to prosecution.

SBA Regulations [Part 103, Sec. 103.13-5(c)] prohibit representatives from charging or proposing to charge any contingent fee for any services performed in connection with an SBA loan unless the amount of such fee bears a necessary and reasonable relationship to the services actually performed; or to charge for any expenses which are not deemed by SBA to have been necessary in connection with the application. The Regulations (Part 120, Sec. 120.104-2) also prohibit the payment of any bonus, brokerage fee or commission in connection with SBA loans.

In line with these Regulations SBA will not approve placement or finder's fees for the use or attempted use of influence in obtaining or trying to obtain an SBA loan, or fees based solely upon a percentage of the approved loan or any part thereof.

Fees which will be approved will be limited to reasonable sums of services actually rendered in connection with the application or the closing, based upon the time and effort required, the qualifications of the representative and the nature and extent of the services rendered by such representatives. Representatives of loan applicants will be required to execute an agreement as to their compensation for services rendered in connection with said loan.

It is the responsibility of the applicant to set forth in the appropriate section of the application the names of all persons or firms engaged by or on behalf of the applicant. Applicants are required to advise the Regional Office in writing the names and fees of any representatives engaged by the applicant subsequent to the filing of the application. This reporting requirement is approved under OMB Approval Number 3245-0016.

Any loan applicant having any questions concerning the payments of fees, or the reasonableness of fees, should communicate with the Field Office where the application is filed.

U.S. GOVERNMENT PRINTING OFFICE : 1993 - 348-097

Appendix A

SBA Field Locations

Region I

Boston Regional Office
155 Federal Street
Boston, MA 02110
(617) 451-2023
FAX (617) 424-5485

Boston District Office
10 Causeway Street, Room 265
Boston, MA 02222-1093
(617) 565-5590
FAX (617) 565-5598

Augusta District Office
40 Western Avenue, Room 512
Augusta, ME 04330
(207) 622-8378
FAX (207) 622-8277

Concord District Office
143 North Main Street, Suite 202
Concord, NH 03301
(603) 225-1400
FAX (603) 225-1409

Hartford District Office
330 Main Street
Hartford, CT 06106
(203) 240-4700
FAX (203) 240-4659

Montpelier District Office
87 State Street, Room 205
Montpelier, VT 05602
(802) 828-4422
FAX (802) 828-4485

Providence District Office
380 Westminster Mall
Providence, RI 02903
(401) 528-4561
FAX (401) 528-4539

Springfield Branch Office
1550 Main Street, Room 212
Springfield, MA 01103
(413) 785-0268
FAX (413) 785-0267

Region II

New York Regional Office
26 Federal Plaza, Suite 31-08
New York, NY 10278
(212) 264-1450
FAX (212) 264-0900

Buffalo District Office
111 West Huron Street, Room 1311
Buffalo, NY 14202
(716) 846-4301
FAX (716) 846-4418

Newark District Office
60 Park Place
Newark, NJ 07102
(201) 645-2434
FAX (201) 645-6265

New York District Office
26 Federal Plaza, Suite 31-00
New York, NY 10278
(212) 264-2454
FAX (212) 264-4963

SBA Field Locations (continued)

Puerto Rico and Virgin Islands
Carlos Chardon Avenue, Suite 691
Hato Rey, PR 00918
(809) 766-5572
FAX (809) 766-5309

Syracuse District Office
100 South Clinton Street, Suite 1071
Syracuse, NY 13260
(315) 423-5383
FAX (315) 423-5370

Elmira Branch Office
333 East Water Street
Elmira, NY 14901
(607) 734-8130
FAX (607) 733-4656

Melville Branch Office
35 Pinelawn Road, Suite 207W
Melville, NY 11747
(516) 454-0750
FAX (516) 454-0769

Rochester Branch Office
100 State Street, Suite 410
Rochester, NY 14614
(716) 263-6700
FAX (716) 263-3146

Albany Post-of-Duty
Corner of Clinton and Pearl, Suite 815
Albany, NY 12207
(518) 472-6300
FAX (518) 472-7138

Camden Post-of-Duty
2600 Mt. Ephraim Avenue
Camden, NJ 08104
(609) 757-5183
FAX (609) 757-5335

St. Croix Post-of-Duty
3013 Golden Rock, Suite 165
St. Croix, VI 00820
(809) 778-5380
FAX (809) 778-1102

St. Thomas Post-of-Duty
3800 Crown Bay
St. Thomas, VI 00802
(809) 774-8530
FAX (809 776-2312

Region III

Philadelphia Regional Office
475 Allendale Road, Suite 201
King of Prussia, PA 19406
(215) 962-3700
FAX (215) 962-3743

Baltimore District Office
10 South Howard Street, Suite 6220
Baltimore, MD 21201-2525
(410) 962-4392
FAX (410) 962-1805

Clarksburg District Office
168 West Main Street
Clarksburg, WV 26301
(304) 623-5631
FAX (304) 623-0023

Philadelphia District Office
475 Allendale Road, Suite 2C1
King of Prussia, PA 19406
(215) 962-3800
FAX (215) 962-3795

Pittsburgh District Office
960 Penn Avenue
Pittsburgh, PA 15222
(412) 644-2780
FAX (412) 644-5446

Richmond District Office
400 North Eighth Street, Rocm 3015
Richmond, VA 23240
(804) 771-2400
FAX (804) 771-8018

SBA Field Locations (continued)

Wilmington Branch Office
910 North King Street, Suite 412
Wilmington, DE 19801
(302) 573-6295
FAX (302) 573-6060

Washington District Office
1110 Vermont Avenue NW, Suite 900
Washington, DC 20036
(202) 606-4000
FAX (202) 606-4225

Charleston Branch Office
550 Eagan Street, Room 309
Charleston, WV 25301
(304) 347-5220
FAX (304) 347-5350

Harrisburg Branch Office
100 Chestnut Street, Room 309
Harrisburg, PA 17101
(717) 782-3840
FAX (717) 782-4839

Wilkes-Barre Branch Office
20 North Pennsylvania Avenue, Room 2327
Wilkes-Barre, PA 18701-3589
(717) 826-6497
FAX (717) 826-6287

Region IV

Atlanta Regional Office
1375 Peachtree Street, NE
Atlanta, GA 30367-8102
(404) 347-2797
FAX (404) 347-2355

Atlanta District Office
1720 Peachtree Road, NW
Atlanta, GA 30309
(404) 347-4749
FAX (404) 347-4745

Birmingham District Office
2121 8th Avenue North, Suite 200
Birmingham, AL 35203-2398
(205) 731-1344
FAX (205) 731-1404

Charlotte District Office
200 North College Street, Suite A2015
Charlotte, NC 28202-2137
(704) 344-6563
FAX (704) 344-6769

Columbia District Office
1835 Assembly Street, Room 358
Columbia, SC 29201
(803) 765-5377
FAX (803) 765-5962

Jackson District Office
101 West Capitol Street, Suite 400
Jackson, MS 39201
(601) 965-4378
FAX (601) 965-4294

Jacksonville District Office
7825 Baymeadows Way, Suite 100-B
Jacksonville, FL 32256-7504
(904) 443-1900
FAX (904) 443-1980

Louisville District Office
600 Dr. M. L. King, Jr. Place, Room 188
Louisville, KY 40202
(502) 582-5971
FAX (502) 582-5009

Miami District Office
1320 South Dixie Highway, Suite 501
Coral Gables, FL 33146-2911
(305) 536-5521
FAX (305) 536-5058

Nashville District Office
50 Vantage Way, Suite 201
Nashville, TN 37228-1500
(615) 736-5881
FAX (615) 736-7232

SBA Field Locations (continued)

Gulfport Branch Office
One Hancock Plaza, Suite 1001
Gulfport, MS 39501-7758
(601) 863-4449
FAX (601) 864-0179

Tampa Post-of-Duty
501 East Polk Street, Suite 104
Tampa, FL 33602-3945
(813) 228-2594
FAX (813) 228-2111

Region V

Chicago Regional Office
300 South Riverside Plaza, Suite 1975 S.
Chicago, IL 60606-6617
(312) 353-5000
FAX (312) 353-3426

Madison District Office
212 East Washington Avenue, Room 213
Madison, WI 53703
(608) 264-5261
FAX (608) 264-5541

Chicago District Office
500 West Madison Street, Suite 1250
Chicago, IL 60661-2511
(312) 353-4528
FAX (312) 886-5108

Minneapolis District Office
100 North 6th Street, Suite 610
Minneapolis, MN 55403-1563
(612) 370-2324
FAX (612) 370-2303

Cleveland District Office
1111 Superior Avenue, Suite 630
Cleveland, OH 44114-2507
(216) 522-4180
FAX (216) 522-2038

Cincinnati Branch Office
525 Vine Street, Suite 870
Cincinnati, OH 45202
(513) 684-2814
FAX (513) 684-3251

Columbus District Office
2 Nationwide Plaza, Suite 1400
Columbus, OH 43215-2592
(614) 469-6860
FAX (614) 469-2391

Milwaukee Branch Office
310 West Wisconsin Avenue, Suite 400
Milwaukee, WI 53203
(414) 297-3941
FAX (414) 297-1377

Detroit District Office
477 Michigan Avenue, Room 515
Detroit, MI 48226
(313) 226-6075
FAX (313) 226-4769

Marquette Branch Office
228 West Washington, Suite 11
Marquette, MI 49885
(906) 225-1108
FAX (906) 225-1109

Indianapolis District Office
429 North Pennsylvania, Suite 100
Indianapolis, IN 46204-1873
(317) 226-7272
FAX (317) 226-7259

Springfield Branch Office
511 West Capitol Avenue, Suite 302
Springfield, IL 62704
(217) 492-4416
FAX (217) 492-4867

SBA Field Locations (continued)

Region VI

Dallas Regional Office
8625 King George Drive, Building C
Dallas, TX 75235-3391
(214) 767-7633
FAX (214) 767-7870

Albuquerque District Office
625 Silver Avenue SW, Suite 320
Albuquerque, NM 87102
(505) 766-1870
FAX (505) 766-1057

Dallas District Office
4300 Amon Carter Boulevard, Suite 114
Ft. Worth, TX 76155
(817) 885-6500
FAX (817) 885-6516

El Paso District Office
10737 Gateway West, Suite 320
El Paso, TX 79935
(915) 540-5676
FAX (915) 540-5636

Houston District Office
9301 Southwest Freeway, Suite 550
Houston, TX 77074-1591
(713) 773-6500
FAX (713) 773-6550

Little Rock District Office
2120 Riverfront Drive, Suite 100
Little Rock, AR 72202
(501) 324-5871
FAX (501) 324-5199

Lower Rio Grande Valley District
222 East Van Buren Street, Room 500
Harlingen, TX 78550-6855
(210) 427-8533
FAX (210) 427-8537

Lubbock District Office
1611 Tenth Street, Suite 200
Lubbock, TX 79401-2693
(806) 743-7462
FAX (806) 743-7487

New Orleans District Office
365 Canal Street, Suite 2250
New Orleans, LA 70130
(504) 589-6685
FAX (504) 589-2339

Oklahoma City District Office
200 North West 5th Street, Suite 670
Oklahoma City, OK 73102
(405) 231-5521
FAX (405) 231-4876

San Antonio District Office
727 East Durango Boulevard, Room A-527
San Antonio, TX 78206-1204
(210) 229-5900
FAX (210) 229-5937

Corpus Christi Branch Office
606 North Carancahua, Suite 1200
Corpus Christi, TX 78476
(512) 888-3331
FAX (512) 888-3418

Austin Post-of-Duty
300 East 8th Street, Room 967
Austin, TX 78701
(512) 482-5288
FAX (512) 482-5290

Marshall Post-of-Duty
505 East Travis, Room 112
Marshall, TX 75670
(903) 935-5257
FAX (903) 935-1248

Shreveport Post-of-Duty
401 Edwards Street, Room 916
Shreveport, LA 71101-5523
(318) 676-3196
FAX (318) 676-3214

SBA Field Locations (continued)

Region VII

Kansas City Regional Office
911 Walnut Street
Kansas City MO 64106
(816) 426-3210
FAX (816) 426-5559

Cedar Rapids District Office
215 4th Avenue SE, Suite 200
Cedar Rapids, IA 52401-1806
(319) 362-6405
FAX (319) 362-7861

Des Moines District Office
210 Walnut Street, Room 749
Des Moines, IA 50309
(515) 284-4422
FAX (515) 284-4572

Kansas City District Office
323 West 8th Street, Suite 501
Kansas City, MO 64105
(816) 374-6708
FAX (816) 374-6759

Omaha District Office
11145 Mill Valley Road
Omaha, NE 68154
(402) 221-4691
FAX (402) 221-3680

St. Louis District Office
815 Olive Street, Room 242
St. Louis, MO 63101
(314) 539-6600
FAX (314) 539-3785

Wichita District Office
100 East English Street, Suite 510
Wichita, KS 67202
(316) 269-6616
FAX (316) 269-6499

Springfield Branch Office
620 South Glenstone Street, Suite 110
Springfield, MO 65802-3200
(417) 864-7670
FAX (417) 864-4108

Region VIII

Denver Regional Office
633 17th Street
Denver, CO 80202
(303) 294-7186
FAX (303) 294-7153

Casper District Office
100 East B Street, Room 4001
Casper, WY 82602-2839
(307) 261-5761
FAX (307) 261-5499

Denver District Office
721 19th Street, Suite 426
Denver, CO 80202-2599
(303) 844-3984
FAX (303) 844-6468

Fargo District Office
657 2nd Avenue North, Room 219
Fargo, ND 58108-3086
(701) 239-5131
FAX (701) 239-5645

Helena District Office
301 South Park, Room 334
Helena, MT 59626
(406) 449-5381
FAX (406) 449-5474

Salt Lake City District Office
125 South State Street, Room 2237
Salt Lake City, UT 84138-1195
(801) 524-5804
FAX (801) 524-4160

Sioux Falls District Office
110 South Phillips Avenue, Suite 200
Sioux Falls, SD 57102-1109
(605) 330-4231
FAX (605) 330-4215

SBA Field Locations (continued)

Region IX

San Francisco Regional Office
71 Stevenson Street
San Francisco, CA 94105-2939
(415) 744-6404
FAX (415) 744-6435

Fresno District Office
2719 North Air Fresno Drive, Suite 107
Fresno, CA 93727-1547
(209) 487-5189
FAX (209) 487-5636

Honolulu District Office
300 Ala Moana Boulevard, Room 2213
Honolulu, HI 96850-4981
(808) 541-2990
FAX (808) 541-2976

Las Vegas District Office
301 East Stewart Street, Room 301
Las Vegas, NV 89125-2527
(702) 388-6611
FAX (702) 388-6469

Los Angeles District Office
330 North Brand Boulevard, Suite 1200
Glendale, CA 91203-2304
(818) 553-3210
FAX (818) 552-3260

Phoenix District Office
2828 North Central Avenue, Suite 800
Phoenix, AZ 85004-1093
(602) 640-2316
FAX (602) 640-2360

San Diego District Office
550 West "C" Street, Suite 550
San Diego, CA 92188-3540
(619) 557-7250
FAX (619) 557-5894

San Francisco District Office
211 Main Street
San Francisco, CA 94105-1988
(415) 744-6820
FAX (415) 744-6812

Santa Ana District Office
901 West Civic Center Drive, Suite 160
Santa Ana, CA 92703-2352
(714) 836-2494
FAX (714) 836-2528

Agana Branch Office
238 Archbishop F. C. Flores Street, Room 508
Agana, GU 96910
(671) 472-7277
FAX (200) 550-7365

Sacramento Branch Office
660 J Street, Suite 215
Sacramento, CA 95814-2413
(916) 498-6410
FAX (916) 498-6422

Reno Post-of-Duty
50 South Virginia Street, Room 238
Reno, NV 89505-3216
(702) 784-5268

Tucson Post-of-Duty
300 West Congress Street, Box FB 33
Tucson, AZ 85701-1319
(602) 670-4759
FAX (602) 670-4763

Ventura Post-of-Duty
6477 Telephone Road, Suite 10
Ventura, CA 93003-4459
(805) 642-1866
FAX (805) 642-9538

Region X

Seattle Regional Office
2601 Fourth Avenue, Suite 440
Seattle, WA 98121-1273
(206) 553-5676
FAX (206) 553-4155

Anchorage District Office
222 West 8th Avenue, Room A36
Anchorage, AK 99513-7559
(907) 271-4022
FAX (907) 271-4545

SBA Field Locations (continued)

Boise District Office
1020 Main Street, Suite 290
Boise, ID 83702-5745
(208) 334-1696
FAX (208) 334-9353

Portland District Office
222 South West Columbia Street, Suite 500
Portland, OR 97201-6695
(503) 326-2682
FAX (503) 326-2808

Seattle District Office
915 Second Avenue, Room 1792
Seattle, WA 98174-1088
(206) 220-6520
FAX (206) 220-6570

Spokane District Office
West 601 First Avenue
Spokane, WA 99204-0317
(509) 353-2800
FAX (509) 353-2829

Disaster Area Regional Offices

DA01 Disaster Area Office – Area 1
360 Rainbow Boulevard South
Niagara Falls, NY 14303-1192
(716) 282-4612
FAX (716) 282-1472

DA02 Disaster Area Office – Area 2
One Baltimore Place, Suite 300
Atlanta, GA 30308
(404) 347-3771
FAX (404) 347-4183

DA03 Disaster Area Office – Area 3
4400 Amon Carter Boulevard, Suite 102
Ft. Worth, TX 76155
(817) 885-7600
FAX (817) 885-7616

DA04 Disaster Area Office – Area 4
1825 Bell Street, Suite 208
Sacramento, CA 95825
(916) 566-7248
FAX (916) 566-7280

Disaster Loan Offices

Reg II: New York Home Loan Servicing Center
201 Varrick Street, Room 628
New York, NY 10014
(212) 620-3722
FAX (212) 620-3730

Reg IV: Birmingham Disaster Loan
2121 8th Avenue North, Suite 200
Birmingham, AL 35203-2398
(205) 731-0441
FAX (205) 731-2765

Reg VI: El Paso Disaster Servicing
10737 Gateway West, Suite 320
El Paso, TX 79935
(915) 540-5166
FAX (915) 540-5636

Reg VI: Little Rock Commercial Loan
2120 Riverfront Drive, Suite 100
Little Rock, AR 72202
(501) 324-5871
FAX (501) 324-5199

Reg IX: Santa Ana Disaster Loan
901 West Civic Center Drive, Suite 160
Santa Ana, CA 92703-2352
(714) 836-2494
FAX (714) 836-2528

Reg IX: Fresno Commercial Loan
2719 North Air Fresno Drive
Fresno, CA 93727-1547
(209) 487-5189;
FAX (209) 487-5803

Appendix B

U.S. Export Assistance Centers

U.S. Export Assistance Centers (USEACs) offer, under one roof, the services and programs of the SBA, the U.S. Department of Commerce, and the Export-Import Bank of the United States, as well as other public/private trade partners. Four initial USEAC sites opened in winter 1994.

BALTIMORE:
World Trade Center
401 East Pratt Street, Suite 2432
Baltimore, MD 21202
(410) 962-4539

CHICAGO:
Xerox Center
55 West Monroe Street, Suite 2440
Chicago, IL 60603
(312) 353-8040

LOS ANGELES:
One World Trade Center, Suite 1670
Long Beach, CA 90831
(310) 980-4550

MIAMI:
Trade Port Building
5600 Northwest 36th Street, 6th Floor
Miami, FL 33166
(305) 526-7425

Notes

Appendix C

Non-Bank Lenders

AT&T Small Business Lending Corporation
44 Whippany Road
Morristown, NJ 07962
(800) 221-7252
FAX (201) 397-4086
Areas of interest: Nationwide

Allied Lending Corp./IDC Financial Corporation
4963 Elm Street, Suite 106
Bethesda, MD 20814
(301) 654-1128
Areas of interest: Nationwide

Business Loan Center
919 Third Avenue, Floor 17
New York, NY 10022-3902
(212) 751-5626
FAX (212) 751-9345
Areas of interest: All states east of the Mississippi
River, including U.S. Virgin Islands

Emergent Business Capital, Inc.
233 North Main Street, Suite 350
Greenville, SC 29606
(803) 232-6197
Areas of interest: Southern and Southwestern
states

The Grow America Fund, Inc.
C/O The National Development Council
41 East 42nd Street, Suite 1500
New York, NY 10017
(212) 682-1106
Areas of interest: Local

Heller First Capital Corporation
650 California Street, 23rd Floor
San Francisco, CA 94108-2604
(415) 274-5700
FAX (415) 274-5744
Areas of interest: West of the Mississippi River

Independence Funding, Inc.
3010 LBJ Freeway, Suite 920
Dallas, TX 75234
(214) 247-1776
Areas of interest: Local

G.E. Small Business Finance Corporation
2055 Craigshire Road, Suite 400
St. Louis, MO 63146
(800) 447-2025
Areas of interest: Nationwide

The Money Store Investment Corporation
3301 C Street, Suite 301
Sacramento, CA 95816
(800) 722-3066
Areas of interest: Nationwide

PMC Capital, Inc.
17290 Preston Road, 3rd Floor
Dallas, TX 75252
(800) 486-3223
Areas of interest: Nationwide

Notes

Appendix D

Microloan Demonstration Program

Intermediary Lenders

Alabama
Elmore Community Action Committee, Inc.
1011 West Tallassee
P.O. Drawer H, Wetumpka, AL 36092
Contact: Marion D. Dunlap
(205) 567-4361
   Service Area: Autauga, Elmore, and Montgomery counties.

Arizona
Chicanos Por La Causa, Inc.
1112 East Buckeye Road, Phoenix, AZ 85034
Contact: Pete Garcia
(602) 257-0700
   Service Area: Urban areas of Maricopa and Pima counties, Graham and Gila counties (including Point of Pines Reservation and the Southwestern area of Fort Apache Reservation), Coconino and Mohave counties (including the Kaibab, Havasupai, and Hualapai Reservations and the Western portions of the Navajo and Hopi Reservations), Yavapai, and La Paz counties.

Arizona
PPEP Housing Development Corp./Micro Industry Credit Rural Organization
802 East 46th Street, Tucson, AZ 85713
Contact: John D. Arnold
(602) 622-3553
   Service Area: Cochise, Santa Cruz, rural Maricopa, rural Pinal, and rural Yuma counties.

Arkansas
Arkansas Enterprise Group
605 Main Street, Suite 203, Arkadelphia, AR 71923
Contact: Brian Kelley
(501) 246-9739
   Service Area: Southern portion of the state including Arkansas, Ashley, Bradley, Calhoun, Chicot, Clark, Cleveland, Columbia, Dallas, Desha, Drew, Garland, Grant, Hempstead, Hot Spring, Howard, Jefferson, Lafayette, Lincoln, Little River, Miller, Monroe, Montgomery, Nevasa, Ouachita, Phillips, Pike, Polk, Pulaski, Saline, Sevier, and Union counties.

Arkansas
Delta Community Development Corp.
675 Eaton Road
P.O. Box 852, Forrest City, AR 72335
Contact: Michael Jackson
(501) 633-9113
   Service Area: Cross, Crittenden, Monroe, Lee, and St. Francis counties.

Arkansas
White River Planning and Development District, Inc.
1652 White Drive
P.O. Box 2396, Batesville, AR 72503
Contact: Van C. Thomas
(501) 793-5233
   Service Area: Cleburne, Fulton, Independence, Izard, Jackson, Sharp, Stone, Van Buren, White, and Woodruff counties.

Microloan Demonstration Program (continued)

California
: Arcata Economic Development Corporation
100 Ericson Court, Suite 100, Arcata, CA 95521
Contact: Kathleen E. Moxon
(707) 822-4616
  Service Area: Del Norte, Humboldt, Mendocino, Siskiyou, and Trinity counties.

California
: Center for Southeast Asian Refugee Resettlement
875 O'Farrell Street, San Francisco, CA 94109
Contact: Vu-Duc Vuong
(415) 885-2743
  Service Area: Alameda, Contra Costa, Marin, Merced, Sacramento, San Francisco, San Joaquin, San Mateo, Santa Clara, and Stanislaus counties.

California
: Coalition for Women's Economic Development
315 West Ninth Street, Suite 705, Los Angeles, CA 90015
Contact: Mari Riddle
(213) 489-4995
  Service Area: Los Angeles County.

California
: Valley Rural Development Corporation
3417 West Shaw, Suite 100, Fresno, CA 93711
Contact: Michael E. Foley
(209) 271-9030
  Service Area: Fresno, Kings, Kern, Stanislaus, Madera, Mariposa, Merced, Tuolumne, and Tulare counties.

Colorado
: Greater Denver Local Development Corporation
1981 Blake Street, Suite 406
P.O. Box 2135, Denver, CO 80206
Contact: Cecilia H. Prinster
(303) 296-9535
  Service Area: City of Denver, and Adams, Arapahoe, Boulder, Denver, and Jefferson counties.

Colorado
: Region 10 LEAP, Inc.
P.O. Box 849, Montrose, CO 81402
Contact: Stan Broome
(303) 249-2436
  Service Area: West Central area including Delta, Gunnison, Hinsdale, Montrose, Ouray, and San Miguel counties.

Connecticut
: New Haven Community Investment Corp.
809 Chapel Street, 2nd Floor, New Haven, CT 06510
Contact: Salvatore J. Brancati, Jr.
(203) 776-6172
  Service Area: Statewide

Delaware
: Wilmington Economic Development Corporation
605-A Market Street Mall, Wilmington, DE 19801
Contact: Edwin H. Nutter, Jr.
(302) 571-9088
  Service Area: New Castle county, in the cities of Wilmington, Newark, New Castle, Middletown, Odessa, and Townsend.

District of Columbia
: ARCH Development Corporation
1227 Good Hope Road SE, Washington, DC 20020
Contact: Duane Gautier
(202) 889-5023
  Service Area: Portions of the District of Columbia commonly referred to as Adams Morgan, Mount Pleasant and Anacostia, Congress Heights, Columbia Heights, and 14th Street Corridor.

Microloan Demonstration Program (continued)

District of Columbia   H Street Development Corporation
611 H Street NE, Washington, DC 20002
Contact: William J. Barrow
(202) 544-8353
    Service Area: Portions of the District of Columbia including specific areas of the Northeast, Southeast, and Northwest quadrants.

Florida   Community Equity Investments, Inc.
302 North Barcelona Street, Pensacola, FL 32501
Contact: Daniel R. Horvath
(904) 444-2234
    Service Area: Western Panhandle including Bay, Calhoun, Escambia, Gadsden, Gulf, Jackson, Holmes, Liberty, Leon, Franklin, Wakulla, Walton, Washington, Okaloosa, and Santa Rosa counties.

Florida   United Gainesville Community Development Corporation, Inc.
505 NW 2nd Avenue
P.O. Box 2518, Gainesville, FL 32602
Contact: Vian M. Cockerham
(904) 376-8891
    Service Area: North Central section including Alachua, Bradford, Columbia, Dixie, Gichrist, Hamilton, Jefferson, LaFayette, Levy, Madison, Marion, Putman, Suwanee, Taylor, and Union counties.

Georgia   Fulton County Development Corp. dba Greater Atlanta Small Business Project
10 Park Place South, Suite 305, Atlanta, GA 30303
Contact: Maurice S. Coakley
(404) 659-5955
    Service Area: Fulton, Dekalb, Cobb, Gwinnett, Fayette, Clayton, Henry, Douglas, and Rockdale counties.

Georgia   Small Business Assistance Corporation
31 West Congress Street, Suite 100, Savannah, GA 31401
Contact: Tony O'Reily
(912) 232-4700
    Service Area: Chatham, Effingham, Bryan, Bulloch, and Liberty counties.

Hawaii   The Immigrant Center
720 North King Street, Honolulu, HI 96817
Contact: Patrician Brandt
(808) 845-3918
    Service Area: Island of Oahu within the City and County of Honolulu.

Idaho   Panhandle Area Council
11100 Airport Drive, Hayden, ID 83835-9743
Contact: Jim Deffenbaugh
(208) 772-0584
    Service Area: Northern Panhandle including Benewah, Bonner, Boundary, Kotenai, and Shoshone counties.

Illinois   Greater Sterling Development Corporation
1741 Industrial Drive, Sterling, IL 61081
Contact: Reid Nolte
(815) 625-5255
    Service Area: City of Sterling and Whiteside and Lee counties.

Illinois   Illinois Development Finance Authority
233 South Wacker Drive, Suite 5310, Chicago, IL 60606
Contact: Philip S. Howe
(312) 793-5586
    Service Area: Statewide with the exceptions of Peoria, Tazwell, Woodford, Whiteside, and Lee counties, the City of Sterling, and those portions of Chicago currently served by WSEP.

Microloan Demonstration Program (continued)

Illinois	The Economic Development Council for the Peoria Area
	124 SW Adams Street, Suite 300, Peoria, IL 61602
	Contact: Michael Kuhns
	(309) 676-7500
		Service Area: Peoria, Tazwell and Woodford counties.

Illinois	The Neighborhood Institute and Women's Self Employment Project
	20 North Clark Street, Suite 400, Chicago, IL 60602
	Contact: Connie Evans, President
	(312) 606-8255
		Service Area: Portions of the City of Chicago.

Indiana	Eastside Community Investments Inc.
	26 North Arsenal Avenue, Indianapolis, IN 46201
	Contact: Dennis J. West
	(317) 637-7300
		Service Area: City of Indianapolis.

Indiana	Metro Small Business Assistance Corp.
	1 NW Martin Luther King, Jr., Boulevard
	Evansville, IN 47708-1869
	Contact: Debra A. Lutz
	(812) 426-5857
		Service Area: Vanderburgh, Posey, Gibson, and Warrick counties.

Iowa	Siouxland Economic Development Corporation
	400 Orpheum Electric Building
	P.O. Box 447, Sioux City, IA 51102
	Contact: Kenneth A. Beekley
	(712) 279-6286
		Service Area: Cherokee, Ida, Monoma, Plymouth, Sioux, and Woodbury counties.

Kansas	South Central Kansas Economic Development District, Inc.
	151 North Volutsia, Wichita, KS 67214
	Contact: Jack E. Alumbaugh
	(316) 683-4422
		Service Areas: Butler, Chautauqua, Cowley, Elk, Greenwood, Harper, Harvey, Kingman, Marion, McPherson, Reno, Rice, Sedgwick, and Sumner counties.

Kansas	Center for Business Innovations, Inc.
	4747 Troost Avenue, Kansas City, MO 64110
	Contact: Robert J. Sherwood
	(816) 561-8567
		Sercice Areas: Wyandotte, Johnson, Kansas City, and Leavenworth.

Kentucky	Kentucky Highlands Investment Corporation
	362 Old Whitley Road, London, KY 40741
	Contact: Jerry A. Rickett
	(606) 864-5175
		Service Area: Bell Clay, Clinton, Harlan, Jackson, Knox, Laurel, McCreary, Pulaski, Rockcastle, Wayne, and Whitley counties.

Kentucky	Purchase Area Development District
	1002 Medical Drive
	P.O. Box 588, Mayfield, KY 42066
	Contact: Henry A. Hodges
	(502) 247-7171
		Service Area: Western Kentucky including Ballard, Calloway, Carlisle, Futon, Graves, Hickman, McCracken, and Marshall counties.

Microloan Demonstration Program (continued)

Louisiana
: Greater Jennings Chamber of Commerce
414 Cary Avenue
P.O. Box 1209, Jennings, LA 70546
Contact: Jerry Arceneaux
(318) 824-0933
    Service Area: Jeff Davis Parish.

Maine
: Coastal Enterprises, Inc.
P.O. Box 268
Water Street, Wiscasset, ME 04578
Contact: Ronald L. Phillips
(207) 882-7552
    Service Area: Statewide excluding Aroostock, Piscataquis, Washington, Oxford, Penobscot, and Hancock counties.

Maine
: Northern Maine Regional Planning Commission
2 South Main Street
P.O. Box 779, Caribou, ME 04736
Contact: Robert P. Clark
(207) 498-8736
    Service Area: Aroostook, Piscataquis, Washington, Penobscot, and Hancock counties.

Maine
: Community Concepts, Inc.
35 Market Square
P.O. Box 278, South Parris, ME 04281
Contact: Charleen M. Chase
(207) 743-7716
    Service Area: Oxford County.

Maryland
: Council for Equal Business Opportunity, Inc.
The Park Plaza
800 North Charles Street, Suite 300, Baltimore, MD 21201
Contact: Michael Gaines
(410) 576-2326
    Service Area: City of Baltimore and Ann Arundel, Baltimore, Carroll, Harford, and Howard counties.

Massachusetts
: Economic Development Industrial Corporation of Lynn
37 Central Square, 3rd Floor, Lynn, MA 01901
Contact: Peter M. DeVeau
(617) 592-2361
    Service Area: City of Lynn.

Massachusetts
: Jobs for Fall River, Inc.
One Government Center, Fall River, MA 02722
Contact: Paul L. Vigeant
(508) 324-2620
    Service Area: City of Fall River.

Massachusetts
: Springfield Business Development Fund
36 Court Street, Room 222, Springfield, MA 01103
Contact: James Asselin
(413) 787-6050
    Service Area: City of Springfield.

Microloan Demonstration Program (continued)

Massachusetts   Western Massachusetts Enterprise Fund
324 Wells Street, Greenfield, MA 01301
Contact: Christopher Sikes
(413) 774-7204
     Service Area: Berkshire and Franklin Counties, the towns of Chester and Chicopes within Hampden County, the towns of Athol, Petersham, Phillipston and Royalston within Worcester County, and the following towns within Hampshire County: Amherst, Chesterfield, Cummington, Easthampton, Goshen, Hadley, Huntington, Middlefield, Northampton, Plainfield, Westhampton, Williamsburg, and Worthington.

Michigan   Ann Arbor Community Development Corp.
2008 Hogback Road, Suite 2A, Ann Arbor, MI 48105
Contact: Michelle Richards Vasquez
(313) 677-1400
     Service Area: Washtenaw County.

Michigan   Detroit Economic Growth Corporation
150 West Jefferson, Suite 1500, Detroit, MI 48226
Contact: Robert W. Spencer
(313) 963-2940
     Service Area: City of Detroit.

Michigan   Flint Community Development Corp.
877 East Fifth Avenue, Building C-1, Flint, MI 48503
Contact: Bobby J. Wells
(810) 239-5847
     Service Area: Genesee County.

Michigan   Northern Economic Initiatives Corp.
1009 West Ridge Street, Marquette, MI 49855
Contact: Richard Anderson
(906) 228-5571
     Service Area: Upper Peninsula including Alger, Baraga, Chippewa, Delta, Dickinson, Gogebic, Houghton, Iron, Keewenaw, Luce, Macinac, Marquette, Menonimee, Ontonagon, and Schoolcraft counties.

Minnesota   Northeast Entrepreneur Fund, Inc.
Olcott Plaza, Suite 140
820 Ninth Street North, Virginia, MN 55792
Contact: Mary Mathews
(218) 749-4191
     Service Area: Koochiching, Itasca, St. Louis, Aitkin, Carlton, Cook, and Lake counties.

Minnesota   Women Venture
2324 University Avenue, St. Paul, MN 55114
Contact: Kay Gudmestad
(612) 646-3808
     Service Area: Cities of Minneapolis and St. Paul and, Andra, Carver, Chisago, Dakota, Hennepin, Isanti, Ramsey, Scott, Washington, and Wright counties.

Minnesota   Minneapolis Consortium of Community Developers
1808 Riverside Avenue, Minneapolis, MN 55454-1035
Contact: Karen Reid
(612) 338-8729
     Service Area: Portions of the City of Minneapolis.

Minnesota   Northwest Minnesota Initiative Fund
722 Paul Bunyan Drive NW, Bemidji, MN 56601
Contact: Tim Wang
(218) 759-2057
     Service Area: Beltrami, Clearwater, Hubbard, Kittsson, Lake of the Woods Mahnomen, Marshall, Norman, Pennington, Polk, Red Lake, and Rousseau counties.

Microloan Demonstration Program (continued)

Mississippi	Delta Foundation 819 Main Street, Greenville, MS 38701 Contact: Harry J. Bowie (601) 335-5291 Service Area: Statewide excluding Issaquena, Sharkey, Humphreys, Madison, Leake, Kemper, Copiah, Hinds, Rankin, Newton, Smith, Jasper, Clarke, Jones, Wayne, and Greene counties.
Mississippi	Friends of Children of Mississippi, Inc. 4880 McWillie Circle, Jackson, MS 39206 Contact: Marvin Hogan (601) 362-1541 Service Area: Issaquena, Sharkey, Humphreys, Madison, Leake, Kemper, Copiah, Hinds, Rankin, Newton, Smith, Jasper, Clarke, Jones, Wayne, and Greene counties.
Missouri	Center for Business Innovations, Inc. 4747 Troost Avenue, Kansas City, MO 64110 Contact: Robert J. Sherwood (816) 561-8567 Service Area: Statewide
Montana	Capital Opportunities/District IX Human Resource Development Council, Inc. 321 East Main Street, Suite 300, Bozeman, MT 59715 Contact: Jeffery Rupp (406) 587-4486 Service Area: Gallatin, Park, and Meagher counties.
Montana	Women's Opportunity and Resource Development, Inc. 127 North Higgins Avenue, Missoula, MT 59802 Contact: Kelly Rosenleaf (406) 543-3550 Service Area: Lake, Mineral, Missoula, Ravalli, and Sanders counties.
Nebraska	Rural Enterprise Assistance Project P.O. Box 406, Walthill, NE 68067 Contact: Don Ralston (402) 846-5428 Service Area: Boone, Brown, Burt, Cass, Cherry, Colfax, Custer, Dixon, Gage, Greeley, Jefferson, Johnson, Keya Paha, Knox, Lancaster, McPherson, Nance, Nemaha, Pierce, Rock, Saline, Saunders, Seward, Thurston, and Wayne counties.
Nebraska	West Central Nebraska Development District, Inc. 710 North Spruce Street P.O. Box 599, Ogailala, NE 69153 Contact: Ronald J. Radil (308) 284-6077 Service Area: Arthur, Chase, Dawson, Dundy, Frontier, Furnas, Gosper, Grant, Hayes, Hitchcock, Hooker, Keith, Lincoln, Logan, Perkins, Red Willow, and Thomas counties.
Nevada	Nevada Women's Fund 210 South Sierra Street, Suite 100, Reno, NV 89501 Contact: Fritsi H. Ericson (702) 786-2335 Service Area: Statewide
New Hampshire	Institute for Cooperative Community Development, Inc. 2500 North River Road, Manchester, NH 03106 Contact: Don Mason (603) 644-3103 Service Area: Statewide excluding Grafton, Carol, and Coos counties.

Microloan Demonstration Program (continued)

New Hampshire
: Northern Community Investment Corp.
c/o 20 Main Street, St. Johnsbury, VT 05819
Contact: Carl J. Garbelotti
(802) 748-5101
  Service Area: Grafton, Carol, and Coos counties.

New Jersey
: Trenton Business Assistance Corp.
Division of Economic Development
319 East State Street, Trenton, NJ 08608-1866
Contact: James Harveson
(609) 989-3509
  Service Area: Portions of the City of Trenton.

New Jersey
: Greater Newark Business Development Consortium
One Newark Center, 22nd Floor, Newark, NJ 07102-5265
Contact: Henry Hayman
(201) 242-6237
  Service Area: Bergen, Essex, Hudson, Middlesex, Monmouth, Morris, Passaic, and Somerset counties with the exception of the city of Jersey City.

New Jersey
: Union County Economic Development Corp.
Liberty Hall Corporate Center
1085 Morris Avenue, Suite 531, Union, NJ 07083
Contact: Maureen Tinen
(908) 527-1166
  Service Area: Union County.

New Jersey
: Jersey City Economic Development Corp.
601 Pavonia Avenue, Jersey City, NJ 07306
Contact: Thomas D. Ahearn
(201) 420-7755
  Service Area: City of Jersey City.

New Mexico
: Women's Economic Self Sufficiency Team
414 Silver South West, Albuquerque, NM 87102-3239
Contact: Agnes Noonan
(505) 848-4760
  Service Area: Statewide

New York
: Adirondack Economic Development Corporation
Trudeau Road, P.O. Box 747, Saranac Lake, NY 12983
Contact: Ernest Hohmeyer
(518) 891-5523
  Service Area: Clinton, Essex, Franklin, Fulton, Hamilton, Herkimer, Jefferson, Lewis, Oneida, Oswego, St. Lawrence, Saratoga, Warren, and Washington counties.

New York
: Hudson Development Corp.
444 Warren Street, Hudson, NY 12534
Contact: Lynda S. Davidson
(518) 828-3373
  Service Area: Columbia County.

New York
: Manhattan Borough Development Corp.
15 Park Row, Suite 510, New York, NY 10038
Contact: Patricia Swann
(212) 791-3660
  Service Area: The borough of Manhattan.

Microloan Demonstration Program (continued)

New York
: Rural Opportunities, Inc.
339 East Avenue, Rochester, NY 14604
Contact: W. Lee Beaulac
(716) 546-7180
  Service Area: Allegheny, Cattaraugua, Cayuga, Chatauqua, Erie, Genessee, Livingston, Niagara, Ontario, Orleans, Senece, Steuben, Wayne, Wyoming, and Yates counties.

North Carolina
: Self-Help Ventures Fund
413 East Chapel Hill Street, Durham, NC 27701
Contact: Robert Schall
(919) 956-8526
  Service Area: Statewide

North Dakota
: Lake Agassiz Regional Council
417 Main Avenue, Fargo, ND 58103
Contact: Irvin D. Rustad
(701) 239-5373
  Service Area: Statewide

Ohio
: Enterprise Development Corporation (formerly Athens Small Business Center, Inc.)
900 East State Street, Athens, OH 45701
Contact: Karen A. Patton
(614) 592-1188
  Service Area: Adams, Ashland, Athens, Belmont, Brown, Carrol, Columbiana, Coshocton, Gallia, Guernsey, Harrison, Highland, Holmes, Jackson, Jefferson, Knox, Lawrence, Meigs, Monroe, Morgan, Muskingum, Nocking, Noble, Perry, Pike, Ross, Scioto, Tuscarawas, Vinton, and Washington counties.

Ohio
: Columbus Countywide Development Corp.
941 Chatham Lane, Suite 207, Columbus, OH 43221
Contact: Mark Barbash
(614) 645-6171
  Service Area: Franklin County and the City of Columbus.

Ohio
: Hamilton County Development Co., Inc.
1776 Mentor Avenue, Cincinnati, OH 45212
Contact: David K. Main
(513) 632-8292
  Service Area: City of Cincinnati and, Adams, Brown, Butler, Clermont, Clinton, Highland, and Warren counties.

Ohio
: Women's Entrepreneurial Growth Orgn. of NE Ohio
58 West Center Street, Suite 228, Akron, OH 44308
Contact: Susan Hale
(216) 535-4523 (also fax number)
  Service Area: Ashtabula, Cuyahoga, Geauga, Lake, Lorain, Mahoning, Medina, Portage, Stark, Summit, Trumbull, and Wayne counties.

Oklahoma
: Rural Enterprises, Inc.
422 Cessna Street, Durant, OK 74701
Contact: Sherry Harlin
(405) 924-5094
  Service Area: Statewide

Oklahoma
: Tulsa Economic Development Corp.
130 North Greenwood Avenue, Suite G, Tulsa, OK 74120
Contact: Frank F. McCrady, III
(918) 585-8332
  Service Area: Adair, Canadian, Cherokee, Cleveland, Craig, Creek, Delaware, Haskell, Hayes, Hughes, Kay, Latimer, Leflore, Lincoln, Logan, McIntosh, Muskogee, Noble, Nowata, Okfuskee, Oklahoma, Okmulgee, Osage, Ottawa, Pawnee, Payne, Pittsburg, Pottawatomie, Rogers, Seminole, Sequoyah, Wagoner, Washington, and Wayne counties including the city of Tulsa.

Microloan Demonstration Program (continued)

Oregon
Cascades West Financial Services, Inc.
408 SW Monroe Street, Corvallis, OR 97333
Contact: Deborah L. Wright
(541) 757-6854
   Service Area: Benton, Clackamas, Hood River, Jefferson, Lane, Lincoln, Linn, Marion, Multnomah, Polk, Tillamook, Wasco, Washington, and Yamhill.

Pennsylvania
The Ben Franklin Technology Center of Southeastern Pennsylvania
3624 Market Street, Philadelphia, PA 19104-2615
Contact: Phillip A. Singerman
(215) 382-0380
   Service Area: Bucks, Chester, Delaware, Montgomery, and Philadelphia counties.

Pennsylvania
The Washington County Council on Economic Development
703 Courthouse Square, Washington, PA 15301
Contact: Malcolm L. Morgan
(412) 228-6816
   Service Area: Southwestern area of Pennsylvania Including Greene, Fayette, and Washington counties.

Pennsylvania
York County Industrial Development Corp.
One Market Way East, York, PA 17401
Contact: David B. Carver
(717) 846-8879
   Service Area: York County.

Puerto Rico
Corp. for the Economic Development of the City of San Juan
Avenue Munos Rivera, #1127, Rio Piedras, PR 00926
Contact: Jesus M. Rivera Viera
(809) 756-5080
   Service Area: Territory wide.

South Carolina
Charleston Citywide Local Development Corporation
496 King Street, Charleston, SC 29403
Contact: Sharon Brennan
(803) 724-3796
   Service Area: City of Charleston.

South Carolina
Santee Lynches Regional Development Corp.
115 North Harvin Street, 4th Floor, Sumter, SC 29151-1837
Contact: James T. Darby, Jr.
(803) 775-7381
   Service Area: Clarendon, Kershaw, Lee, and Sumter counties.

South Dakota
Northeast South Dakota Energy Conservation Corporation
414 Third Avenue East, Sisseton, SD 57262
Contact: Arnold Petersen
(605) 698-7654
   Service Area: Beadle, Brown, Buffalo, Campbell, Clark, Codington, Day, Edmunds, Faulk, Grant, Hand, Hyde, Jerauld, Kingsbury, McPherson, Marshall, Miner, Potter, Roberts, Sanborn, Spink, and Walworth counties.

Tennessee
South Central Tennessee Development District
815 South Main Street
P.O. Box 1346, Columbia, TN 38402
Contact: Joe Max Williams
(615) 318-2040
   Service Area: Bedford, Coffee, Franklin, Giles, Hickman, Lawrence, Lewis, Lincoln, Marshall, Maury, Moore, Perry, and Wayne counties.

Microloan Demonstration Program (continued)

Texas
Business Resource Center Incubator
4601 North 19th Street, Waco, TX 76708
Contact: Curtis Cleveland
(817) 754-8898
Service Area: Bell, Bosque, Coryell, Falls, Hill, and McLennan counties.

Texas
San Antonio Local Development Corp.
100 Military Plaza
4th Floor City Hall, San Antonio, TX 78205
Contact: Robert Nance
(210) 299-8080
Service Area: Atascosa, Bandera, Bexar, Comal, Frio, Gillespie, Guadalupe, Karnes, Kendall, Kerr, Medina, and Wilson counties.

Texas
Southern Dallas Development Corporation
1402 Crinth, Suite 1150, Dallas, TX 75215
Contact: Jim Reid
(214) 428-7332
Service Area: Portions of the City of Dallas.

Utah
Utah Technology Finance Corporation
177 East 100 South, Salt Lake City, UT 84111
Contact: Todd Clark
(801) 364-4346
Service Area: Carbon, Emery, Grand, Iron, Juab, Milard, Salt Lake County, San Juan, Sanpete, Sevier, Tooele, Washington, and parts of Utah and Weber counties.

Vermont
Economic Development Council of Northern Vermont, Inc.
155 Lake Street, St. Albans, VT 05478
Contact: Connie Stanley-Little
(802) 524-4546
Service Area: Chittenden, Franklin, Grand Isle, Lamoilee, and Washington counties.

Vermont
Northern Community Investments Corporation
20 Main Street, St. Johnsbury, VT 05819
Contact: Carl J. Garbelotti
(802) 748-5101
Service Area: Caledonia, Essex, and Orleans counties.

Virginia
Ethiopian Community Development Council, Inc.
1038 South Highland Street, Arlington, VA 22204
Contact: Tsehaye Teferra
(703) 685-0510
Service Area: Prince William, Arlington and Fairfax counties and the cities of Alexandria and Falls Church.

Virginia
Business Development Centre, Inc.
147 Mill Ridge Road, Lynchburg, VA 24502
Contact: Karen Mauch
(804) 582-6100
Service Area: Amherst, Appomattox, Bedford, Campell counties, cities of Lynchburg and Bedford, and the Town of Amherst.

Virginia
People, Incorporated of Southwest Virginia
988 West Main Street, Abingdon, VA 24210
Contact: Robert G. Goldsmith
(703) 628-9188
Service Area: Buchanan, Dickenson, Lee, Russell, Scott, Washington, Wise counties and the cities of Bristol and Norton.

Microloan Demonstration Program (continued)

Washington
: Snohomish County Private Industry Council
917 134th Street SW, Suite A-10, Everett, WA 98204
Contact: Emily Duncan
(206) 743-9669
   Service Area: Adams, Chelan, Douglas, Grant, King, Kittitas, Klickitat, Okanogan, Pierce, Skagit, Snohomish, Whatcom, and Yakima counties.

Washington
: Tri-Cities Enterprise Association
2000 Logston Boulevard, Richland, WA 99352
Contact: Dallas E. Breamer
(509) 375-3268
   Service Area: Benton and Franklin counties.

West Virginia
: Ohio Valley Industrial and Business Development Corp.
12th and Chapline Streets, Wheeling, WV 26003
Contact: Terry Burkhart
(304) 232-7722
   Service Area: Marshall, Ohio, Wetzel, Brooke, Hancock, and Tyler counties.

Wisconsin
: Advocap, Inc.
19 West First Street
P.O. Box 1108, Fond du Lac, WI 54936
Contact: Richard Schlimm
(414) 922-7760
   Service Area: Fond du Lac and Winnebago counties.

Wisconsin
: Impact Seven, Inc.
100 Digital Drive, Clear Lake, WI 54005
Contact: William Bay
(715) 263-2532
   Service Area: Statewide with the exceptions of Fond du Lac, Kenosha, Milwaukee, Oasukee, Racine, Walworth, Waukesha, Washington, and Winnebago counties, and inner city Milwaukee.

Wisconsin
: Northwest Side Community Development Corp.
5174 North Hopkins Avenue, Milwaukee, WI 53209
Contact: Howard Snyder
(414) 462-5509
   Service Area: Inner City Milwaukee.

Wisconsin
: Women's Business Initiative Corporation
3112 West Highland Boulevard, Milwaukee, WI 53208
Contact: Becky Pileggi
(414) 933-3231
   Service Area: Kenosha, Milwaukee, Oazukee, Racine, Walworth, Washington, and Waukesha counties.

Technical Assistance Grant Recipients

Alaska
: Southeast Alaska Small Business Development Center
400 Willoughby Avenue, Suite 211, Juneau, AK 99801-1724
Contact: Charles M. Northrip
(907) 463-3789
   Service Area: Through SBDC system, the Alaska Panhandle.

California
: Women's Initiative for Self Employment
450 Mission Street, Suite 402, San Francisco, CA 94105
Contact: Etienne LeGrand
(415) 247-9473
   Service Area: Defined sectors of the San Francisco Bay area.

Microloan Demonstration Program (continued)

Connecticut
American Women's Economic Development Corporation
Plaza West Office Centers
200 West Main Street, Suite 140, Stamford, CT 06902
Contact: Fran Polak
(203) 326-7914
Service Area: SW corner of state including Ansonia, Beacon Falls, Bethel, Bridgeport, Bridgewater, Brookfield, Danbury, Darien, Derby, Easton, Fairfield, Greenwich, Milford, Monroe, New Canaan, New Fairfield, New Milford, Newtown, Norwalk, Oxford, Redding, Ridgefield, Seymour, Shelton, Sherman, Stamford, Stratford, Trumbull, Weston, Westport, and Wilton counties.

District of Columbia
American Women's Economic Development Corporation
Washington D.C. Regional Training Center
1250 24th Street NW, Suite 120, Washington, DC 20037
Contact: Susan P. Bari
(202) 857-0091
Service Area: District of Columbia.

Florida
Lee County Employment & Economic Development Corporation
2121 West 1st Street, Rear,
P.O. Box 2285, Fort Myers, FL 33902-2285
Contact: Roy H. Kennix
(813) 337-2300
Service Area: Community Redevelopment Areas of Lee County including Charleston Park, Dunbar, Harlem Heights, North Fort Myers, and State Road 80.

Illinois
Women's Business Development Center
8 South Michigan Avenue, Suite 400, Chicago, IL 60603
Contact: Linda Darragh
(312) 853-3477
Service Area: Boone, Cook, DeKalb, DuPage, Kane, Kankakee, Kendall, Lake, McHenry, Will, and Winnebago counties.

Indiana
Hoosier Valley Economic Development Corp.
1613 East 8th Street
P.O. Box 843, Jeffersonville, IN 47131-0843
Contact: Jerry L. Stephenson
(812) 288-6451
Service Area: Clark, Crawford, Floyd, Harrison, Orange, Scott, and Washington counties.

Iowa
Institute for Social and Economic Development
1901 Broadway, Suite 313, Iowa City, IA 52240
Contact: John F. Else
(319) 338-2331
Service Area: Statewide

Kansas
Great Plains Development, Inc.
100 Military Plaza, Suite 128
P.O. Box 1116, Dodge City, KS 67801
Contact: Carlyle Kienne
(316) 227-6406
Service Area: State of Kansas.

Kentucky
Community Ventures Corporation
200 West Vine Street, Fifth Floor, Lexington, KY 40507
Contact: Kevin R. Smith
(606) 281-5475
Service Area: Anderson, Bourbon, Clark, Fayette, Harrison, Jessamine, Nicholas, Scott, and Woodford counties.

Microloan Demonstration Program (continued)

Massachusetts
Jewish Vocational Service, Inc.
105 Chauncy Street, 6th Floor, Boston, MA 02111
Contact: Barbara S. Rosenbaum
(617) 451-8147
  Service Area: Greater Boston with particular emphasis on the Mattapan (Boston), North Dorchester (Boston), and Central Square (Cambridge) neighborhoods.

Michigan
Cornerstone Alliance
185 East Main, Benton Harbor, Berrien County, MI 49022-4440
Contact: D. Jeffrey Noel
(616) 925-6100
  Service Area: The city of Benton Harbor and Berrien County.

Minnesota
Neighborhood Development Center, Inc.
663 University Avenue, St. Paul, MN 55104
Contact: Mihailo Temali
(612) 290-8150
  Service Area: Districts 3, 5, 6, 8, 9, and 16 of the City of St. Paul.

Missouri
Community Development Corporation of Kansas City
2420 East Linwood Boulevard, Suite 400, Kansas City, MO 64109
Contact: Donald Maxwell
(816) 924-5800
  Service Area: Cass, Clay, Platte, Ray, and Jackson counties.

Montana
Montana Department of Commerce – SBDC Division
1424 9th Avenue, P.O. Box 200501, Helena, MT 59620-0501
Contact: Gene Marcille
(406) 444-4780
  Service Area: Through the SBDC network, Cascade, Chouteau, Fergus, Glacier, Golden Valley, Judity Basin, Musselshell, Petroleum, Pondera, Teton, Toole, and Wheatland counties, and the Blackfeet, Flathead, and Fort Peck Reservations, and the Crow, Fort Belknap, Northern Cheyenne, and Rocky Boys Reservations and their Trust Lands.

Nebraska
Omaha Small Business Network, Inc.
2505 North 24th Street, Omaha, NE 68110
Contact: John R. Cochran
(402) 346-8262
  Service Area: Areas within the City of Omaha known as the North Omaha and South Omaha Target Areas.

New Jersey
New Jersey Small Business Development Center
180 University Avenue, Newark, NJ 07102-1895
Contact: Andrew B. Rudczynski
(201) 648-5950
  Service Area: Through the SBDC network, statewide.

New Mexico
New Mexico Community Development Loan Fund
P.O. Box 705, Albuquerque, NM 87103-0705
Contact: Vangie Gabaldon
(505) 243-3196
  Service Area: Statewide

New York
Brooklyn Economic Development Corporation
30 Flatbush Avenue, Suite 420, Brooklyn, NY 11217-1197
Contact: Joan Bartolomeo
(718) 522-4600
  Service Area: The five boroughs of New York City.

Microloan Demonstration Program (continued)

North Carolina
North Carolina Economic Development Center, Inc.
4 North Blount Street, 2nd Floor, Raliegh, NC 27601
Contact: Billy Ray Hall
(919) 715-2725
   Service Area: Statewide

Ohio
Women Entrepreneurs, Incorporated
36 East Fourth Street, Suite 925, Cincinnati, OH 45202
Contact: Peg Moertil
(513) 684-0700
   Service Area: Brown, Butler, Clermont, Hamilton, and Warren counties.

Pennsylvania
Philadelphia Commercial Development Corporation
1315 Walnut Street, Suite 600, Philadelphia, PA 19107
Contact: Curtis Jones
(215) 790-2200
   Service Area: Bucks, Montgomery, Philadelphia, Chester, and Delaware counties.

Texas
Corpus Christi Chamber of Commerce/SBDC
1201 North Shoreline, P.O. Box 640, Corpus Christi, TX 78403
Contact: Robert R. Carey
(512) 882-6161
   Service Area: Nueces and San Patricio counties.

Vermont
Champlain Valley Office of Economic Opportunity, Inc.
191 North Street, Burlington, VT 05401
Contact: Robert Kiss
(802) 862-2771
   Service Area: State of Vermont.

Virginia
The Commonwealth of VA Department of Economic Development
1021 East Cary Street, Richmond, VA 23219
Contact: David V. O'Donnell
(804) 371-8253
   Service Area: Through the SBDC network, the State of Virginia.

Notes

Appendix E

Certified and Preferred Lenders

Certified Lenders Program (CLP) participants have no asterisk before the lender's name. Certified lenders have been delegated partial authority from the SBA. All loan applications must be reviewed by a local SBA office. This review must be completed within three business days. Usually, total processing time, including your lender's full review, is less than two weeks.

Preferred Lenders Program (PLP) participants have an asterisk (*) before the lender's name. PLP participants have been delegated full authority by the SBA and can decide unilaterally on SBA participation for eligible business loans. Preferred lenders do not require that your loan be reviewed by the SBA before they can make a decision. Usually, a decision can be made within one business week.

REGION I

CONNECTICUT

Danbury	Nutmeg Federal Savings and Loan Association	Hartford	*First National Bank of New England Mechanics Savings Bank
Hamden	*AT&T Small Business Lending Corporation (SBLC) LaFayette American Bank and Trust	New Haven	Founders Bank
		West Hartford	First Bank of West Hartford

MAINE

Augusta	*AT&T SBLC *Key Bank of Central Maine	Bangor	Merrill Merchants Bank
		Portland	Fleet Bank of Maine

MASSACHUSETTS

Boston	Fleet Bank of MA, N.A. *Massachusetts Business Development Corp. USTrust	Norwood	Norwood Cooperative Bank
		Rockland	*Rockland Trust Company
		Waltham	*Bank of Boston
		Westboro	*AT&T SBLC
Danvers	*Danvers Savings Bank	Whitinsville	UniBank for Savings
Fitchburg	Safety Fund National Bank	Worcester	Commerce Bank and Trust Company *Flagship Bank & Trust Company
Framingham	*Shawmut Bank of Boston The Money Store Investment Corp.		
Hyannis	*Cape Cod Bank and Trust Company		

NEW HAMPSHIRE

Berlin	The Berlin City Bank	Dover	Southeast Bank for Savings
Concord	Concord Savings Bank	Keene	CFX Bank

Certified and Preferred Lenders (continued)

NEW HAMPSHIRE (continued)

Keene	Granite Bank	Nashua	Fleet Bank-NH
Lebanon	Landmark Bank		N.F.S. Savings Bank
Manchester	Bank of New Hampshire	Peterborough	*AT&T SBLC
	*First NH Bank		Peterborough Savings Bank
	New Dartmouth Bank	Portsmouth	The First National Bank of Portsmouth
	New Hampshire Business Development Corporation		

RHODE ISLAND

Providence	*AT&T SBLC	Providence	Rhode Island Hospital Trust National Bank
	*The Citizens Trust Company		
	Fleet National Bank		
	Home Loan and Investment Association		

VERMONT

Barre	Granite Savings Bank & Trust	Manchester Ctr.	Factory Point National Bank
Brattleboro	First Vermont Bank & Trust	Morrisville	*Union Bank
	Vermont National Bank	Northfield	Northfield Savings Bank
Burlington	Bank of Vermont	Rutland	*Green Mountain Bank
	*Chittenden Bank	St. Albans	*Franklin Lamoille Bank
	*The Howard Bank	Woodstock	Bank of Woodstock
	*The Merchant's Bank		
Charlotte	*The Money Store Investment Corporation		

REGION II

NEW JERSEY

Annandale	First Community Bank	North Brunswick	Farrington Bank
Cherry Hill	Commercial Bank	North Plainfield	*Valley National Bank
Chatham	Summit Bank	Parsippany	*AT&T SBLC
Flemington	*Prestige State Bank	Pennington	*CoreStates/New Jersey National Bank
Hackensack	United Jersey Bank	Somerset	*New Era Bank
Iselin	*AT&T SBLC	Union	*The Money Store of New York
Jackson	*Garden State Bank	Woodbury	First Fidelity Bank, N.A. New Jersey
Jamesburgh	*AT&T SBLC	Wayne	*The Ramapo Bank
Mount Laurel	Midlantic Bank	Hasbrouck, NY	*Bank of New York (National Community Division)
Newark	National Westminister Bank NJ		

NEW YORK

Albany	*Fleet Bank of New York	Buffalo	Key Bank of New York
	Key Bank, N.A.		*Manufacturers and Traders Trust Co.
	*New York Business Development Corporation		*Marine Midland Bank
		Canandaigua	The Canandaigua National Bank and Trust Co.
Bath	The Bath National Bank		
Buffalo	*Fleet Bank of New York	Castile	Bank of Castile

Certified and Preferred Lenders (continued)

NEW YORK (continued)

Cortland	First National Bank of Cortland
Dewitt	Community Bank, N.A.
East Hampton	The Bank of the Hamptons
Elmira	Chemung Canal Trust Co.
Fayetteville	*AT&T SBLC
Geneva	*The National Bank of Geneva
Glens Falls	*Glens Falls National Bank and Trust Company
Islandia	Long Island Commercial Bank
Ithaca	Thompkins County Trust Company
Little Falls	Herkimer County Trust Co.
Melville	*AT&T SBLC
	The Bank of New York
	Fleet Bank
Newburgh	Key Bank of New York
New Hyde Park	State Bank of Long Island
New York City	Broadway National Bank
	*Chase Manhattan Bank, N.A.
New York City	Chemical Community Development Inc.
	*Citibank, N.A.
	*National Westminster Bank
	Republic National Bank
N.Y. City/Bronx	New York National Bank
Norwich	The National Bank and Trust Co. of Norwich
Rochester	Chase Lincoln First Bank, N.A.
Rosslyn Heights	*The Money Store Investment Corporation
Solvay	Solvay Bank
Syracuse	*Marine Midland Bank
	OnBank & Trust Co.
Uniondale	European American Bank
Warsaw	Wyoming County Bank
White Plains	Reliance Bank
Williamsville	G.E. Small Business Finance Corporation

PUERTO RICO

Hato Rey	Banco Santander Puerto Rico
San Juan	*Banco Popular de Puerto Rico

REGION III

DELAWARE

Newark	*Delaware Trust Company
Wilmington	Mellon Bank (DE), N.A.
Wilmington	Wilmington Trust Company

DISTRICT OF COLUMBIA (Washington, DC SMSA)

Washington, DC	Adams National Bank
	*Allied Lending Corporation
Washington, DC	Franklin National Bank of Washington

MARYLAND

Baltimore	*AT&T SBLC
	*First National Bank of Maryland
	*Maryland National Bank
	Provident Bank of Maryland
Baltimore	*Signet Bank
Greenbelt	Suburban Bank of Maryland
Owings Mills	Key Federal Savings Bank
Union, NJ	The Money Store Investment Corporation

PENNSYLVANIA

Annandale, NJ	First Community Bank
Blue Bell	*AT&T SBLC
DuBois	S & T Bank
Erie	*Integra National Bank/North
Erie	Mellon Bank (North)
	*PNC Bank (Northwest)
Ft. Washington	*The Money Store Investment
Harrisburg	Mellon Bank (Commonwealth Region), N.A.

Certified and Preferred Lenders (continued)

PENNSYLVANIA (continued)

Harrisburg	Pennsylvania National Bank
Hermitage	*First National Bank of PA
Horsham	Frankford Bank
Laceyville	Grange National Bank of Wyoming County
Narbeth	Royal Bank of Pennsylvania
New Castle	First Western Bank, N.A.
Philadelphia	*Corestate Bank, N.A.
	*Mellon Bank, N.A. / Mellon PSFS
Pittsburgh	*AT&T SBLC
	Integra Bank/Pittsburgh
	Mellon Bank, N.A.
Pittsburgh	*PNC Bank
Pittston	Commonwealth Bank, a division of Meridian Bank
Reading	*Meridian Bank
Scranton	PNC Bank, Northeast PA
Sharon	First Western Bank, FSB
Souderton	*Union National Bank
State College	Mellon Bank (Central)
Unionville	*Integra National Bank/South
Wilkes Barre	Mellon Bank

VIRGINIA

Fairfax	The George Mason Bank
Hampton	*AT&T SBLC
Reston	Patriot National Bank of Reston
Richmond	Crestar
	*The Money Store Investment Corporation
Richmond	NationsBank of Virginia, N.A.
Vienna	*AT&T SBLC
Virginia Beach	Commerce Bank
Washington, DC	Allied Lending Corporation

WEST VIRGINIA

Clarksburg	Bank One, West Virginia
Huntington	*Bank One
Morgantown	One Valley Bank of Morgantown, Inc.
Wheeling	Wheeling National Bank

REGION IV

ALABAMA

Anniston	SouthTrust Bank of Calhoun County
Birmingham	AmSouth Bank, N.A.
	*AT&T SBLC
	*Compass Bank
	First Commercial Bank
	*The Money Store Investment Corporation
	SouthTrust Bank of Alabama-Birmingham, N.A.
Dothan	Southland Bancorporation
	Southtrust Bank of Dothan
Florence	First National Bank of Florence
Fultondale	Bank of Alabama
Guntersville	The Home Bank
Huntsville	SouthTrust Bank of Huntsville
Montgomery	First Montgomery Bank
	South Trust Bank, N.A.
Opelika	Farmers National Bank
Opp	Southtrust Bank of Covington County
Selma	Peoples Bank & Trust Co.

FLORIDA

Boca Raton	*AT&T SBLC
	First United Bank
Clearwater	*Citizens Bank of Clearwater
Fernandina Beach	First Coast Community Bank
Ft. Walton Bch.	First National Bank and Trust
Jacksonville	Community Savings Bank
	First Guaranty Bank & Trust Company
Longwood	*Liberty National Bank
	The Money Store Investment Corporation
Miami	International Bank of Miami Ocean Bank
	Ocean Bank
	*Sun Bank/Miami, N.A.
Naples	BancFlorida A FSB
Newport Richey (Tampa)	*AT&T SBLC
No. Miami Beach	First Western SBLC, Inc.
Panama City	*AT&T SBLC
	Bay Bank and Trust Co.

Certified and Preferred Lenders (continued)

FLORIDA (continued)

Panama City	*Emergent Business Capital, Inc.
	*First National Bank of Northwest Floridia
Pensacola	Liberty Bank
Ponte Vedra Beach	Ponte Vedra National Bank
Port Charlotte	Charlotte State Bank
Sarasota	Enterprise National Bank of Sarasota
	West Coast Bank
St. Petersburg	United Bank of Pinellas
Tampa	NationsBank
	Southern Commerce Bank
West Palm Beach	*Barnett Bank of Palm Beach
Winter Garden	BankFirst
Elizabethton, TN	Citizens Bank

GEORGIA

Atlanta	*AT&T SBLC
	*The Business Development Corporation of Georgia
	*Commercial Bank of Georgia
	Fidelity National Bank
	*Georgia Bankers Bank
	*Metro Bank
	*Nations Bank of Georgia
	The Summit National Bank
Augusta	Bankers First Savings Bank, FSB
Blairsville	Union County Bank
Byron	Middle Georgia Bank
Cordele	*First State Bank & Trust
Cornelia	Habersham Bank
Kennesaw	*AT&T SBLC
Lawrenceville	*AT&T SBLC
Macon	*First South Bank
Marietta	*Bank South
Morrow	Southern Crescent Bank
Norcross	*First Capital Bank Norcross
Savannah	*The Coastal Bank
Snellville	Eastside Bank & Trust
Tucker	Mountain National Bank
Woodstock	First National Bank of Cherokee
Dallas, TX	First Western SBLC
Glenn Allen, VA	The Money Store Investment Corporation

KENTUCKY

Florence	The Fifth Third Bank
Lexington	*AT&T SBLC
	Bank One, Lexington
Louisville	Liberty National Bank
	PNC Bank – Kentucky
Louisville	National City Bank
Mount Sterling	Exchange Bank of Kentucky
Murray	*Peoples Bank of Murray
Pikeville	Pikeville National Bank & Trust Company

MISSISSIPPI

Batesville	Batesville Security Bank
Biloxi	The Jefferson Bank
Grenada	Union Planters Bank
Gulfport	*AT&T SBLC
	Hancock Bank
Jackson	Deposit Guaranty National Bank
Jackson	Trustmark National Bank
McComb	Pike County National Bank
Picayune	First National Bank of Picayune
Starkville	National Bank of Commerce of Mississippi
Tupelo	*Bank of Mississippi

NORTH CAROLINA

Charlotte	*AT&T SBLC
	Bank of Mecklenburg
	First Union National Bank of North Carolina
	NationsBank of North Carolina
Durham	Central Carolina Bank & Trust Company
	Self-Help Credit Union
Gastonia	First Community Bank
Granite Falls	Bank of Granite
Lumberton	Southern National Bank of North Carolina
Raleigh	First Citizens Bank & Trust Co.
	Triangle East Bank
Rocky Mount	Centura Bank
Whiteville	United Carolina Bank
Wilson	Branch Banking & Trust Company
Winston-Salem	*Wachovia Bank & Trust Company, N.A.
Glen Allen, VA	The Money Store Investment Corporation

Certified and Preferred Lenders (continued)

SOUTH CAROLINA

Atlanta, GA	Vine Street Trust	Columbia	*NationsBank
Charleston	Bank of Charleston		Wachovia Bank of SC
Columbia	Bank of Columbia	Greenville	Carolina First Bank
	*Business Development Corporation of SC	Lexington	The Lexington State Bank
	Emergent Business Capital, Inc.	Orangeburg	First National Bank
	*First Citizens Bank	Spartanburg	Spartanburg National Bank
	The Money Store Investment Corporation		

TENNESSEE

Brentwood	Brentwood National Bank	Knoxville	Third National Bank of East Tennessee
Chattanooga	American National Bank & Trust Company	Memphis	Union Planters National Bank
	Marion Trust and Banking Co.		United American Bank
	Volunteer Bank and Trust Company	Nashville	*AT&T SBLC
Columbia	First Farmers & Merchants National Bank		First American National Bank, N.A.
Elizabethton	*Citizens Bank		NationsBank of Tennessee
Jacksboro	The First State Bank		Third National Bank

REGION V

ILLINOIS

Addison	Oxford Bank and Trust	Homewood	Bank of Homewood
Aurora	Merchants Bank of Aurora	La Grange	Bank One, Chicago
	Old Second National Bank of Aurora	Lincoln	State Bank of Lincoln
Bellwood	The Bank of Bellwood	Maywood	Maywood-Proviso State Bank
Blue Island	The First National Bank of Blue Island	Naperville	First Colonial Bank of DuPage County
Chicago	*AT&T SBLC		Firstar Bank West, N.A.
	Albany Bank and Trust Company, N.A.	Norridge	Plaza Bank Norridge
	American National Bank and Trust Co.	O'Fallon	First Bank of Illinois
	First National Bank of Chicago	Palatine	*AT&T SBLC
	Foster Bank	Park Ridge	First State Bank of Park Ridge
	Harris Trust & Savings Bank		NBD Park Ridge Bank
	*The Money Store Investment Corporation	Pekin	*First State Bank of Pekin
	*South Central Bank & Trust	Rockford	Bank One, Rockford
	*The South Shore Bank of Chicago	Roselle	Harris Bank Roselle
Decatur	Soy Capital Bank and Trust Company	Springfield	*First of American Bank
Danville	Palmer American National Bank		Bank One, Springfield
Evergreen Park	*G.E. Small Business Finance Corporation	Urbana	*Busey First National Bank
Elgin	*Union National Bank & Trust of Elgin		Central Illinois Bank
Fairview Heights	*Central Bank	West Frankfort	*Banterra Bank of West Frankfort

INDIANA

Covington	Bank of Western Indiana	Indianapolis	G.E. Small Business Finance Corporation
Evansville	Citizens National Bank of Evansville		The Money Store Investment Corporation
Fort Wayne	Fort Wayne National Bank		National City Bank
	NBD Summit Bank		NBD Bank, Indiana
	*Huntington National Bank of Indiana	LaPorte	First Citizens Bank, N.A.
Indianapolis	*AT&T SBLC	South Bend	First Source Bank of Southbend
	Bank One Indianapolis		Society National Bank
	*Busey Bank	Whiting	Centier Bank

Certified and Preferred Lenders (continued)

MICHIGAN

Bay City	*Chemical Bank – Bay Area	Midland	*Chemical Bank & Trust Company
Detroit	Comerica Bank	Owosso	*Chemical Bank-Key State
Flint	Citizens Commercial and Savings Bank	Traverse City	*The Empire National Bank of Traverse City
Grand Rapids	*United Bank of Michigan		*Old Kent Bank – Traverse City
Kalamazoo	First of America Bank-Michigan, N.A.	Troy	*AT&T SBLC
	Old Kent Bank – Southwest		NBD Bank, N.A.
Lansing	*Michigan National Bank		

MINNESOTA

Bloomington	*Firstar Bank of Minnesota, N.A.	Pipestone	First National Bank of Pipestone
Edina	*First Bank National Association	St. Cloud	*First American Bank, N.A.
Minneapolis	*AT&T SBLC		Zapp Bank
	*Norwest Bank, Minnesota, N.A.	West St. Paul	Signal Bank, Inc.
	Riverside Bank	Young America	State Bank of Young America
Morris	Morris State Bank		

OHIO

Akron	Bank One, Akron, N.A.	Dayton	Society Bank – Dayton area
	First National Bank of Akron	Dublin	*The Money Store Investment Company
Bedford Heights	Bank One, Cleveland	Elyria	Elyria Savings and Trust National Bank
Cincinnati	North Side Bank and Trust Company		Premier Bank & Trust
	PNC Bank, Cincinnati	Lorain	*Lorain National Bank
Cleveland	American National Bank	Mineral Ridge	*AT&T SBLC
	Society National Bank	Newark	The Park National Bank
Columbus	*Bank One, Columbus, N.A.	Piqua	The Fifth Third Bank of Western Ohio
	*The Huntington National Bank	Salineville	The Citizens Banking Company
	Society Bank	Toledo	*Mid American National Bank and Trust Co.
Dayton	Bank One, Dayton, N.A.		National City Bank, Northwest
	*National City Bank		The Fifth Third Bank of Northwestern Ohio

WISCONSIN

Appleton	Firstar Bank, Appleton	Manitowoc	Associated Bank Lakeshore, N.A.
	*Valley Bank		First National Bank of Manitowoc
Eau Claire	*Firstar Bank Eau Claire	Menomonee	*Associated Bank of Menomonee Falls
	M&I Community State Bank, Eau Claire	Milwaukee	*Bank One, Milwaukee
Fond du Lac	*Firstar of Fond du Lac		First Bank, Milwaukee
Germantown	*AT&T SBLC		*Firstar Bank of Milwaukee
Green Bay	Associated Bank, Green Bay		Marshall and Ilsley Bank of Milwaukee
	Firstar Bank, Green Bay	Neenah	Associated Bank, N.A.
	Norwest Bank	Oshkosh	Firstar Bank Oshkosh, N.A.
Madison	Bank One, Madison	Sheboygan	*Firstar Bank Sheboygan
	*Firststar Bank of Madison	Sturgeon Bay	Baylake Bank
	M&I Madison Bank	Wausau	*M&I First American National Bank
	Valley Bank Madison	West Bend	Bank One, West Bend

Certified and Preferred Lenders (continued)

REGION VI

ARKANSAS

Arkadelphia	Elk Horn Bank & Trust	Jonesboro	Citizens Bank of Jonesboro
Batesville	Worthen National Bank	Little Rock	Arkansas Capital Corporation
Bentonville	Worthen National Bank of NWA/Bentonville		First Commercial Bank, N.A.
Camden	Worthen National Bank of Camden		Metropolitan National Bank
Clarksville	Arkansas State Bank		Worthen National Bank of Arkansas
Conway	First National Bank of Conway	Mongolia	First National Bank of Arkansas
El Dorado	First Financial Bank	No. Little Rock	National Bank of Arkansas
	First National Bank of El Dorado		The Twin City Bank
Fayetteville	McIlroy Bank & Trust	Pine Bluff	Simmons First National Bank
	Worthen National Bank of NW Arkansas	Pocahontas	Bank of Pocahontas
Fort Smith	City National Bank of Fort Smith	Rogers	First National Bank
	Merchants National Bank	Russellville	Worthen National Bank of Russellville
Hot Springs	Worthern National Bank of Hot Springs	Searcy	First National Bank of Searcy

LOUISIANA

Abbeville	Gulf Coast Bank	Monroe	Central Bank
Baton Rouge	City National Bank		First American Bank
	Guaranty Bank and Trust Co.	Morgan City	First National in St. Mary Parish
	Premier Bank, N.A.	New Orleans	First National Bank of Commerce
Eunice	Tri-Parish Bank		Gulf Coast Bank and Trust Co.
Gonzales	Bank of Gonzales		Whitney National Bank
Harvey	Schwegmann Bank and Trust Co.	Plattenville	Bayoulands Bank
Kenner	Metro Bank	Port Allen	Bank of West Baton Rouge
Lafayette	First National Bank	Ruston	Ruston State Bank
Metairie	Hibernia National Bank in Jefferson Parish	Shreveport	Commercial National Bank
	Jefferson Guaranty Bank		Pioneer Bank
	Omni Bank		

NEW MEXICO

Albuquerque	*AT&T SBLC	Hobbs	Lea County State Bank
	*Bank of America, FSB	Las Cruces	Bank of the Rio Grande, N.A.
	*First Security Bank		*Citizens Bank of Las Cruces
	Sunwest Bank of Albuquerque		*United New Mexico Bank at Las Cruces
	*United New Mexico Bank at Albuquerque		Western Bank
Belen	First National Bank of Belen	Santa Fe	Bank of Santa Fe
Carlsbad	*Western Commerce Bank	Taos	First State Bank of Taos
Clovis	Sunwest Bank	Tucumcari	The First National Bank of Tucumcari
	Western Bank of Clovis		

OKLAHOMA

Broken Arrow	First National Bank and Trust	Ponca City	*Pioneer Bank & Trust
Midwest City	Community Bank and Trust	Poteay	Central National Bank
Oklahoma City	*BancFirst	Stillwater	*Stillwater National Bank and Trust Company
	Bank of Oklahoma, N.A.		
	Boatmen's First National Bank	Tonkawa	*First National Bank of Tonkawa
	First National Bank	Tulsa	Bank IV Oklahoma, N.A. of Tulsa
	Liberty Bank & Trust Co. of Oklahoma City		Boatmen's First National Bank
	Rockwell Bank, N.A.		Woodland Bank

Certified and Preferred Lenders (continued)

TEXAS

Abilene	First National Bank of Abilene	Harlingen	The Harlingen State Bank
	Security State Bank	Houston	Allied Lending Corporation
Amarillo	Amarillo National Bank		*AT&T SBLC
	The First National Bank of Amarillo		Bank of America-Nevada
Arlington	Bank One Texas, N.A.		Bank of North Texas
Austin	Cattlemen's State Bank		Bank One, Texas
	Hill County Bank		Charter National Bank-Houston
	*Horizon Savings Association		Comerica Bank-Texas
	Liberty National Bank		Compass Bank
	Texas Bank		Enterprise Bank
	Texas Commerce Bank		First Bank Houston
Baytown	Citizens Bank and Trust Company		First Interstate Bank
Beaumont	Bank One, Texas, N.A.		First Western SBLC
Bellaire	Park National Bank		Frost National Bank
Brownsville	International Bank of Commerce, N.A.		Great Southwest Bank, FSB
	Mercantile Bank, N.A.		Harrisburg Bank
	*Texas Commerce Bank-Brownsville		Heller First Capital Corp.
Bryan	Victoria Bank & Trust		Houston Independent Bank
College Station	Commerce National Bank		Independence Bank
Converse	Converse National Bank		Klein Bank
Corpus Christi	*American National Bank		Langham Creek National Bank
	Bank of Corpus Christi		Lockwood National Bank
	Citizens State Bank		Merchants Bank
	First Commerce Bank		Metrobank, N.A.
	Frost National Bank		The Money Store Investment Corporation
Dallas	Abrams Centre National Bank		NationsBank
	*AT&T SBLC		Northwest Bank
	*Bank One Texas, N.A.		OmniBank, N.A.
	Comerica Bank-Texas		*Park National Bank
	*Equitable Bank		*QuestStar Bank
	First Texas Bank		Southwest Bank of Texas
	*First Western SBLC, Inc.		Sterling Bank
	*Gateway National Bank		Sunbelt National Bank
	*Heller First Capital Corp.		Texas Capital Bank, N.A.
	Independence Funding Co., Ltd. (IFC)		Texas Central Bank
	*The Money Store Investment Corporation		Texas Commerce Bank
	State Bank and Trust Company		Texas Guaranty Bank
	Texas Commerce Bank	Hutto	Hutto State Bank
El Paso	*Bank of the West	Idalou	Security Bank
	*The Bank of El Paso	Irving	*Bank of America, NV
	First Commercial Capital		*Bank of the West
	*Montwood National Bank		Irving National Bank
	NationsBank	Katy	Community Bank
	State National Bank		First Bank
	Sunwest Bank of El Paso	Kerrville	First National Bank
	Texas Commerce Bank of El Paso, N.A.	Kilgore	*Kilgore First National Bank
Fort Davis	Fort Davis State Bank	Lampasas	First National Bank of Lampasas
Fort Worth	Citizens National Bank	LaPorte	Bayshore National Bank of LaPorte
	*Bank of North Texas	Laredo	South Texas National Bank
	Southwest Bank	League City	League City Bank and Trust
Galveston	Bank of Galveston	Los Fresnos	*First Bank Los Fresnos
Garland	*Central Bank	Lubbock	American State Bank
	Security Bank		*First National Bank at Lubbock
Grapevine	*AT&T SBLC		Lubbock National Bank
Harlingen	Harlingen National Bank		Plains National Bank

Certified and Preferred Lenders (continued)

TEXAS (continued)

Mansfield	Overton Bank and Trust, N.A.	San Antonio	Frost National Bank / Corpus Christi
McAllen	Inter National Bank		Groos Bank
	Texas State Bank		Heller First Capital Corp.
Midland	Midland American Bank		G.E. Small Business Finance Corp.
	Texas National Bank of Midland		*The Money Store Investment Corporation
Missouri City	*First National Bank of Missouri City		Texas Bank, N.A.
Navasoto	First Bank		Nationsbank of Texas, N.A.
North Richland Hills	Liberty Bank		Plaza Bank
Odessa	First State Bank of Odessa		Security National Bank
	*Texas Bank – Odessa		Valley-Hi Bank
Pharr	Lone Star National Bank	San Marcos	State Bank and Trust Co.
Plainview	First National Bank of Plainview	Scherta	Schertz Bank
Plano	Plano Bank & Trust	Seguin	First Commercial Bank
San Angelo	Bank of the West	Sonora	First National Bank of Sonora
	Southwest Bank	Sundown	Sundown State Bank
San Antonio	Bank of America, NV	Tomball	Texas National Bank
	Bank One, Texas, N.A.	Victoria	Citizens National Bank
	Broadway National Bank	Weatherford	*Texas Bank, Weatherford
	First Western SBLC	Wolfforth	American Bank of Commerce
	First Interstate Bank, N.A.		

REGION VII

IOWA

Ames	Firstar Bank Ames	Fort Dodge	Norwest Bank Iowa, N.A.
Cedar Rapids	*Firstar Bank Cedar Rapids	Iowa City	Iowa State Bank and Trust Company
Davenport	*Norwest Bank Iowa, N.A.	Maquoketa	Maqucketa State Bank
Des Moines	Bankers Trust Company	Marion	Farmers State Bank
	Boatmen's Bank Iowa, N.A.	Newton	Hawkeye Bank of Jasper County
	*Brenton National Bank of Des Moines	Oskaloosa	Mahaska State Bank
	Firstar Bank Des Moines	Sioux Center	American State Bank
	*Hawkeye Bank & Trust of Des Moines	Spencer	Boatmen's National Bank of Northwest Iowa
	*Norwest Bank Des Moines, N.A.	Storm Lake	Commercial Trust and Savings Bank
Dubuque	Dubuque Bank and Trust Company	West Des Moines	*West Des Moines State Bank

KANSAS

Dodge City	Fidelity State Bank & Trust Company	Neodesha	First National Bank of Neodesha
	First National Bank and Trust Company in Dodge City	Olathe	Bank IV Olathe
			First National Bank
Great Bend	Farmers Bank & Trust	Overland Park	Metcalf State Bank
Hayes	*Emprise Bank, N.A.		UMB Bank Kansas
Haysville	Intrust Bank	Topeka	Commerce Bank & Trust
Hutchinson	Emprise Bank, N.A.	Ulysses	Grant County State Bank
Kansas City	*Guaranty Bank & Trust	Wichita	American National Bank
Lawrence	Mercantile Bank of Lawrence		*Bank IV Wichita
Liberal	First National Bank of Liberal		Emergent Business Capital, Inc.
Manhattan	*AT&T SBLC		Emprise Bank
Merriam	*United Kansas Bank and Trust		Intrust Bank
Newton	Midland National Bank		Union National Bank

Certified and Preferred Lenders (continued)

MISSOURI

Brentwood	Magna Bank of Missouri	Springfield	*The Boatmen's National Bank of Southern Missouri
Carthage	*Boatmen's Bank of Carthage		Citizens National Bank of Springfield
Clayton	*The Money Store Investment Corporation		*Commerce Bank of Springfield
Columbia	Capital Bank of Columbia		*First City National Bank
Independence	Standard Bank and Trust Co.		Mercantile Bank of Springfield
Jefferson City	Exchange National Bank of Jefferson City	St. Louis	*AT&T SBLC
	The Central Trust Bank		*Emergent Business Capital, Inc.
Joplin	Mercantile Bank and Trust Co. of Joplin		Boatmen's National Bank of St. Louis
Kansas City	Bannister Bank & Trust		G.E. Small Business Finance Corporation
	Boatmen's First National Bank of Kansas City		*Mertcantile Bank, St. Louis, N.A.
	Country Club Bank		United Missouri Bank of St. Louis, N.A.
	First National Bank of Platte County	Washington	Bank of Washington
	United Missouri Bank of Kansas City, N.A.		

NEBRASKA

Blair	The Washington County Bank	North Platte	First National Bank of North Platte
Fremont	Fremont National Bank and Trust Co.	Omaha	American National Bank
Lincoln	*FirsTier Bank, N.A.		*Douglas County Bank & Trust
	National Bank of Commerce		First National Bank of Omaha
	*Union Bank and Trust Co.		Norwest Bank Nebraska, N.A.

REGION VIII

COLORADO

Alamosa	The First National Bank in Alamosa	Englewood	Emergent Business Capital, Inc.
Aurora	Aurora National Bank		First Commercial Bank, N.A. dba First Commercial Capital Corp.
	*The Money Store Investment Corporation	Estes Park	Park National Bank
Breckenridge	The Bank, N.A.	Evergreen	The Bank
Broomfield	Eagle Bank	Golden	Golden Bank of Colorado
Clifton	Alpine Bank, Grand Junction	Grand Junction	Bank of Grand Junction
Colorado Springs	State Bank and Trust		Grand Valley National Bank
Denver	Key Bank of Colorado	Hotchkiss	The First State Bank of Hotchkiss
	Colorado National Bank	Lakewood	Bank One, Denver, N.A.
	G.E. Small Business Finance Corp.	Loveland	Bank One, Fort Collins/Loveland, N.A.
	Norwest Bank Denver	Montrose	Bank One, Montrose – Main
	Vectra Bank		Norwest Bank Montrose, N.A.
Durango	Durango National Bank	Steamboat Springs	First National Bank of Steamboat Springs
Englewood	*AT&T SBLC		

MONTANA

Bigfork	Flathead Bank of Bigfork	Helena	Mountain West Bank
Billings	First Bank, N.A.		Valley Bank of Helena
	*First Interstate Bank of Commerce	Kalispell	*Norwest Bank Kalispell, N.A.
	*Norwest Bank Billings		Valley Bank of Kalispell
	Yellowstone Bank	Livingston	First National Park Bank
Bozeman	First Security Bank of Bozeman	Missoula	*AT&T SBLC
	*Montana Bank of Bozeman		*First Security Bank of Missoula
Great Falls	Norwest Bank Great Falls		Montana Bank of South Missoula

Certified and Preferred Lenders (continued)

MONTANA (continued)

Polson	First Citizens Bank	Whitefish	*Mountain Bank
Sidney	Richland Bank and Trust		

NORTH DAKOTA

Bismarck	Bank Center First	Grand Forks	Community National Bank
	United Bank of Bismarck		First American Bank
Devils Lake	The First National Bank		First National Bank of Grand Forks
Dickinson	American State Bank and Trust of Dickinson	Mandan	First Southwest Bank of Mandan
	Liberty National Bank and Trust	Minot	First American Bank West
Fargo	Community First National Bank		First Western Bank of Minot
	Norwest Bank North Dakota, N.A.	West Fargo	First National Bank North Dakota
	State Bank of Fargo	Williston	American State Bank and Trust Company

SOUTH DAKOTA

Belle Fourche	*Pioneer Bank and Trust	Pierre	First National Bank
Brookings	First National Bank in Brookings	Rapid City	*Rushmore State Bank
Burke	First Fidelity Bank	Sioux Falls	First Bank of South Dakota, N.A.
Custer	First Western Bank		First National Bank in Sioux Falls
Huron	Farmers & Merchants Bank		Marquette Bank of South Dakota, N.A.
Milbank	Dakota State Bank		Norwest Bank Sioux Falls, N.A.
Philip	First National Bank		Western Bank
Pierre	American State Bank	Sturgis	The First Western Bank Sturgis
	BankWest, N.A.	Yankton	First Dakota National Bank

UTAH

Ogden	Bank of Utah	Salt Lake City	*First Security Bank
Salt Lake City	Bank One		*Guardian State Bank
	Brighton Bank		*Key Bank
	First Interstate Bank of UT		*Zions First National Bank, N.A.

WYOMING

Casper	Hilltop National Bank	Cody	Shoshone First Bank
	Norwest Bank Wyoming	Gillette	First National Bank of Gillette
Cheyenne	*Key Bank		

REGION IX

ARIZONA

Phoenix	*AT&T SBLC	Phoenix	M&I Thunderbird Bank
	*Bank One, Arizona		National Bank of Arizona
	*First Interstate Bank of Arizona, N.A.		Republic National Bank
	*G.E. Small Business Finance Corporation	Scottsdale	Bank of Arizona

Certified and Preferred Lenders (continued)

CALIFORNIA

Anaheim	Landmark Bank	Redding	North Valley Bank
Auburn	*The Bank of Commerce, N.A.		Redding Bank of Commerce
Bakersfield	*San Joaquin Bank	Rolling Hills	*AT&T SBLC
Borrego Springs	Borrego Springs Bank	Rosemead	General Bank
Cameron Park	Western Sierra National Bank	Sacramento	*The Money Store Investment Corporation
Carlsbad	*Capital Bank of Carlsbad		*Sacramento Commercial Bank
Chula Vista	Pacific Commerce Bank		Sacramento First National Bank
Concord	Tracy Federal Bank	Salinas	First National Bank of Central CA
Coronado	Bank of Coronado	San Clemente	Mariners Bank
Cupertino	*Cupertino National Bank	San Diego	*Bank of Commerce
Discovery Bay	*AT&T SBLC		*Bank of Southern California
El Centro	*Valley Independent Bank		*G.E. Small Business Finance Corp.
Encinitas	San Dieguito National Bank		*North County Bank
Escondido	First Pacific National Bank		Peninsula Bank of San Diego
Eureka	*U.S. Bank of California		Rancho Santa Fe National Bank
Fallbrook	*Fallbrook National Bank		San Diego Trust & Savings Bank
Fresno	Bank of Fresno		Union Bank
	*Regency Bank	San Francisco	*Commercial Bank of San Francisco
Goleta	Goleta National Bank		*Heller First Capital
Hemet	Valley Merchants Bank	San Jose	*California Business Bank
Huntington Beach	*AT&T SBLC		*Comerica Bank
	Liberty National Bank		*San Jose National Bank
Inglewood	Imperial Bank	San Leandro	*Bay Bank of Commerce
LaPalma	Frontier Bank	San Luis Obispo	Commerce Bank of San Luis Obispo
Los Angeles	City National Bank		*First Bank of San Luis Obispo
	Hanmi Bank	Santa Cruz	*Coast Commercial Bank
	First Interstate Bank of California	Santa Rosa	*National Bank of Redwoods
	*National Bank of California		*Sonoma National Bank
	Wilshire State Bank	Sherman Oaks	*American Pacific State Bank
Modesto	Modesto Banking Co.		Transworld Bank
	*Pacific Valley National Bank	Truckee	*Truckee River Bank
Montebello	Farfield Bank	Tustin	*Eldorado Bank
Monterey	*Monterey County Bank	Van Nuys	Industrial Bank
Ontario	Western Community Bank	West Covina	*California State Bank
Orange	*Orange National Bank	Yorba Linda	Bank of Yorba Linda
Rancho Cordova	*Bank of America Community Development Bank		

HAWAII

Honolulu	*Bank of Hawaii	Honolulu	City Bank
	Central Pacific Bank		First Hawaiian Bank

NEVADA

Las Vegas	American Bank of Commerce	Las Vegas	First Security Bank of Nevada
	*AT&T SBLC		Nevada State Bank
	*Bank of America Nevada	San Diego, CA	G.E. Small Business Finance Corp.
	*First Interstate Bank of Nevada, N.A.		

Appendix E: Certified and Preferred Lenders **187**

Certified and Preferred Lenders (continued)

REGION X

ALASKA

Anchorage	Bank of America, FSB First National Bank of Anchorage Key Bank of Alaska	Anchorage Fairbanks	National Bank of Alaska Northrim Bank Denali State Bank

IDAHO

Boise	American Bank of Commerce Farmers and Merchants State Bank First Interstate Bank of Idaho *First Security Bank of Idaho	Boise Coeur d'Alene Eugene, OR	*Key Bank of Idaho *West One Bank *AT&T SBLC Bank of America, FSB

OREGON

Eugene Lake Oswego Medford Portland	Pacific Continental Bank The Bank of Newport *Western Bank *AT&T SBLC *Bank of America, FSB	Portland	*First Interstate Bank of Oregon, N.A. *Key Bank of Oregon *The Money Store Investment Corporation *U.S. National Bank of Oregon

WASHINGTON

Englewood, CO Aberdeen Bellevue Chelan Coupeville Duvall Lynnwood Olympia Everett Ferndale Issaquah Kennewick Lacey	*AT&T SBLC The Bank of Grays Harbor *The Money Store Investment *North Cascades National Bank Whidbey Island Bank Valley Community Bank *City Bank *Centennial Bank American First National Bank Frontier Bank Whatcom State Bank *AT&T SBLC American National Bank *First Community Bank of Washington	Seattle Snohomish Spokane Tacoma Tukwila Westboro Yakima	First Interstate Bank of Washington, N.A. *Key Bank of Washington Pacific Northwest Bank *Seattle-First National Bank *U.S. Bank of Washington West One Bank Washington *First Heritage Bank *Inland Northwest Bank Sterling Savings Association *Washington Trust Bank North Pacific Bank National Bank of Tukwila *AT&T SBLC *Pioneer National Bank

Appendix F

Small Business Investment Companies

Regular SBICs — Licensed Since June 1994

	LICENSE NUMBER & DATE	PRIVATE CAPITAL	SBA LEVERAGE	INVESTMENT POLICY
Anthem Capital, L.P. William M. Gust, II, Manager 16 South Calvert Street, Suite 800 Baltimore, MD 21202 (410) 625-1510 FAX (410) 625-1735	03/73-0200 09/26/94	25,000,000	0	Diversified
Aspen Ventures West II, L.P. Alexander Cilento/David Crocket, Managers 1000 Fremont Avenue, Suite V Los Altos, CA 94024 (415) 917-5670 FAX (415) 917-5677	09/79-0400 11/08/94	12,295,918	0	Diversified
AVI Capital, L.P. P. Wolken, B. Weinman and B. Grossi, Managers One First Street, Suite 12 Los Altos, CA 94022 (415) 949-9862 FAX (415) 949-8510	09/79-0402 02/06/95			
Bay Partners SBIC, L.P. John Freidenrich and Neal Dempsey, Managers 10600 North De Anza Boulevard, Suite 100 Cupertino, CA 95014 (408) 725-2444 FAX (408) 446-4502	09/79-0404 07/28/95			
Blue Ridge Investors, L.P. Edward C. McCarthy, Manager 300 North Greene Street, Suite 2100 Greensboro, NC 27401 (910) 370-0576 FAX (910) 274-4984	04/74-0262 07/28/95			
Canaan SBIC, L.P. Gregory Kopchinsky, Manager 105 Rowayton Avenue Rowayton, CT 06853 (203) 855-0400 FAX (203) 854-9117	01/71-0361 09/26/94	14,650,000	0	Diversified

Small Business Investment Companies (continued)

	License Number & Date	Private Capital	SBA Leverage	Investment Policy
Canaan SBIC, L.P. (Main Office: Rowayton, CT) Eric Young, Manager 2884 Sand Hill Road Menlo Park, CA 94025 (415) 854-8082 FAX (415) 854-8127				
DFW Capital Partners, L.P. Donald F. DeMuth, Manager Glenpointe Center East, 5th Floor 300 Frank W. Burr Blvd. Teaneck, NJ 07666 (201) 836-2233 FAX (201) 836-5666	02/72-0556 09/19/94	10,000,000	0	Electronics, Computer Apply, Healthcare
Eos Partners SBIC, L.P. Marc H. Michel, Manager 520 Madison Avenue, 42nd Floor New York, NY 10022 (212) 832-5814 FAX (212) 832-5805	02/72-0552 09/19/94	14,629,500	0	Diversified
Exeter Equity Partners, L.P. Keith Fox/Timothy Bradley/Jeff Weber 10 East 53rd Street New York, NY 10022 (212) 872-1170 FAX (212) 872-1198	02/72-0559 12/22/94	13,127,300	0	Diversified
First Commerce Capital, Inc. William Harper, Manager 821 Gravier Street, Suite 1027 New Orleans, LA 70119 (504) 561-1491 FAX (504) 561-1779	06/06-0308 07/29/94	24,000,000	0	Diversified
First Legacy Fund, Inc. Jonathan Ledecky, Manager 1400 34th Street NW Washington, DC 20007 (202) 659-1100 FAX (202) 342-7474	03/03-0199 07/14/94	3,000,000	0	Diversified
Fleet Equity Partners VI, L.P. Robert Van Degna/Habib Y. Gorgi, Managers 111 Westminister, 4th Floor Providence, RI 02903 (401) 278-6770 FAX (401) 278-6387	01/01-0362 01/11/95	10,000,000	0	Diversified
Furman Selz SBIC, L.P. Brian Friedman, Manager 230 Park Avenue New York, NY 10169 (212) 309-8200 FAX (212) 692-9608	02/72-0551 08/22/94	22,315,000	0	Diversified

Small Business Investment Companies (continued)

	License Number & Date	Private Capital	SBA Leverage	Investment Policy
Gateway Partners, L.P. John S. McCarthy 8000 Maryland Avenue, Suite 1190 St. Louis, MO 63105 (314) 721-5707 FAX (314) 721-5135	07/77-0097 01/23/95	7,500,000	0	Diversified
Hanifen Imhoff Mezzanine Fund, L.P. Edward C. Brown, Manager 1125 17th Street, Suite 1820 Denver, CO 80202 (303) 291-5209 FAX (303) 291-5327	08/08-0149 07/26/94	14,700,000	4,970,000	Diversified
KCEP I, L.P. Paul H. Henson, Manager 4200 Somerset Drive, Suite 101 Prairie Village, KS 66208 (913) 649-1771 FAX (913) 649-2125	07/77-0096 09/19/94	11,000,000	0	Diversified
Kline Hawkes California SBIC, L.P. Frank R. Kline, Manager 11726 San Vincente Boulevard, Suite 300 Los Angeles, CA 90049 (310) 442-4700 FAX (310) 442-4707	09/79-0403 07/28/95			
LEG Partners SBIC, L.P. Lawrence E. Golub, Manager 230 Park Avenue, 21st Floor New York, NY 10169 (212) 207-1585 FAX (212) 207-1579	02/72-0560 04/06/95			
Mercury Capital, L.P. David W. Elenowitz, Manager 650 Madison Avenue New York, NY 10022 (212) 838-0888 FAX (212) 838-7598	02/72-0557 09/26/94	18,800,000	0	Manufacturing & Distribution
MidMark Capital, L.P. Denis Newman, Manager 466 Southern Boulevard Chatham, NJ 07928 (201) 822-2999 FAX (201) 822-8911	02/72-0558 09/26/94	15,000,000	0	Manufacturing, Distribution, & Service Ind.
Needham Capital SBIC, L.P. John Michaelson, Manager 400 Park Avenue New York, NY 10022 (212) 705-0291 FAX (212) 371-8418	02/72-0553 09/19/94	7,500,000	0	

Small Business Investment Companies (continued)

	License Number & Date	Private Capital	SBA Leverage	Investment Policy
North Atlantic Venture Fund II, L.P. David M. Coit, Manager 70 Center Street Portland, ME 04101 (207) 772-1001 FAX (207) 772-3257	01/71-0359 09/19/94	5,380,000	0	Diversified
North Dakota SBIC, L.P. David R. Schroder, Manager 417 Main Avenue, Suite 401 Fargo, ND 58103 (701) 237-6132 FAX (701) 293-7819	08/78-0150 05/09/95			
Norwest Equity Partners V, L.P. John F. Whaley, Manager 2800 Piper Jaffrey Tower Minneapolis, MN 55402 (612) 667-1667 FAX (612) 667-1660	05/05-0222 02/06/95			
Novus Ventures, L.P. Daniel D. Tompkins, Manager 20111 Stevens Creek Boulevard, Suite 130 Cupertino, CA 95014 (408) 252-3900 FAX (408) 252-1713	09/79-0401 11/08/94	5,000,000	0	Diversified
Odyssey Partners SBIC, L.P. Alain Oberrotman, Manager 31 West 52nd Street New York, NY 10019 (212) 708-0641 FAX (212) 708-0735	02/72-0554 09/19/94	45,400,000	0	Diversified
Pacific Capital Stephen F. 109	04/04-0261 05/22/95			
	'89	10,600,000	0	Software, Healthcare, Special Retail
		7,500,000	0	Medical Devices Healthcare

Small Business Investment Companies (continued)

	License Number & Date	Private Capital	SBA Leverage	Investment Policy
Prospect Street NYC Discovery Fund, L.P. Richard E. Omohundro, Chief Executive Officer 250 Park Avenue, 17th Floor New York, NY 10177 (212) 490-0480 FAX (212) 490-1566	02/72-0561 05/23/95			
RFE Investment Partners V, L.P. James A. Parsons, General Partner 36 Grove Street New Canaan, CT 06840 (203) 966-2800 FAX (203) 966-3109	02/72-0555 09/19/94	35,714,000	0	Diversified
River Cities Capital Fund, L.P. R. Glen Mayfield, Manager 221 East Fourth Street, Suite 2250 Cincinnati, OH 45202 (513) 621-9700 FAX (513) 579-8939	05/75-0221 09/26/94	11,600,000	0	Manufacturers, Distributors, Broadcasting
SBIC Partners, L.P. Gregory Forrest/Jeffrey Brown, Managers 201 Main Street, Suite 2302 Fort Worth, TX 76102 (714) 729-3222 FAX (714) 729-3226	06/76-0309 08/22/94	30,000,000	0	Diversified
Seacoast Capital Partners, L.P. Mr. Eben Moulton, Manager 55 Ferncroft Road Danvers, MA 01923 (508) 777-3866 FAX (508) 750-1301	01/01-0358 08/22/94	30,000,000	17,000,000	Diversified
Shaw Venture Partners III, L.P. Ralph R. Shaw, Manager 400 Southwest Sixth Avenue, Suite 1100 Portland, OR 97204 (503) 228-4884 FAX (503) 227-2471	10/10-0190 09/2694	30,075,188	0	Software, Biotech, Medical Devices
Shenandoah Venture Capital, L.P. Thomas E. Loehr, President 208 Capitol Street, Suite 300 Charleston, WV 25301 (304) 344-1796 FAX (304) 344-1798	03/03-0201 06/01/95			
Sorrento Growth Partners I, L.P. Robert Jaffee, Manager 4225 Executive Square, Suite 1450 San Diego, CA 92037 (619) 452-6400 FAX (619) 452-7607	09/79-0398 09/19/94	10,587,338	0	Diversified

Small Business Investment Companies (continued)

	License Number & Date	Private Capital	SBA Leverage	Investment Policy
UBS Partners, Inc. Justin S. Maccarone, President 299 Park Avenue New York, NY 10171 (212) 821-6490 FAX (212) 821-6333	02/02-0562 05/24/95			
Walden-SBIC, L.P. Arthur S. Berliner, Manager 750 Battery Street, 7th Floor San Francisco, CA 94111 (415) 391-7225 FAX (415) 391-7262	09/79-0399 09/19/94	20,000,000	0	Computer Software Peripherals, Special Retail
Zero Stage Capital V, L.P. Paul Kelley, Manager Kendall Square 1010 Main Street, 17th Floor Cambridge, MA 02142 (617) 876-5355 FAX (617) 876-1248	01/71-0360 09/26/94	10,800,000	0	Diversified

Small Business Investment Companies (continued)

Active Regular Small Business Investment Companies — (SBICs Licensed Before June 1994)

	License Number & Date	Private Capital	SBA Leverage	Investment Policy

Alabama

First SBIC of Alabama
David C. DeLaney, President
16 Midtown Park East
Mobile, AL 36606
(334) 476-0700
FAX (334) 476-0026

04/04-0143
07/20/78

2,166,700

6,500,000

Diversified

Hickory Venture Capital Corporation
J. Thomas Noojin, President
200 West Court Square, Suite 100
Huntsville, AL 35801
(205) 539-1931
FAX (205) 539-5130

04/04-0235
03/28/85

18,750,000

5,000,000

Diversified

Arizona

First Commerce & Loan, L.P.
Ross M. Horowitz, GP & Manager
5620 North Kolb, #260
Tucson, AZ 85715
(602) 298-2500
FAX (602) 745-6112

09/09-0386
10/19/90

1,012,000

1,000,000

Diversified

First Interstate Equity Corp.
Edmund G. Zito, President
100 West Washington Street
Phoenix, AZ 85003
(602) 528-6647
FAX (602) 440-1320

09/09-0379
02/01/89

1,000,000

0

Diversified

Sundance Venture Partners, L.P.
(Main Office: Cupertino, CA)
Gregory S. Anderson, Vice President
2828 North Central Avenue, Suite 1275
Phoenix, AZ 85004
(602) 279-1101
FAX (408) 257-8111

Arkansas

Small Business Investment Capital, Inc.
Charles E. Toland, President
12103 Interstate 30
P.O. Box 3627
Little Rock, AR 72203
(501) 455-6599
FAX (501) 455-6556

06/06-0175
03/06/75

1,150,000

3,250,000

Grocery Stores

Small Business Investment Companies (continued)

	License Number & Date	Private Capital	SBA Leverage	Investment Policy

California

BT Capital Partners, Inc.
(Main Office: New York, NY)
300 South Grand Avenue
Los Angeles, CA 90071

BankAmerica Ventures 950 Tower Lane, Suite 700 Foster City, CA 94404 (415) 378-6000 FAX (415) 378-6040	09/14-0009 01/29/60	100,714,475	0	Diversified

Citicorp Venture Capital, Ltd.
(Main Office: New York, NY)
2 Embarcadero Place
2200 Geny Road, Suite 203
Palo Alto, CA 94303
(415) 424-8000

Draper Associates, a California L.P. Timothy C. Draper, President 400 Seaport Court, Suite 250 Redwood City, CA 94063 (415) 599-9000 FAX (415) 599-9726	09/09-0242 09/12/79	2,015,000	6,000,000	Diversified
Hall, Morris & Drufva II, L.P. Ronald J. Hall, Managing Director 25401 Cabbot Road, Suite 116 Laguna Hills, CA 92653 (714) 707-5096 FAX (714) 707-5121	09/09-0224 07/05/78	32,117,778	0	Diversified
Imperial Ventures, Inc. Ray Vadalma, Manager 9920 South LaCienega Boulevard P.O. Box 92991, Los Angeles, CA 90009 Inglewood, CA 90301 (310) 417-5710 FAX (310) 417-5874	09/09-0203 08/31/78	8,001,731	0	Diversified
Jupiter Partners John M. Bryan, President 600 Montgomery Street, 35th Floor San Francisco, CA 94111 (415) 421-9990 FAX (415) 421-0471	09/12-0079 10/26/62	3,253,720	3,760,000	50% in Electronic Manufacturing
Marwit Capital Corp. Martin W. Witte, President 180 Newport Center Drive, Suite 200 Newport Beach, CA 92660 (714) 640-6234 FAX (714) 759-1363	09/02-0175 05/03/62	1,300,707	0	Diversified

Small Business Investment Companies (continued)

	License Number & Date	Private Capital	SBA Leverage	Investment Policy
Merrill Pickard Anderson & Eyre I Steven L. Merrill, President 2480 Sand Hill Road, Suite 200 Menlo Park, CA 94025 (415) 854-8600 FAX (415) 854-0345	09/09-0271 11/26/80	28,083,735	0	Diversified
Pacific Mezzanine Fund, L.P. David C. Woodward, General Partner 88 Kearny Street, Suite 1850 San Francisco, CA 94108 (415) 362-6776 FAX (415) 781-1314	09/09-0397 03/24/94	5,100,000	0	Diversified
Ritter Partners William C. Edwards, President 150 Isabella Avenue Atherton, CA 94027 (415) 854-1555 FAX (415) 854-5015	09/12-0075 10/18/62	3,228,802	3,510,000	50% in Electronic Manufacturing
Sundance Venture Partners, L.P. Larry J. Wells, General Partner 10600 North DeAnza Boulevard, Suite 215 Cupertino, CA 95014 (408) 257-8100 FAX (408) 257-8111	09/09-0387 04/23/90	6,021,414	13,920,000	Diversified
Union Venture Corp. Robert S. Clarke, President 445 South Figueroa Street P.O. Box 3100 Los Angeles, CA 90071 (213) 236-4092 FAX (213) 629-5328	09/12-0145 09/30/67	24,789,708	0	Diversified
VK Capital Company Franklin Van Kasper, General Partner 600 California Street, Suite 1700 San Francisco, CA 94108 (415) 391-5600 FAX (415) 397-2744	09/09-0365 02/07/86	1,050,505	500,000	Diversified

Connecticut

	License Number & Date	Private Capital	SBA Leverage	Investment Policy
AB SBIC, Inc. Adam J. Bozzuto, President 275 School House Road Cheshire, CT 06410 (203) 272-0203 FAX (203) 272-9978	01/01-0280 11/17/76	1,000,000	1,000,000	Grocery Stores

Small Business Investment Companies (continued)

	License Number & Date	Private Capital	SBA Leverage	Investment Policy
Capital Resource Co. of Connecticut Morris Morgenstein, General Partner 2558 Albany Avenue West Hartford, CT 06117 (203) 236-4336 FAX (203) 232-8161	01/01-0285 03/23/77	1,365,000	3,665,000	Diversified
Central Texas SBI Corporation David E. Erb, Contact Person One Canterbury Green 201 Broad Street, 2nd Floor Stamford, CT 06901 (203) 352-4506 FAX (203) 352-4184	01/10-0076 03/29/62	600,000	0	Diversified
Financial Opportunities, Inc. Ms. Robin Munson, Manager One Vision Drive Enfield, CT 06082 (203) 741-4444 FAX (203) 741-9716	01/04-0113 10/17/74	1,900,000	4,220,000	Diversified
First New England Capital, L.P. Richard C. Klaffky, President 100 Pearl Street Hartford, CT 06103 (203) 293-3333 FAX (203) 293-3338	01/01-0344 03/25/88	4,968,553	3,500,000	Diversified
Marcon Capital Corp. Martin A. Cohen, President 10 John Street Southport, CT 06490 (203) 259-7233 FAX (203) 259-9428	01/01-0277 10/23/75	826,550	2,400,000	Diversified
RFE Capital Partners, L.P. Robert M. Williams, Managing Partner 36 Grove Street New Canaan, CT 06840 (203) 966-2800 FAX (203) 966-3109	01/01-0307 07/01/80	9,800,000	8,000,000	Diversified

Delaware

	License Number & Date	Private Capital	SBA Leverage	Investment Policy
PNC Capital Corp. Gary J. Zentner, President 300 Delaware Avenue, Suite 304 Wilmington, DE 19801 (302) 427-5895 FAX (302) 427-5810	03/03-0152 08/12/82			

Small Business Investment Companies (continued)

	License Number & Date	Private Capital	SBA Leverage	Investment Policy

District of Columbia

Allied Investment Corporation
Cabell Williams, President
1666 K Street NW, Suite 901
Washington, DC 20006
(202) 331-1112
FAX (202) 659-2053

03/04-0003
04/23/59

12,593,334   30,850,000   Diversified

Allied Investment Corporation II
William F. Dunbar, President
1666 K Street NW, Suite 901
Washington, DC 20006
(202) 331-1112
FAX (202) 659-2053

03/03-0196
03/20/91

10,000,000   0   Diversified

Legacy Fund Limited Partnership
John Ledecky, Manager & General Partner
1400 34th Street, Suite 800
Washington, DC 20007
(202) 965-2020
FAX (202) 342-7474

03/03-0193
04/16/92

12,000,000   0   Diversified

Florida

Allied Investment Corporation
(Main Office: Washington, D.C.)
Executive Office Center, Suite 305
2770 North Indian River Boulevard
Vero Beach, FL 32960
(407) 778-5556
FAX (202) 659-2053

J & D Capital Corp.
Jack Carmel, President
12747 Biscayne Boulevard
North Miami, FL 33181
(305) 893-0303
FAX (305) 891-2339

04/04-0188
07/09/80

1,150,106   2,560,000   Diversified

Market Capital Corp.
Donald Kolvenbach, President
1102 North 28th Street
P.O. Box 31667
Tampa, FL 33631-3667
(813) 247-1357
FAX (813) 248-5531

04/05-0086
03/24/64

786,000   1,200,000   Grocery Stores

Western Financial Capital Corporation
(Main Office: Dallas, TX)
AmeriFirst Bank Building, 2nd Floor South
18301 Biscayne Boulevard
North Miami Beach, FL 33160
(305) 933-5858
FAX (305) 931-3054

Small Business Investment Companies (continued)

	License Number & Date	Private Capital	SBA Leverage	Investment Policy

Georgia

Cordova Capital Partners, L.P.
Paul DiBella/Ralph Wright, Managers
3350 Cumberland Circle, Suite 970
Atlanta, GA 30339
(770) 951-1542
FAX (770) 955-7610

04/04-0260
03/24/94

8,112,500

0

Diversified

North Riverside Capital Corporation
Tom Barry, President
50 Technology Park/Atlanta
Norcross, GA 30092
(404) 446-5556
FAX (404) 446-8627

04/04-0230
08/24/84

3,010,500

0

Diversified

Hawaii

Bancorp Hawaii SBIC
Robert Paris, President
111 South King Street, Suite 1060
Honolulu, HI 96813
(808) 537-8613
FAX (808) 521-7602

09/09-0340
02/17/84

2,000,000

0

Diversified

Illinois

Continental Illinois Venture Corp.
John Willis, President
209 South LaSalle Street
Mail: 231 South LaSalle Street
Chicago, IL 60693
(312) 828-8023
FAX (312) 987-0887

05/07-0078
04/02/70

116,000,000

0

Diversified

First Capital Corp. of Chicago
J. Mikesell Thomas, President
Three First National Plaza, Suite 1330
Chicago, IL 60670
(312) 732-5400
FAX (312) 732-4098

05/07-0042
06/08/61

103,100,000

0

Diversified

Heller Equity Capital Corporation
John M. Goense, President
500 West Monroe Street
Chicago, IL 60661
(312) 441-7200
FAX (312) 441-7378

05/02-0401
09/19/80

17,621,472

0

Diversified

Small Business Investment Companies (continued)

	License Number & Date	Private Capital	SBA Leverage	Investment Policy
Walnut Capital Corp. Burton W. Kanter, Chairman of the Board Two North LaSalle Street, Suite 2200 Chicago, IL 60602 (312) 269-1700 FAX (312) 269-1747	05/02-0430 11/07/83	7,321,800	12,000,000	Diversified

Indiana

	License Number & Date	Private Capital	SBA Leverage	Investment Policy
1st Source Capital Corporation Eugene L. Cavanaugh, Jr., Vice President 100 North Michigan Street P.O. Box 1602, South Bend, IN 46634 South Bend, IN 46601 (219) 235-2180 FAX (219) 235-2719	05/05-0194 12/23/83	2,500,000	0	Diversified
Cambridge Ventures, L.P. Ms. Jean Wojtowicz, President 8440 Woodfield Crossing, #315 Indianapolis, IN 46240 (317) 469-9704 FAX (317) 469-3926	05/05-0218 07/06/92	3,046,150	0	Diversified
Circle Ventures, Inc. Carrie Walkup, Manager 26 North Arsenal Avenue Indianapolis, IN 46201 (317) 636-7242 FAX (317) 637-7581	05/05-0171 08/19/83	1,000,000	500,000	Diversified

Iowa

	License Number & Date	Private Capital	SBA Leverage	Investment Policy
MorAmerica Capital Corporation David R. Schroder, President 101 2nd Street SE, Suite 800 Cedar Rapids, IA 52401 (319) 363-8249 FAX (319) 363-9683	07/07-0006 09/30/59	5,520,000	10,290,000	Diversified

Kansas

	License Number & Date	Private Capital	SBA Leverage	Investment Policy
Kansas Venture Capital, Inc. Rex E. Wiggins, President 6700 Antioch Plaza, Suite 460 Overland Park, KS 66204 (913) 262-7117 FAX (913) 262-3509	07/07-0077 06/17/77	9,549,116	0	Diversified

Small Business Investment Companies (continued)

	License Number & Date	Private Capital	SBA Leverage	Investment Policy
Kentucky				
Mountain Ventures, Inc. L. Ray Moncrief, Executive Vice President 362 Old Whitley Road P.O. Box 1738 London, KY 40743-1738 (606) 864-5175 FAX (606) 864-5194	04/04-0145 12/19/78	1,640,000	0	Diversified
Louisiana				
Premier Venture Capital Corporation G. Lee Griffin, President 451 Florida Street Baton Rouge, LA 70821 (504) 332-4421 FAX (504) 334-7929	06/06-0169 02/21/74	4,260,639	0	Diversified
Maryland				
Greater Washington Investments, Inc. Haywood Miller, Manager 39 West Montgomery Avenue Rockville, MD 20850 (301) 738-3939 FAX (301) 738-7949	03/04-0011 02/09/60	5,000,000	14,500,000	Diversified
Massachusetts				
BancBoston Ventures, Incorporated Frederick M. Fritz, President 100 Federal Street Mail: P.O. Box 2016 Stop 01-31-08 Boston, MA 02110 (617) 434-2442 FAX (617) 434-1153	01/01-0001 05/08/59	75,000,000	0	Diversified
Business Achievement Corporation Michael L. Katzeff, President 1172 Beacon Street, Suite 202 Newton, MA 02161 (617) 965-0550 FAX (617) 345-7201	01/01-0055 08/08/63	550,000	1,610,000	Diversified
Chestnut Street Partners, Inc. David D. Croll, President 75 State Street, Suite 2500 Boston, MA 02109 (617) 345-7220 FAX (617) 345-7201	01/01-0339 12/03/86	4,000,000	5,000,000	Diversified

Small Business Investment Companies (continued)

	License Number & Date	Private Capital	SBA Leverage	Investment Policy
First Capital Corp. of Chicago (Main Office: Chicago, IL) One Financial Center, 27th Floor Boston, MA 02111 (617) 457-2500 FAX (617) 457-2506				
Mezzanine Capital Corporation David D. Croll, President 75 State Street, Suite 2500 Boston, MA 02109 (617) 345-7200 FAX (617) 345-7201	01/01-0341 05/28/87	30,000,000	25,000,000	Diversified
Northeast SBI Corp. Joseph Mindick, Treasurer 130 New Market Square, Suite 1 Boston, MA 02118 (617) 267-3983 FAX (617) 442-0101	01/01-0275 05/07/74	378,802	1,130,000	Diversified
Pioneer Ventures, L.P. Leigh Michl, General Partner 60 State Street, 19th Floor Boston, MA 02109 (617) 742-7825 FAX (617) 742-7315	01/01-0337 11/20/86	5,609,745	4,950,000	Diversified
UST Capital Corp. Arthur F. Snyder, President 40 Court Street Boston, MA 02108 (617) 726-7000 FAX (617) 723-9414	01/01-0027 10/06/61	1,752,800	1,501,000	Diversified

Michigan

Capital Fund, Inc. Barry Wilson, President 6412 Centurion Drive, Suite 150 Lansing, MI 48917 (517) 323-7772 FAX (517) 323-1999	05/05-0219 09/08/93	2,500,000	0	Expansion
White Pines Capital Corporation Mr. Ian Bund, President & Manager 2929 Plymouth Road, Suite 210 Ann Arbor, MI 48105 (313) 747-9401 FAX (313) 747-9704	05/05-0217 02/25/92	1,750,000	0	Diversified

Small Business Investment Companies (continued)

	License Number & Date	Private Capital	SBA Leverage	Investment Policy

Minnesota

FBS SBIC, Limited Partnership
Richard Rinkoff, Manager
601 Second Avenue South, 16th Floor
Minneapolis, MN 55402
(612) 973-0988
FAX (612) 973-0203

09/09-0345
09/27/84

11,183,321

0

Diversified

Northwest Venture Partners
Daniel J. Haggerty, Managing General Partner
2800 Piper Jaffray Tower
222 South Ninth Street
Minneapolis, MN 55402
(612) 667-1650
FAX (612) 667-1660

05/05-0182
10/13/83

24,016,106

0

Diversified

Norwest Equity Partners IV
Robert F. Zicarelli, General Partner
2800 Piper Jaffray Tower
222 South Ninth Street
Minneapolis, MN 55402
(612) 667-1650
FAX (612) 667-1660

05/05-0210
08/02/89

104,934,738

0

Diversified

Norwest Growth Fund, Inc.
Daniel J. Haggerty, President
2800 Piper Jaffray Tower
222 South Ninth Street
Minneapolis, MN 55402
(612) 667-1650
FAX (612) 667-1660

05/08-0006
02/25/60

28,982,360

1,000,000

Diversified

Missouri

Bankers Capital Corp.
Raymond E. Glasnapp, President
3100 Gillham Road
Kansas City, MO 64109
(816) 531-1600
FAX (816) 531-1334

07/07-0075
02/12/76

632,000

710,000

Diversified

CFB Venture Fund I, Inc.
James F. O'Donnell, Chairman
11 South Meramec, Suite 1430
St. Louis, MO 63105
(314) 746-7427
FAX (314) 746-8739

07/09-0002
10/15/59

6,000,000

0

Diversified

CFB Venture Fund II, L.P.
James F. O'Donnell, Chairman
11 South Meramec, Suite 1430
St. Louis, MO 63105
(314) 746-7427
FAX (314) 746-8739

07/07-0095
03/02/93

3,336,061

0

Diversified

Small Business Investment Companies (continued)

	License Number & Date	Private Capital	SBA Leverage	Investment Policy
MorAmerica Capital Corporation (Main Office: Cedar Rapids, IA) Commerce Tower Building 911 Main Street, Suite 2724A Kansas City, MO 64105 (816) 842-0114 FAX (816) 471-7339				
United Missouri Capital Corporation Noel Shull, Manager 1010 Grand Avenue P.O. Box 419226, Kansas City, MO 64141 Kansas City, MO 64106 (816) 860-7914 FAX (816) 860-7143	07/07-0091 09/21/84	2,500,000	0	Diversified

Nebraska

United Financial Resources Corp. Joan Boulay, Manager 7401 "F" Street P.O. Box 1131, Omaha, NE 68101 Omaha, NE 68127 (402) 339-7300 FAX (402) 734-0650	07/07-0087 07/07/83	500,000	500,000	Grocery Stores

Nevada

Atalanta Investment Company, Inc. L. Mark Newman, Chairman of the Board 601 Fairview Boulevard Incline Village, NV 89451 (702) 833-1836 FAX (702) 833-1890	02/02-0357 06/22/79	4,359,961	0	Diversified

New Jersey

CIT Group/Venture Capital, Inc. Colby W. Collier, Manager 650 CIT Drive Livingston, NJ 07039 (201) 740-5429 FAX (201) 740-5555	02/02-0547 06/01/92	11,900,000	0	Diversified
ESLO Capital Corp. Leo Katz, President 212 Wright Street Newark, NJ 07114 (201) 242-4488 FAX (201) 643-6062	01/01-0300 05/31/79	688,323	1,300,000	Diversified

Small Business Investment Companies (continued)

	License Number & Date	Private Capital	SBA Leverage	Investment Policy
Tappan Zee Capital Corporation Jack Birnberg, President 201 Lower Notch Road Little Falls, NJ 07424 (201) 256-8280 FAX (201) 256-2841	02/02-0209 11/16/63	1,000,000	2,700,000	66% Real Estate

New York

	License Number & Date	Private Capital	SBA Leverage	Investment Policy
399 Venture Partners William Comfort, Chairman 399 Park Avenue, 14th Floor/Zone 4 New York, NY 10043 (212) 559-1127 FAX (212) 888-2940	02/02-0514 02/02/89	100,000,000	0	Diversified
Argentum Capital Partners, LP Daniel Raynor, Chairman 405 Lexington Avenue, 54th Floor New York, NY 10174 (212) 949-8272 FAX (212) 949-8294	02/02-0535 01/31/90	3,000,000	4,800,000	Diversified
BT Capital Partners, Inc. Heidi Silverstein, Vice President 280 Park Avenue—32 West New York, NY 10017 (212) 250-8084 FAX (212) 250-7651	02/02-0295 11/10/72	119,998,033	18,000,000	Diversified
Barclays Capital Investors Corp. Graham McGahen, President 222 Broadway, 7th Floor New York, NY 10038 (212) 412-3937 FAX (212) 412-6780	02/02-0549 10/03/91	5,000,000	0	Diversified
CB Investors, Inc. Edward L. Kock, III, President 270 Park Avenue, 5th Floor New York, NY 10017 (212) 270-3220 FAX (212) 270-2327	02/02-0501 11/06/86	20,000,000	0	Diversified
CIBC Wood Gundy Ventures, Inc. Gordon Muessel, Vice President 425 Lexington Avenue, 9th Floor New York, NY 10017 (212) 856-3713 FAX (212) 697-1554	02/02-0540 10/26/90	32,911,000	0	Diversified

Small Business Investment Companies (continued)

	License Number & Date	Private Capital	SBA Leverage	Investment Policy
CMNY Capital II, L.P. Robert G. Davidoff, General Partner 135 East 57th Street, 26th Floor New York, NY 10022 (212) 909-8432 FAX (212) 980-2630	02/02-0515 06/30/89	4,000,000	4,500,000	Diversified
Chase Manhattan Capital Corporation Gustav H. Koven, President 1 Chase Plaza–7th Floor New York, NY 10081 (212) 552-6275 FAX (212) 552-2807	02/02-0228 08/02/62	50,000,105	0	Diversified
Chemical Venture Capital Associates Jeffrey C. Walker, Managing General Partner 270 Park Avenue, 5th Floor New York, NY 10017 (212) 270-3220 FAX (212) 270-2327	02/02-0479 10/22/84	168,914,772	0	Diversified
Citicorp Venture Capital, Ltd. William Comfort, Chairman of the Board 399 Park Avenue, 14th Floor/Zone 4 New York, NY 10043 (212) 599-1127 FAX (212) 527-2496	02/02-0266 12/18/67	127,197,602	0	Diversified
Edwards Capital Company Michael Kowalsky, Chief Executive Officer Two Park Avenue, 20th Floor New York, NY 10016 (212) 686-5449 FAX (212) 213-6234	02/02-0366 06/22/79	7,200,000	24,950,000	Transportation
Exeter Venture Lenders, L.P. Keith Fox, Manager 10 East 53rd Street New York, NY 10022 (212) 872-1170 FAX (212) 872-1198	02/02-0548 02/07/94	13,600,000	0	Diversified
First Wall Street SBIC, L.P. Alan Farkas, General Partner 26 Broadway, Suite 1320 New York, NY 10004 (212) 742-3770 FAX (212) 742-3776	02/02-0524 02/01/89	3,050,000	9,000,000	Diversified
Fundex Capital Corp. Howard Sommer, President 555 Theodore Fremd Avenue, C-200 Rye, NY 10580 (516) 466-8551 FAX (914) 967-6522	02/02-0340 05/18/78	2,258,659	6,650,000	Diversified

Small Business Investment Companies (continued)

	License Number & Date	Private Capital	SBA Leverage	Investment Policy
Genesee Funding, Inc. Stuart Marsh, President & CEO 70 Linden Oaks, 3rd Floor Rochester, NY 14625 (716) 383-5550 FAX (716) 383-5305	02/02-0499 11/26/86	1,000,000	600,000	Diversified
IBJS Capital Corp. Peter D. Matthy, President One State Street, 8th Floor New York, NY 10004 (212) 858-2000 FAX (212) 858-2768	02/02-0539 05/25/90	5,000,000	0	Diversified
InterEquity Capital Partners, L.P. Irwin Schlass, President 220 Fifth Avenue, 12th Floor New York, NY 10001 (212) 779-2022 FAX (212) 779-2103	02/02-0545 12/17/90	2,990,941	5,000,000	Diversified
J. P. Morgan Investment Corporation David M. Cromwell, Managing Director 60 Wall Street New York, NY 10260 (212) 483-2323	02/03-0185 12/10/87	50,294,000	0	Diversified
KOCO Capital Company, L.P. Albert Pastino, President 111 Radio Circle Mount Kisco, NY 10549 (914) 242-2324 FAX (914) 241-7476	02/02-0550 03/25/94	5,000,000	0	Diversified
M & T Capital Corp. Philip A. McNeill, Vice President One Fountain Plaza, 9th Floor Buffalo, NY 14203 (716) 848-3800 FAX (716) 848-3424	02/02-0268 12/29/67	10,007,486	0	Diversified
NYBDC Capital Corp. Robert W. Lazar, President 41 State Street P.O. Box 738 Albany, NY 12207 (518) 463-2268 FAX (518) 463-0240	02/02-0303 11/02/73	500,000	350,000	Diversified
NatWest USA Capital Corporation Phillip Krall, General Manager 175 Water Street, 27th Floor New York, NY 10038 (212) 602-1200 FAX (212) 602-2149	02/02-0492 02/06/86	20,000,000	0	Diversified

Business Investment Companies (continued)

	License Number & Date	Private Capital	SBA Leverage	Investment Policy
Norwood Venture Corp. Mark R. Littell, President 1430 Broadway, Suite 1607 New York, NY 10018 (212) 869-5075 FAX (212) 869-5331	02/02-0403 08/18/80	5,000,000	15,070,000	Diversified
Paribas Principal Incorporated Steven Alexander, President 787 Seventh Avenue, 33rd Floor New York, NY 10019 (212) 841-2000 FAX (212) 841-2146	02/02-0526 08/02/89	3,000,000	0	Diversified
Pyramid Ventures, Inc. Brian Talbot, Vice President 130 Liberty Street, 31st Floor New York, NY 10006 (212) 250-9571 FAX (212) 250-7651	02/02-0507 06/26/87	23,000,000	0	Diversified
Sterling Commercial Capital, Inc. Harvey L. Granat, President 175 Great Neck Road–Suite 408 Great Neck, NY 11021 (516) 482-7374 FAX (516) 487-0781	02/02-0517 10/03/88	5,000,000	12,000,000	Diversified
TLC Funding Corp. Phillip G. Kass, President 660 White Plains Road Tarrytown, NY 10591 (914) 332-5200 FAX (914) 332-5660	02/02-0380 02/29/80	1,750,000	1,044,000	Laundries and Dry Cleaning
Vega Capital Corp. Ron Linden, President 80 Business Park Drive, Suite 201 Armonk, NY 10504 (914) 273-1025 FAX (914) 273-1028	02/02-0270 08/05/68	2,402,861	4,780,000	Diversified
Winfield Capital Corp. Stanley M. Pechman, President 237 Mamaroneck Avenue White Plains, NY 10605 (914) 949-2600 FAX (914) 949-7195	02/02-0292 04/19/72	1,250,000	3,750,.000	Diversified

Small Business Investment Companies (continued)

	LICENSE NUMBER & DATE	PRIVATE CAPITAL	SBA LEVERAGE	INVESTMENT POLICY
North Carolina				
First Union Capital Partners, Inc. Kevin J. Roche, Senior Vice President One First Union Center, 18th Floor 301 South College Street Charlotte, NC 28288 (704) 374-6487 FAX (704) 374-6711	03/03-0188 02/15/90	13,180,025	0	Diversified
NationsBanc Capital Corporation (Main Office: Dallas, TX) 100 North Tryon, 7th Floor Charlotte, NC 28255 (704) 386-8063 FAX (704) 386-6432	02/07/94			
NationsBanc SBIC Corp. J. Michael Pitchford, Interim President 901 West Trade Street, Suite 1020 Charlotte, NC 28202 (704) 386-7720 FAX (704) 386-6662	04/04-0232 07/19/84	2,500,000	0	Diversified
Springdale Venture Partners, L.P. S. Epes Robinson, General Partner 2039 Queens Road East Charlotte, NC 28207 (704) 344-8290 FAX (704) 386-6695	04/04-0231 07/19/84	9,871,553	0	Diversified
Ohio				
Banc One Capital Partners Corporation (Main Office: Dallas, TX) 10 West Broad Street, Suite 200 Columbus, OH 43215				
Clarion Capital Corp. Morton A. Cohen, President Ohio Savings Plaza, Suite 510 1801 East 9th Street Cleveland, OH 44114 (216) 687-1096 FAX (216) 694-3545	05/07-0023 09/25/68	6,970,219	8,790,000	Diversified
Key Equity Capital Corporation Raymond Lancaster, President 127 Public Square, 6th Floor Cleveland, OH 44114 (216) 689-5776 FAX (216) 689-3204	05/06-0011 12/09/60	40,624,630	0	Diversified

Small Business Investment Companies (continued)

	License Number & Date	Private Capital	SBA Leverage	Investment Policy
National City Capital Corporation William H. Schecter, President & General Manager 1965 East Sixth Street, Suite 400 Cleveland, OH 44114 (216) 575-2491 FAX (216) 575-3355	05/05-0137 02/08/79	12,783,791	0	Diversified

Oklahoma

Alliance Business Investment Company Barry Davis, President 17 East Second Street One Williams Center, Suite 2000 Tulsa, OK 74172 (918) 584-3581 FAX (918) 582-3403	06/10-0012 08/12/59	3,480,502	2,560,000	Diversified
BancFirst Investment Corp. T. Kent Faison, Manager 101 North Broadway P.O. Box 26788 Oklahoma City, OK 73126 (405) 270-1000 FAX (405) 270-1089	06/06-0306 04/01/94	2,500,000	0	Diversified

Oregon

Northern Pacific Capital Corporation Joseph P. Tennant, President 937 SW 14th Street, Suite 200 P.O. Box 1658 Portland, OR 97207 (503) 241-1255 FAX (503) 299-6653	10/13-0014 01/18/62	1,141,464	1,000,000	Diversified
U.S. Bancorp Capital Corporation Gary Patterson, President 111 SW Fifth Avenue, Suite 1450 Portland, OR 97204 (503) 275-5710 FAX (503) 275-7565	10/10-0174 03/05/81	13,028,892	0	Diversified

Pennsylvania

CIP Capital, L.P. Winston Churchill, Jr., Manager 20 Valley Stream Parkway, Suite 265 Malvern, PA 19355 (610) 695-8380 FAX (610) 695-8388	03/03-0195 10/03/91	6,658,278	7,000,000	Diversified

Small Business Investment Companies (continued)

	License Number & Date	Private Capital	SBA Leverage	Investment Policy
Enterprise Venture Cap Corp. of Pennsylvania Don Cowie, CEO 111 Market Street Johnstown, PA 15901 (814) 535-7597 FAX (814) 535-8677	03/03-0179 09/11/85	1,147,649	0	Diversified
Fidelcor Capital Corp. Elizabeth T. Crawford, President Fidelity Building, 11th Floor 123 South Broad Street Philadelphia, PA 19109 (215) 985-3722 FAX (215) 985-7282	03/03-0184 01/14/88	5,100,000	0	Diversified
First SBIC of California (Main Office: Costa Mesa, CA) Daniel A. Dye, Contact P.O. Box 512 Washington, PA 15301 (412) 223-0707 FAX (714) 546-8021				
Meridian Venture Partners Raymond R. Rafferty, General Partner The Fidelity Court Building 259 Radnor-Chester Road, Suite 140 Radnor, PA 19087 (610) 254-2999 FAX (610) 254-2996	03/03-0181 02/24/87	24,886,449	0	Diversified

Rhode Island

	License Number & Date	Private Capital	SBA Leverage	Investment Policy
Domestic Capital Corp. Nathaniel B. Baker, President 815 Reservoir Avenue Cranston, RI 02910 (401) 946-3310 FAX (401) 943-6708	01/01-0333 12/11/84	500,000	1,000,000	Diversified
Fleet Venture Resources, Inc. Robert M. Van Degna, President 111 Westminster Street, 4th Floor Providence, RI 02903 (401) 278-6770 FAX (401) 278-6387	01/01-0067 12/18/67	35,007,068	0	Diversified
Moneta Capital Corp. Arnold Kilberg, President 285 Governor Street Providence, RI 02906 (401) 454-7500 FAX (401) 455-3636	01/01-0322 05/04/84	2,002,500	6,000,000	Diversified

Small Business Investment Companies (continued)

	License Number & Date	Private Capital	SBA Leverage	Investment Policy
Richmond Square Capital Corporation Harold I. Schein, President 1 Richmond Square Providence, RI 02906 (401) 521-3000 FAX (401) 751-3940	01/01-0349 01/31/90	3,025,000	0	Diversified
Wallace Capital Corp. Lloyd W. Granoff, President 170 Westminister Street, Suite 300 Providence, RI 02903 (401) 273-9191 FAX (401) 273-9648	01/01-0338 12/22/86	2,015,000	2,750,000	Diversified

South Carolina

	License Number & Date	Private Capital	SBA Leverage	Investment Policy
Charleston Capital Corporation Henry Yaschik, President 111 Church Street P.O. Box 328 Charleston, SC 29402 (803) 723-6464 FAX (803) 723-1047	04/04-0042 06/21/61	1,487,424	2,000,000	Diversified
The Floco Investment Company, Inc. William H. Johnson, Sr., President Highway 52 North P.O. Box 919, Lake City, SC 29560 Scranton, SC 29561 (803) 389-2731 FAX (803) 389-4199	04/04-0032 07/05/61	588,400	0	Food Retailers

Tennessee

	License Number & Date	Private Capital	SBA Leverage	Investment Policy
Equitas, L.P. D. Shannon LeRoy, President of CGP 2000 Glen Echo Road, Suite 100 Nashville, TN 37215 (615) 383-8673 FAX (615) 383-8693	04/04-0259 11/05/93	4,484,848	0	Diversified
Sirrom Capital, L.P. George M. Miller, II, Manager 500 Church Street, Suite 200 Nashville, TN 37219 (615) 256-0701 FAX (615) 726-1208	04/04-0258 05/14/92	18,300,798	34,000,000	Diversified

Small Business Investment Companies (continued)

	License Number & Date	Private Capital	SBA Leverage	Investment Policy

Texas

AMT Capital, Ltd.
Tom H. Delimitros, CGP
8204 Elmbrook Drive, Suite 101
Dallas, TX 75247
(214) 905-9760
FAX (214) 905-9761

| | 06/06-0304 10/07/91 | 2,196,969 | 0 | Diversified |

Alliance Business Investment Company
(Main Office: Tulsa, OK)
911 Louisiana
One Shell Plaza, Suite 3990
Houston, TX 77002
(713) 224-8224
FAX (713) 659-8070

Banc One Capital Partners Corporation
Michael J. Endres, President
300 Crescent Court, Suite 1600
Dallas, TX 75201
(214) 979-4360
FAX (214) 979-4355

| | 06/06-0188 12/08/76 | 34,942,000 | 15,200,000 | Diversified |

Capital Southwest Venture Corp.
William R. Thomas, President
12900 Preston Road, Suite 700
Dallas, TX 75230
(214) 233-8242
FAX (214) 233-7362

| | 06/10-0065 07/13/61 | 14,229,271 | 15,000,000 | Diversified |

The Catalyst Fund, Ltd.
Richard L. Herrman, Manager
Three Riverway, Suite 770
Houston, TX 77056
(713) 623-8133
FAX (713) 623-0473

| | 06/06-0303 05/08/91 | 5,000,000 | 1,500,000 | Diversified |

Charter Venture Group, Incorporated
Winston C. Davis, President
2600 Citadel Plaza Drive, Suite 600
P.O. Box 4525
Houston, TX 77008
(713) 622-7500
FAX (713) 552-8446

| | 06/06-0237 10/10/80 | 1,685,000 | 1,000,000 | Diversified |

Citicorp Venture Capital, Ltd.
(Main Office: New York, NY)
717 North Harwood, Suite 2920-LB87
Dallas, TX 75201
(214) 880-9670
FAX (214) 953-1495

Small Business Investment Companies (continued)

	License Number & Date	Private Capital	SBA Leverage	Investment Policy
HCT Capital Corp. Vichy Woodward Young, Jr., President 4916 Camp Bowie Boulevard, Suite 200 Fort Worth, TX 76107 (817) 763-8706 FAX (817) 377-8049	06/06/-0305 11/01/91	1,000,000	300,000	Diversified
Houston Partners, SBIP Harvard Hill, President, CGP Capital Center Penthouse, 8th Floor 401 Louisiana Houston, TX 77002 (713) 222-8600 FAX (713) 222-8932	06/06-0290 11/19/85	2,521,587	2,800,000	Diversified
Mapleleaf Capital, Ltd. Patrick A. Rivelli, Manager Three Forest Plaza, Suite 1300 12221 Merit Drive Dallas, TX 75251 (214) 239-5650 FAX (214) 701-0024	06/06-0239 10/06/80	5,000,000	3,000,000	Diversified
NationsBanc Capital Corporation Walter W. Walker, President 901 Main Street, 66th Floor Dallas, TX 75202 (214) 508-0932 FAX (214) 508-0985	06/10-0059 06/26/61	36,000,044	0	Diversified
SBI Capital Corp. William E. Wright, President P.O. Box 570638, Houston, TX 77257 Houston, TX 77057 (713) 975-1188 FAX (713) 975-l302	06/06-0244 10/22/81	2,250,000	1,700,000	Diversified
Stratford Capital Group, Inc. Michael D. Brown, President 200 Crescent Court, Suite 1650 Dallas, TX 75201 (214) 740-7377 FAX (214) 740-7340	06/06-0307 05/19/94	5,000,000	0	Diversified
UNCO Ventures, Ltd. Walter Cunningham, Managing Partner 520 Post Oak Boulevard, Suite 130 Houston, TX 77027 (713) 622-9595 FAX (713) 622-9007	06/06-0297 09/30/88	3,000,000	3,000,000	Diversified

Small Business Investment Companies (continued)

	License Number & Date	Private Capital	SBA Leverage	Investment Policy
Ventex Partners, Ltd. Richard S. Smith, President 1000 Louisiana, Suite 1095 Houston, TX 77002 (713) 659-7860 FAX (713) 659-7855	06/06-0219 11/01/79	19,857,026	0	Diversified
Victoria Capital Corp. Darrell Cooper, Interim President One O'Connor Plaza Victoria, TX 77902 (512) 573-5646 FAX (512) 574-5236	06/10-0019 05/08/61	3,000,000	0	Diversified
Victoria Capital Corp. (Main Office: Victoria, TX) Jeffrey P. Blanchard, Vice President 750 East Mulberry, #305 Box 15616 San Antonio, TX 78212 (210) 736-4233 FAX (210) 736-5449				
Western Financial Capital Corporation Andrew S. Rosemore, President 17290 Preston Road, Suite 300 Dallas, TX 75252 (214) 380-0044 FAX (214) 380-1371	04/04-0183 02/22/80	5,546,744	14,280,000	Medical

Utah

First Security Business Investment Corp. Louis D. Alder, Manager 79 South Main Street, Suite 800 Salt Lake City, UT 84111 (801) 246-5737 FAX (801) 246-5424	08/08-0147 10/18/93	5,000,000	0	Diversified
Wasatch Venture Corporation W. David Hemingway, Manager 1 South Main Street, Suite 1000 Salt Lake City, UT 84133 (801) 524-8939 FAX (801) 524-8941	08/08-0148 04/15/94	4,500,000	0	Diversified

Vermont

Green Mountain Capital, L.P. Michael Sweatman, General Manager RD 1, Box 1503 Waterbury, VT 05676 (802) 244-8981 FAX (802) 244-8990	01/01-0357 03/29/93	2,842,391	0	Diversified

Small Business Investment Companies (continued)

	License Number & Date	Private Capital	SBA Leverage	Investment Policy
Queneska Capital Corporation Albert W. Coffrin, III, President 123 Church Street Burlington, VT 05401 (802) 865-1806 FAX (802) 865-1891	01/01-0345 04/25/88	1,500,000	0	Diversified

Virginia

Walnut Capital Corp.
(Main Office: Chicago, IL)
8000 Tower Crescent Drive, Suite 1070
Vienna, VA 22182
(703) 448-3771
FAX (703) 448-7751

West Virginia

Anker Capital Corporation Thomas Loehr, Manager 208 Capital Street, Suite 300 Charleston, WV 25301 (304) 344-1794 FAX (304) 344-1798	03/03-0198 05/16/94	2,500,000	0	Diversified
WestVen Limited Partnership Thomas E. Loehr, President 208 Capitol Street, Suite 300 Charleston, WV 25301 (304) 344-1794 FAX (304) 344-1798	03/03-0197 11/01/93	2,500,000	0	

Wisconsin

Banc One Venture Corp. H. Wayne Foreman, President 111 East Wisconsin Avenue Milwaukee, WI 53202 (414) 765-2274 FAX (414) 765-2235	05/05-0195 05/02/84	13,005,000	1,000,000	Diversified
Bando-McGlocklin SBIC George Schonath, Chief Executive Officer 13555 Bishops Court, Suite 205 Brookfield, WI 53005 (414) 784-9010 FAX (414) 784-3426	05/05-0147 09/02/80	24,421,525	15,020,000	Diversified
Capital Investments, Inc. James R. Sanger, President 1009 West Glen Oaks Lane, Suite 103 Mequon, WI 53092 (414) 241-0303 FAX (414) 241-8451	05/07-0003 05/25/59	4,783,245	10,730,000	Diversified

Small Business Investment Companies (continued)

	License Number & Date	Private Capital	SBA Leverage	Investment Policy
M & I Ventures Corp. John T. Byrnes, President 770 North Water Street Milwaukee, WI 53202 (414) 765-7910 FAX (414) 765-7850	05/05-0202 08/19/85	16,048,370	0	Diversified
MorAmerica Capital Corporation (Main Office: Cedar Rapids, IA) 600 East Mason Street Milwaukee, WI 53202 (414) 276-3839 FAX (414) 276-1885				
Polaris Capital Corp. Richard Laabs, President 2525 North 124th Street, Suite 200 Brookfield, WI 53005 (414) 789-5780 FAX (414) 789-5799	05/05-0212 02/09/90	2,114,759	2,460,000	Diversified

Small Business Investment Companies (continued)

Active Specialized Small Business Investment Companies
These companies are oriented toward minority investments.

	LICENSE NUMBER & DATE	PRIVATE CAPITAL	SBA LEVERAGE	INVESTMENT POLICY
Alabama				
Alabama Capital Corporation David C. DeLaney, President 16 Midtown Park East Mobile, AL 36606 (334) 476-0700 FAX (334) 476-0026	04/04-5203 07/28/81	1,550,000	3,150,000	Diversified
Alabama Small Business Investment Co. Harold Gilchrist, Manager 1732 5th Avenue North Birmingham, AL 35203 (205) 324-5231 FAX (205) 324-5234	04/04-5243 04/05/88	1,005,000	2,000,000	Diversified
FJC Growth Capital Corporation William B. Noojin, Manager 200 West Court Square, Suite 750 Huntsville, AL 35801 (205) 922-2918 FAX (205) 922-2909	04/04-5254 03/07/91	2,167,401	2,000,000	Diversified
California				
Allied Business Investors, Inc. Jack Hong, President 428 South Atlantic Boulevard, Suite 201 Monterey Park, CA 91754 (818) 289-0186 FAX (818) 289-2369	09/09-5309 12/29/82	600,000	1,200,000	Diversified
Ally Finance Corp. Percy P. Lin, President 9100 Wilshire Boulevard, Suite 408 Beverly Hills, CA 90212 (310) 550-8100 FAX (310) 550-6136	09/09-5299 06/04/82	600,000	950,000	Diversified
Asian American Capital Corporation Jennie Chien, Manager 1251 West Tennyson Road, Suite #4 Hayward, CA 94544 (510) 887-6888 FAX (510) 887-6897	09/09-5279 02/23/81	516,200	500,000	Diversified
Astar Capital Corp. George Hsu, President 9537 East Gidley Street Temple City, CA 91780 (818) 350-1211 FAX (818) 443-5874	09/09-5370 11/06/86	1,020,000	4,080,000	Diversified

Small Business Investment Companies (continued)

	License Number & Date	Private Capital	SBA Leverage	Investment Policy
Bentley Capital John Hung, President 592 Vallejo Street, Suite #2 San Francisco, CA 94133 (415) 362-2868 FAX (415) 398-8209	09/09-5375 08/27/87	1,500,000	5,960,000	Diversified
Best Finance Corporation Vincent Lee, General Manager 4929 West Wilshire Boulevard, Suite 407 Los Angeles, CA 90010 (213) 937-1636 FAX (213) 937-6393	09/09-5369 06/24/87	1,510,000	4,530,000	Diversified
Calsafe Capital Corp. Ming-Min Su, President, Director & Manager 245 East Main Street, Suite 107 Alhambra, CA 91801 (818) 289-3400 FAX (818) 300-8025	09/09-5380 12/28/88	1,010,000	2,020,000	Diversified
Charterway Investment Corporation Tien Chen, President One Wilshire Building 624 South Grand Avenue, Suite 1600 Los Angeles, CA 90017 (213) 689-9107 FAX (213) 689-9108	09/09-5338 04/04/84	1,597,336	3,000,000	Diversified
Far East Capital Corp. Tom Wang, Manager 977 North Broadway, Suite 401 Los Angeles, CA 90012 (213) 687-1361 FAX (213) 626-7497	09/09-5383 06/26/89	1,025,000	1,500,000	Diversified
First American Capital Funding, Inc. Chuoc Vota, President 10840 Warner Avenue, Suite 202 Fountain Valley, CA 92708 (714) 965-7190 FAX (714) 965-7193	09/09-5332 05/02/84	823,250	1,646,000	Diversified
Fulcrum Venture Capital Corporation Brian Argrett, President 300 Corporate Pointe, Suite 380 Culver City, CA 90230 (310) 645-1271 FAX (310) 645-1272	09/03-5135 07/05/78	2,000,000	2,000,000	Diversified
LaiLai Capital Corp. Danny Ku, President 223 East Garvey Avenue, Suite 228 Monterey Park, CA 91754 (818) 288-0704 FAX (818) 288-4101	09/09-5285 11/24/82	1,125,000	3,375,000	Diversified

Small Business Investment Companies (continued)

	License Number & Date	Private Capital	SBA Leverage	Investment Policy
Magna Pacific Investments David Wong, President 330 North Brand Boulevard, Suite 670 Glendale, CA 91203 (818) 547-0809 FAX (818) 547-9303	09/09-5362 12/03/85	1,080,000	2,160,000	Diversified
Myriad Capital, Inc. Chuang-I Lin, President 701 South Atlantic Boulevard, Suite 302 Monterey Park, CA 91754 (818) 570-4548 FAX (818) 570-9570	09/09-5272 09/16/80	1,334,530	5,338,120	Diversified
Opportunity Capital Corporation J. Peter Thompson, President 2201 Walnut Avenue, Suite 210 Fremont, CA 94538 (510) 795-7000 FAX (510) 494-5439	09/12-5155 09/23/71	2,526,043	2,180,500	Diversified
Opportunity Capital Partners II, L.P. J. Peter Thompson, General Partner 2201 Walnut Avenue, Suite 210 Fremont, CA 94538 (510) 795-7000 FAX (510) 494-5439	09/09-5396 05/07/93	1,556,161	0	Diversified
Positive Enterprises, Inc. Kwok Szeto, President 1489 Webster Street, Suite 228 San Francisco, CA 94115 (415) 885-6600 FAX (415) 928-6363	09/09-5256 06/06/80	505,000	505,000	Diversified
San Joaquin Business Investment Group Inc. Eugene Waller, President 1900 Mariposa Mall, Suite 100 Fresno, CA 93721 (209) 233-3580 FAX (209) 233-3709	09/09-5376 04/23/88	1,000,000	2,000,000	Diversified
South Bay Capital Corporation John Wang, Manager 5325 East Pacific Coast Highway Long Beach, CA 90804 (310) 597-3285 FAX (310) 498-7167	09/09-5382 10/25/89	1,020,000	0	Diversified
Western General Capital Corporation Alan Thian, President 13701 Riverside Drive, Suite 610 Sherman Oaks, CA 91423 (818) 986-5038 FAX (818) 905-9220	09/09-5381 08/02/89	1,000,000	1,000,000	Diversified

Small Business Investment Companies (continued)

	License Number & Date	Private Capital	SBA Leverage	Investment Policy

Connecticut

TSG Ventures, Inc.
Duane Hill, President
1055 Washington Boulevard, 10th Floor
Stamford, CT 06901
(203) 363-5344
FAX (203) 363-5340

02/02-5286
05/07/71 — 10,550,000 — 10,295,000 — Diversified

District of Columbia

Allied Capital Financial Corp.
Cabell Williams, President
1666 K Street NW, Suite 901
Washington, DC 20006
(202) 331-1112
FAX (202) 659-2053

03/03-5163
08/09/83 — 8,900,000 — 25,950,000 — Diversified

Broadcast Capital, Inc.
John E. Oxendine, President
1771 N Street NW, Suite 421
Washington, DC 20036
(202) 429-5393
FAX (202) 496-9259

03/03-5147
11/26/80 — 3,350,000 — 5,800,000 — Communications Media

Minority Broadcast Investment Corp.
Walter L. Threadgill, President
1001 Connecticut Avenue NW, Suite 622
Washington, DC 20036
(202) 293-1166
FAX (202) 293-1181

03/03-5142
08/07/79 — 1,000,100 — 2,000,100 — Communications Media

Florida

Allied Capital Financial Corp.
(Main Office: Washington, DC)
Executive Office Center, Suite 305
2770 North Indian River Boulevard
Vero Beach, FL 32960
(407) 778-5556
FAX (202) 569-9303

BAC Investment Corp.
Gregory Hobbs, Manager
6600 NW 27th Avenue
Miami, FL 33217
(305) 693-5919
FAX (305) 693-7450

04/04-5249
05/01/89 — 1,144,000 — 0 — Diversified

PMC Investment Corporation
(Main Office: Dallas, TX)
AmeriFirst Bank Building, 2nd Floor South
18301 Biscayne Boulevard
North Miami Beach, FL 33160
(305) 933-5858
FAX (305) 931-3054

Small Business Investment Companies (continued)

	License Number & Date	Private Capital	SBA Leverage	Investment Policy

Georgia

First Growth Capital, Inc.
Vijay K. Patel, President/Manager
1-75 & GA 42, Best Western Plaza
P.O. Box 815
Forsyth, GA 31029
(912) 994-9260
FAX (912) 994-1280

04/04-5251
11/16/89

1,060,000   2,945,000   Diversified

Renaissance Capital Corporation
Anita P. Stephens, President
34 Peachtree Street NW, Suite 2610
Atlanta, GA 30303
(404) 658-9061
FAX (404) 658-9064

04/04-5236
12/05/86

1,155,500   500,000   Diversified

Hawaii

Pacific Venture Capital, Ltd.
Dexter J. Taniguchi, President
222 South Vineyard Street
Honolulu, HI 96813
(808) 521-6502
FAX (808) 521-6541

09/09-5182
06/25/75

1,250,000   700,000   Diversified

Illinois

The Combined Fund, Inc.
John Eggemeyer, Director
915 East Hyde Park Boulevard
Chicago, IL 60615
(312) 363-0300
FAX (312) 363-6816

05/07-5080
05/04/71

1,100,250   2,729,000   Diversified

The Neighborhood Fund, Inc.
David Shyrock, President
25 East Washington Boulevard, Suite 2015
Chicago, IL 60649
(312) 753-5670
FAX (312) 493-6609

05/05-5124
04/03/78

980,000   1,450,000   Diversified

Peterson Finance and Investment Company
James S. Rhee, President
3300 West Peterson Avenue, Suite A
Chicago, IL 60659
(312) 539-0502
FAX (312) 583-6714

05/05-5176
02/07/84

1,035,000   1,035,000   Diversified

Polestar Capital, Inc.
Wallace Lennox, President
180 North Michigan Avenue, Suite 1905
Chicago, IL 60601
(312) 984-9875
FAX (312) 984-9877

05/07-5083
12/22/70

6,334,750   6,888,000   Diversified

Small Business Investment Companies (continued)

	License Number & Date	Private Capital	SBA Leverage	Investment Policy

Kentucky

Equal Opportunity Finance, Inc.
David A. Sattich, President
420 South Hurstbourne Parkway, Suite 201
Louisville, KY 40222
(502) 423-1943
FAX (502) 423-1945

04/05-5096
09/24/70

3,670,292

1,600,000

Diversified

Maryland

Security Financial and Investment Corp.
7720 Wisconsin Avenue, Suite 207
Bethesda, MD 20814
(301) 951-4288

03/03-5158
12/29/83

535,500

1,500,000

Diversified

Syncom Capital Corp.
Terry L. Jones, President
8401 Colesville Road, #300
Silver Spring, MD 20910
(301) 608-3207

03/03-5137
07/10/78

2,250,000

1,000,000

Communications
Media

Massachusetts

The Argonauts MESBIC Corporation
Kevin Chen, General Manager
929 Worcester Road
Framingham, MA 01701
(508) 820-3430
FAX (508) 872-3741

01/01-5343
06/17/88

1,140,237

2,000,000

Diversified

Commonwealth Enterprise Fund Inc.
Gabrielle Greene, Manager
10 Post Office Square, Suite 1090
Boston, MA 02109
(617) 482-1881
FAX (617) 482-7129

01/01-5356
05/28/92

1,500,000

0

Diversified

Transportation Capital Corporation
(Main Office: New York, NY)
45 Newbury Street, Suite 207
Boston, MA 02116
(617) 536-0344
FAX (212) 949-9836

Small Business Investment Companies (continued)

	License Number & Date	Private Capital	SBA Leverage	Investment Policy

Michigan

Dearborn Capital Corporation
Edwin M. Sweda, President
c/o Ford Motor Credit Corporation
The American Road
Dearborn, MI 48121
(313) 337-8577
FAX (313) 248-1252

05/05-5135
12/14/78

5,449,897

5,200,000

Diversified

Metro-Detroit Investment Company
William J. Fowler, President
30777 Northwestern Highway, Suite 300
Farmington Hill, MI 48334
(810) 851-6300
FAX (810) 851-9551

05/05-5126
06/01/78

2,000,000

6,000,000

Grocery Stores

Motor Enterprises, Inc.
James Kobus, Manager
General Motors Building
2044 West Grand Boulevard, Room 11-119
Detroit, MI 48202
(313) 556-4273
FAX (313) 974-4499

05/15-5024
04/13/70

1,500,000

2,000,000

Diversified

Minnesota

Capital Dimensions Ventures Fund, Inc.
Dean R. Pickerell, President
Two Appletree Square, Suite 335
Minneapolis, MN 55425
(612) 854-3007
FAX (612) 854-6657

05/05-5134
01/29/79

7,342,662

6,278,200

Diversified

Milestone Growth Fund, Inc.
Esperanza Guerrero, President
75 South 5th Street, Suite 705
Minneapolis, MN 55402
(612) 338-0090
FAX (612) 338-1172

05/05-5213
12/27/89

2,018,807

1,300,000

Diversified

Mississippi

Sun-Delta Capital Access Center, Inc.
Howard Boutte, Jr., Vice President
819 Main Street
Greenville, MS 38701
(601) 335-5291
FAX (601) 335-5293

04/04-5175
09/25/79

1,258,100

0

Diversified

Small Business Investment Companies (continued)

	License Number & Date	Private Capital	SBA Leverage	Investment Policy

New Jersey

Capital Circulation Corporation
Judy Kao, Manager
2035 Lemoine Avenue, Second Floor
Fort Lee, NJ 07024
(201) 947-8637
FAX (201) 585-1965

02/02-5484
03/28/85 — 1,000,000 — 2,000,000 — Diversified

Rutgers Minority Investment Company
Oscar Figueroa, President
180 University Avenue, 3rd Floor
Newark, NJ 07102
(201) 648-5627
FAX (201) 648-1110

02/02-5283
07/28/70 — 1,826,000 — 0 — Diversified

Transpac Capital Corporation
Tsuey Tang Wang, President
1037 Route 46 East
Clifton, NJ 07013
(201) 470-8855
FAX (201) 470-8827

02/02-5502
05/28/87 — 1,000,000 — 4,000,000 — Diversified

New York

American Asian Capital Corporation
Howard H. Lin, President
130 Water Street, Suite 6-L
New York, NY 10005
(212) 422-6880

02/02-5316
11/12/76 — 503,000 — 500,000 — Diversified

Capital Investors & Management Corp.
Rose Chao, Manager
210 Canal Street, Suite 611
New York, NY 10013
(212) 964-2480
FAX (212) 349-9160

02/02-5363
02/06/80 — 1,300,000 — 1,450,000 — Diversified

East Coast Venture Capital, Inc.
Zindel Zelmanovitch, President
313 West 53rd Street, Third Floor
New York, NY 10019
(212) 245-6460
FAX (212) 265-2962

02/02-5470
07/14/86 — 1,060,454 — 3,000,000 — Diversified

Elk Associates Funding Corporation
Gray C. Granoff, President
747 Third Avenue
New York, NY 10017
(212) 421-2111
FAX (212) 421-3488

02/02-5377
07/24/80 — 5,405,118 — 14,197,140 — Transportation

Small Business Investment Companies (continued)

	License Number & Date	Private Capital	SBA Leverage	Investment Policy
Empire State Capital Corporation Dr. Joseph Wu, President 170 Broadway, Suite 1200 New York, NY 10038 (212) 513-1799 FAX (212) 513-1892	02/02-5543 02/05/91	2,100,000	4,200,000	Diversified
Esquire Capital Corp. Wen-Chan Chin, President 69 Veterans Memorial Highway Commack, NY 11725 (516) 462-6946 FAX (516) 864-8152	02/02-5520 02/14/89	1,266,200	2,450,000	Diversified
Exim Capital Corp. Victor K. Chun, President 241 5th Avenue, 3rd Floor New York, NY 10016 (212) 683-3375 FAX (212) 689-4118	02/02-5351 01/05/79	660,000	1,950,000	Diversified
Fair Capital Corp. Rose Chao, Manager 210 Canal Street, Suite 611 New York, NY 10013 (212) 964-2480 FAX (212) 349-9160	02/02-5437 09/27/82	625,000	500,000	Diversified
First County Capital, Inc. Zenia Yuan, President 135-14 Northern Boulevard, 2nd Floor Flushing, NY 11354 (718) 461-1778 FAX (718) 461-1835	02/02-5519 03/31/89	1,000,000	1,000,000	Diversified
Flushing Capital Corp. Frank J. Mitchell, President 39-06 Union Street, Room 202 Flushing, NY 11354 (718) 886-5866 FAX (718) 939-7761	02/02-5516 12/24/90	1,000,000	1,000,000	Diversified
Freshstart Venture Capital Corporation Zindel Zelmanovich, President 313 West 53rd Street, 3rd Floor New York, NY 10019 (212) 265-2249 FAX (212) 265-2962	02/02-5447 02/24/83	1,540,597	4,990,000	Diversified
Hanam Capital Corp. Robert Schairer, President 38 West 32nd Street, Suite 1512 New York, NY 10001 (212) 564-5225 FAX (212) 564-5307	02/02-5497 05/06/87	1,402,000	2,400,000	Diversified

Small Business Investment Companies (continued)

	License Number & Date	Private Capital	SBA Leverage	Investment Policy
Ibero American Investors Corp. Emilio Serrano, President 104 Scio Street Rochester, NY 14604 (716) 262-3440 FAX (716) 262-3441	02/02-5369 09/28/79	2,576,471	3,088,659	Diversified
International Paper Capital Formation, Inc. (Main Office: Memphis, TN) Frank Polney, Manager Two Manhattanville Road Purchase, NY 10577 (914) 397-1578 FAX (914) 397-1909				
Medallion Funding Corporation Alvin Murstein, President 205 East 42nd Street, Suite 2020 New York, NY 10017 (212) 682-3300 FAX (212) 983-0351	02/02-5393 06/23/80	11,234,000	21,733,712	Transportation
Pierre Funding Corp. Elias Debbas, President 805 Third Avenue, 6th Floor New York, NY 10022 (212) 888-1515 FAX (212) 688-4252	02/02-5396 01/22/81	2,761,473	7,108,173	Transportation
Situation Ventures Corporation Sam Hollander, President 56-20 59th Street Maspeth, NY 11378 (718) 894-2000 FAX (718) 326-4642	02/02-5323 02/16/77	1,000,200	3,000,000	Diversified
Transportation Capital Corp. Mark Hornstein, President 315 Park Avenue South, 10th Floor New York, NY 10010 (212) 598-3225 FAX (212) 598-3102	02/02-5388 06/23/80	6,560,000	14,113,333	Diversified
Triad Capital Corp. of New York Oscar Figueroa, Manager of Rutgers Inv. 305 Seventh Avenue, 20th Floor New York, NY 10001 (212) 243-7360 FAX (212) 243-7647	02/02-5455 11/25/83	545,253	500,000	Diversified
Trusty Capital Inc. Yungduk Hahn, President 350 Fifth Avenue, Suite 2026 New York, NY 10118 (212) 736-7653 FAX (212) 629-3019	02/02-5512 05/01/89	1,025,000	2,025,000	Diversified

Small Business Investment Companies (continued)

	License Number & Date	Private Capital	SBA Leverage	Investment Policy
United Capital Investment Corp. Paul Lee, President 60 East 42nd Street, Suite 1515 New York, NY 10165 (212) 682-7210 FAX (212) 573-6352	02/02-5480 02/05/85	1,448,417	2,800,000	Diversified
Venture Opportunities Corporation A. Fred March, President 150 East 58th Street, 16th Floor New York, NY 10155 (212) 832-3737 FAX (212) 223-4912	02/04-5151 12/01/78	1,825,000	4,575,000	Diversified

Ohio

Cactus Capital Company Edward C. Liu, President 6660 North High Street, #1B Worthington, OH 43085 (614) 436-4060 FAX (614) 436-4060	05-05-5210 09/22/89	1,100,000	1,100,000	Diversified
Enterprise Ohio Investment Company Steven Budd, President 8 North Main Street Dayton, OH 45402 (513) 226-0457 FAX (513) 222-7035	05/05-5153 07/29/81	525,000	500,000	Diversified

Pennsylvania

Greater Philadelphia Venture Capital Corp. Fred S. Choate, Manager 351 East Conestoga Road, Room 203 Wayne, PA 19087 (215) 688-6829 FAX (215) 254-8958	03/03-5112 03/31/72	760,981	1,432,800	Diversified

Puerto Rico

North America Investment Corporation Rita V. de Fajardo, President Mercantil Plaza Building, Suite 813 P.O. Box 1831, Hato Rey Sta., PR 00919 Hato Rey, PR 00919 (809) 754-6178 FAX (809) 754-6181	02/02-5308 11/07/74	1,181,250	1,250,000	Diversified

Small Business Investment Companies (continued)

	License Number & Date	Private Capital	SBA Leverage	Investment Policy

Tennessee

International Paper Capital Formation, Inc.
Bob J. Higgins, V. P. and Controller
International Place II
6400 Poplar Avenue
Memphis, TN 38197
(901) 763-6282
FAX (901) 763-7278

04/02-5432
11/05/81

1,000,000

1,000,000

Diversified

Tennessee Venture Capital Corporation
William E. Farris, Chairman
201 4th Avenue North
P.O. Box 305110
Nashville, TN 37230-5110
(615) 748-4291
FAX (615) 259-4119

04/04-5176

500,000

500,000

Diversified

Valley Capital Corp.
Lamar J. Partridge, President
Suite 212, Krystal Building
100 W. Martin Luther King Boulevard
Chattanooga, TN 37402
(615) 265-1557
FAX (615) 265-1588

04/04-5216
10/08/82

1,145,000

1,000,000

Diversified

West Tennessee Venture Capital Corporation
Frank Banks, President
5 North Third Street
Memphis, TN 38103
(901) 522-9237
FAX (901) 527-6091

04/04-5218
12/16/82

1,250,000

0

Diversified

Texas

Alliance Enterprise Corporation
Donald R. Lawhorne, President
North Central Plaza 1, Suite 710
12655 North Central Expressway
Dallas, TX 75243
(214) 991-1597
FAX (214) 991-1647

03/03-5066
10/20/71

3,030,200

2,700,000

Diversified

Chen's Financial Group, Inc.
Samuel S. C. Chen, President
10101 Southwest Freeway, Suite 370
Houston, TX 77074
(713) 772-8868
FAX (713) 772-2168

06/06-5281
03/05/84

1,500,000

3,000,000

Diversified

Small Business Investment Companies (continued)

	License Number & Date	Private Capital	SBA Leverage	Investment Policy
MESBIC Financial Corp. of Houston Atillio Galli, President of Alliance Cap 401 Studewood, Suite 200 Houston, TX 77007 (713) 869-4061 FAX (713) 869-4462	06/06-5180 11/12/76	1,726,701	1,679,000	Diversified
MESBIC Ventures, Inc. Donald R. Lawhorne, President 12655 North Central Expressway, Suite 710 Dallas, TX 75243 (214) 991-1597 FAX (214) 991-1647	06/10-5153 02/26/70	4,213,282	9,400,000	Diversified
North Texas MESBIC, Inc. Allan Lee, President 12770 Coit Road, Suite 240 Dallas, TX 75251 (214) 991-8060 FAX (214) 991-8061	06/06-5302 07/11/91	1,033,202	3,100,000	Diversified
PMC Investment Corporation Mr. Andrew S. Rosemore, President 17290 Preston Road, Suite 300 Dallas, TX 75252 (214) 380-0044 FAX (214) 380-1371	04/04-5240 11/28/86	5,000,000	9,000,000	Diversified
Tower Ventures, Inc. Donald R. Lawhorne, President North Central Plaza 1 12655 North Central Expressway, Suite 710 Dallas, TX 75243 (214) 991-1597 FAX (214) 991-1647	06/05-5104 06/30/75	2,000,000	3,000,000	Diversified
United Oriental Capital Corporation Jai Min Tai, President 908 Town & Country Boulevard, Suite 310 Houston, TX 77024 (713) 461-3909 FAX (713) 465-7559	06/06-5254 07/07/82	1,000,000	3,700,000	Diversified

Virginia

Continental SBIC Arthur Walters, President 4141 North Henderson Road, Suite 8 Arlington, VA 22203 (703) 527-5200 FAX (703) 527-3700	03/03-5191 10/19/90	1,200,000	0	Diversified

Small Business Investment Companies (continued)

	License Number & Date	Private Capital	SBA Leverage	Investment Policy
East West United Investment Company Dung Bui, President 1568 Spring Hill Road, Suite 100 McLean, VA 22102 (703) 442-0150 FAX (703) 442-0156	03/03-5125 01/22/76	500,000	1,000,000	Diversified

Wisconsin

	License Number & Date	Private Capital	SBA Leverage	Investment Policy
Future Value Ventures, Incorporated William P. Beckett, President Plaza East Office Center, Suite 711 330 East Kibourn Avenue Milwaukee, WI 53203 (414) 278-0377 FAX (414) 278-7321	05/05-5198 11/09/84	2,532,307	1,000,000	Diversified

Glossary

accounts payable — A list of current business debts or liabilities that must be paid in the future (usually within one year).

accounts receivable — A list of the amounts a business is owed by others for merchandise or services sold, representing current assets.

accrual basis accounting — By this long-established and widely used principle, revenue and expenses are recognized when a service is performed or goods are delivered, regardless of when payment is received or made. This method allows what accountants call the matching of revenues and associated expenses. Revenue example: If a store sells $500 worth of tires in a day, $500 of revenue is earned and entered in the books even though the proceeds of the sale may not be collected for a month or more. Expense example: If a store clerk earns a $10 commission on the day of the tire sale, this expense to the business is recorded that day even though it may not actually be paid until the next payroll day. Compare: cash basis accounting.

aging the receivables — A method of determining the quality of accounts receivable by listing the accounts' length of time on the books — 30, 60, 90, 120, or more days. An excess of past due accounts may indicate ineffective collection methods and, thus, poor management.

amortization — To liquidate on an installment basis; the process of gradually paying off a liability over a period of time, such as a mortgage which is amortized by periodically paying off part of it.

appreciation — Any increase from the acquisition price of a fixed asset to current appraised market value. However, for financial statement purposes, appreciation is not considered because of three accounting concepts: (1) the objectivity principle, which would necessitate an appraisal of each asset's market value per accounting period — a costly and highly variable endeavor; (2) the continuity assumption — that fixed assets are acquired for continuing business operations and not for resale; and (3) the principle of conservatism, which states that given a choice of values, an accountant always chooses the more conservative.

assets — The valuable resources, or properties and property rights, owned by an individual or business enterprise.

balance sheet	A detailed listing of assets, liabilities, and owner's equity accounts (net worth) showing the financial position of a company at a specific time.
bank of record	The financial institution where you have been doing business.
capital	Capital funds are those funds which are needed for the base of a business. Usually these funds are put into the business in a fairly permanent form such as in fixed assets, plant, and equipment, or are used in other ways which are not recoverable in the short run unless the entire business is sold. See also: working capital.
capital equipment	Equipment used to manufacture a product, provide a service, or sell and deliver merchandise. Such equipment is not sold in the normal course of business, but will be used and worn out or consumed over time as business is conducted.
cash basis accounting	As its name implies, this method recognizes revenue and expenses only when cash payment is actually received or made. Because it does not allow matching, the cash basis does not always provide an accurate picture of profitability and is less commonly used than the accrual basis. Compare: accrual basis accounting.
cash flow	The supply of money continuously received from operations and the supply continuously disbursed to pay business expenses. See also: negative cash flow.
collateral	Property you pledge as a guarantee for repayment of money, which may include a mortgage on the land and building being financed and liens on machinery, equipment, and fixtures.
compensating balances	Cash balances kept on deposit at a bank, usually non-interest bearing, which are taken into consideration when a bank decides what interest rate it will charge for a loan.
current assets	Cash or other items that will normally be turned into cash within one year, and assets that will be used up in the operations of a business within one year.
current liabilities	Amounts owed that will normally be paid off within one year. Such items include accounts payable, wages payable, taxes payable, the current portion of a long-term debt, and interest and dividends payable.
current ratio	A ratio of a business' current assets to its current liabilities. Because a current ratio includes the value of inventories that have not been sold, it does not offer the best evaluation of a business' current status. The "quick" ratio, covering the most liquid of current assets, produces a better evaluation. See also: quick ratio.
debenture	A bond or other debt obligation usually backed only by the integrity or general credit of an issuing borrower and not secured by a lien or any specific asset.

debt	Debt refers to borrowed funds, whether from your own coffers, other individuals, banks, or institutions. It is generally secured with a note, which in turn may be secured by a lien against property or other assets. Ordinarily, a note indicates repayment and interest provisions, which vary greatly in both amount and duration, depending upon the purpose, source, and term of the loan. Some debt is convertible; that is, it may be changed into direct ownership of a portion of a business under stated conditions.
depreciation	A universal accounting assumption holds that all fixed assets — with the exception of land — deteriorate, wear out, or become obsolete. This process represents a decline in value that is called depreciation. It is calculated by apportioning an asset's original acquisition price, less any expected salvage, over the asset's expected years of useful life. (For accounting purposes, land is always valued at its original purchase price.)
equity	Equity is an owner's investment in a business. Unlike capital, equity is what remains after the liabilities of the company are subtracted from the assets — thus it may be greater than or less than the capital invested in the business. Equity investment carries with it a share of ownership and usually a share in the profits, as well as some say in how the business is managed.
equity financing	Equity financing is raised by selling a portion of a firm's ownership interest to an outsider of the business.
fixed assets	Those terms of a permanent nature, required for the normal conduct of a business, and not converted into cash during a normal fiscal period. Examples include building, machinery, and furniture.
fixed (long-term) liabilities	Liabilities that will not mature during the next accounting period.
gross profit	Net sales (sales minus returned merchandise, discounts, or other allowances) minus the cost of goods sold.
guaranty (or guarantee)	A pledge by a third party to repay a loan in the event that the borrower cannot repay it.
income statement	A statement of income and expenses for a given period of time.
inventory	The materials owned and held by a business, including new materials, intermediate products and parts, work-in-progress, and finished goods, intended either for internal consumption or for sale.
line of credit	If a business has seasonal or cyclical needs for cash, a line of credit may work for it. A business may need to pay off the line for a 30-day period each 12 months, just to show that it doesn't need the loan for long-term financing.
liquidity	A term used to describe the solvency of a business, which has special reference to the degree of readiness in which assets can be converted into cash without a loss. Also called cash position. If a business' current assets cannot be converted into cash to meet current liabilities, the firm is said to be illiquid.

loan agreement A document that states what a business can and cannot do as long as it owes money to a lender — usually a bank. A loan agreement may place restrictions on owners' salaries or dividends, amount of other debt, working capital limits, sales, or number of added personnel.

loans Debt money for private business is usually in the form of bank loans. Depending on the lender's policy, a loan can be secured with business assets or unsecured. An unsecured loan is backed by the faith the bank has in the borrower's ability to repay the loan.

negative cash flow Cash receipts that are insufficient to meet ongoing operating expenditures.

net worth An owner's equity in a given business represented by the excess of total assets over the total amounts owed to outside creditors (total liabilities) at a given moment in time. Also, the net worth of an individual as determined by deducting the amount of all of his or her personal liabilities from the total value of his or her personal assets. Generally, net worth refers to tangible items and does not include such things as goodwill.

note In a basic business loan, a note represents a debt that will be repaid, or substantially reduced 30, 60, or 90 days later at a stated interest rate. Notes are short-term, and unless they are made under a line of credit, a separate loan application is needed for each loan and each renewal.

prime rate A benchmark interest rate that an individual bank may establish and sometimes use to compute an appropriate rate of interest for a particular loan contract. This rate is based on numerous factors, including the bank's supply of funds, its administrative costs, and competition from other credit suppliers.

pro forma A projection or estimate of what may result in the future from actions in the present. A pro forma financial statement is one that shows how the actual operations of a business will turn if certain assumptions are realized.

profit The excess of the selling price over costs and expenses incurred in making a sale. Also, the reward to the entrepreneur for the risks assumed by him or her in the establishment, operation, and management of a given enterprise or undertaking.

quick ratio Cash plus other assets that can be used immediately (converted to cash) should approach or exceed current liabilities. The formula used to determine the ratio is:

cash + accounts receivable + marketable securities = current liabilities

The quick ratio is one of the most important credit barometers used by lending institutions, because it indicates the ability of a business enterprise to meet its current obligations. See also: current ratio.

rates (fixed) Loan rates that will be fixed (remain the same) for the life of a loan. These types of loan rates are generally associated with long-term, fixed asset financing.

rates (variable) Variable loan rates will generally change monthly or quarterly and be based on some index, such as the bank's prime rate. Variable rates can increase or decrease during the life of a loan depending on what happens to the index rate the loan is based on. A typical variable rate quote is the prime rate plus 2%. Variable rates will usually be quoted for short-term financing, such as working capital loans, accounts receivable financing, or short-term equipment loans.

revolving credit A contractual agreement allowing a customer to borrow funds when needed, up to a specified maximum amount for a limited period of time.

secured loan A loan for which the lender's interest is protected by collateral pledged by the borrower. The collateral can be any marketable asset.

take-over The acquisition of one business by another business.

term loans Either secured or unsecured, usually for periods of more than a year to as many as 20 years. Term loans are paid off like a mortgage: "x" amount of dollars per month for "x" amount of years. The most common uses of term loans are for equipment and other fixed asset purposes, working capital, and real estate.

working capital The difference between total current assets and total current liabilities. The result is a pool of resources readily available to maintain normal business operations.

Notes

Index

A

accountants and attorneys 39, 43, 45
America Online 29
applicants 35–38, 41–42, 47, 66, 89, 121
    academic schools 36
    aliens 37
    disabled individuals 43, 77–78
    farms and agricultural businesses 37
    fishing vessels 37
    franchises 36, 89, 91, 99, 101–102, 108–110, 112, 116
    gambling activities 36
    illegal activities 36
    lending activities 36
    manufacturing businesses 33, 84
    medical facilities 37
    pyramid sales plans 36
    real estate investment firms 35
    recreational facilities and clubs 37
    speculative activities 35
    veterans 3, 8, 22, 42–43
    women-owned 21–22
Applicant's Agreement of Compliance, SBA Form 601 142–143
Application for Business Loan, SBA Form 4 40, 42, 47–51, 67, 91–95, 122–125
Application for Small Business Loan (Short Form), SBA Form 4 86–87
Application for Business Loan (Up to $100,000), SBA Form 4-L 88
application process 13, 40
    pre-application 4
    specific loan programs, related to 68–85
    supplemental instructions for *SBA Form 4* 47
appraisals 4, 39–40, 45, 47, 144
Associate Administrator for Investment 20
Association of Industrial Engineers 5
AT&T Small Business Lending Corporation 14–16

B

balance sheet 4, 41, 45, 91, 102, 121, 133, 144
bank of record 13–16
borrowing basics 1
    cash contribution 2
    collateral 1–2, 18–19, 39–40, 53–54
    management 1–2, 14
    repayment ability 2
business financial information 41–42

business loan application 1–4, 9, 13–16, 40–45, 91–95, 121–125
    existing business case history 89
    loan processing, 7(a) Program 66–67
    new business case history 89
business plan 2, 5–6, 9, 41–44, 46–47, 137
    credit decision based on 34
    guidelines for writing a successful plan 43
    home-based businesses 5
    outline 44, 46
    retailers 5, 16, 33, 47, 192, 194, 213
    sample 137
    small construction firms 5
    small manufacturers 5
    small service firms 5
business relocations 44–45
buyer/seller, close relationship of 45
buying and selling a business 5

C

capital [See "working capital"]
capital equipment 91, 115
CAPLines Short-Term Working Capital Lines of Credit Program 84
cash flow 1, 41–42, 57–59
    pro forma 91, 106–108
    your cash contribution 2–4
Certificate of Competency (COC) Program 27–28
Certified Lenders Program (CLP) 66–68
    nationwide listing 175–188
    restrictions on CAPLines 84
chamber of commerce 5, 7, 20, 23
change of ownership loan 35, 37, 44–45
Checklist for Going into Business 5
closing costs 39
collateral 1–2, 18–19, 39–40, 53–54, 91, 101
Commerce Business Daily (CBD) 26, 29
Compensation Agreement, SBA Form 159 43, 62–63, 91, 117–118, 121, 145–146
competitive analysis 46
conflict of interest 67
Consolidated Farm Service Agency 37
construction businesses 5, 23, 33
Contract Loan Program 42, 71

conventional bank loan 9, 13
counseling 4–6, 9–10, 20–22

D

debt-to-equity ratios 7
declination letters 42
Defense Loan & Technical Assistance (DELTA) Program 22
disabled individuals 43, 77–78
Dun and Bradstreet's *Key Business Ratios* 7

E

eligibility
    general requirements for SBA loans 33–38
    PLP and CLP 66–67
    SBIC 19
    secondary loan programs 68–84
Encyclopedia of Associations 7
equity guidelines 3
existing business 89
Export Assistance Centers (EACs) 22–23, 155
Export Working Capital Loan Program 81

F

farms and agricultural businesses 37
Fast-Track Loan Program 69
Federation of Business and Professional Women 5
fees
    and closing 39
    for professional help 43
Financial Statement Spread Sheet 41, 60–61
financial statements 34, 40–41, 55–56, 60–61, 91, 96–97, 108, 121, 126–130
fishing vessels 37
forms, SBA
    Applicant's Agreement of Compliance, SBA Form 601 142–143
    Application for Business Loan, SBA Form 4 48–51, 92–95, 122–125
    Application for Small Business Loan (Short Form), SBA Form 4 86–87
    Application for Business Loan (Up to $100,000), SBA Form 4-L 88

forms, SBA (continued)
Compensation Agreement, SBA Form 159 62–63, 117–118, 145–146
Monthly Cash Flow Projection, Form 1100 57–59
PASS Application, SBA Form 1167 30–31
Personal Financial Statement, SBA Form 413 55–56, 96–97, 126–129
Schedule of Collateral, SBA Form 4 Schedule A 53–54
Statement of Personal History, SBA Form 912 52, 98, 130–131
franchises 36, 89, 90–119

G
gambling activities 36
government contracts 25–29
government guarantee 3, 13–14, 25, 39, 70, 99
    general eligibility requirements for SBA loans 33

H
Handicapped Assistance Loan (HAL) Program 38, 77–79

I
IRS 41–42, 116
illegal activities 36
income projection 136
    pro forma cash flow 91, 106
    pro forma profit and loss 91, 104
income tax returns 40–41, 91, 116, 144
interest rates
    SBA loans 38–39
    SBIC financing 18–19
    secondary loan programs 68–84
    7(a) Program 66
international marketing 22
International Trade Loan Program 83
inventory 65, 89–90, 99–102, 112–114, 136

L
lender options
    bank of record 13–16
    microloan lenders 13, 16–17

lender options (continued)
    non-bank lenders 13–16
    venture capital companies 14
lending activities 36
letters of interest 137
loan application [See "business loan application"]
loan package 3, 6, 9, 34
    how to properly prepare a 40, 89
    processing time 39
    seeking professional help 43
local library 7, 29
LowDoc Loan Program 68, 70–71

M
machinery and equipment 38, 65, 89, 101, 120–121, 132–133, 137
management 1–2, 14, 110–111
Management and Technical Assistance 7(j) Program 22
manufacturing businesses 33, 84
marketing plan 46
maturity, loan 38–39
    and secondary loan programs 72, 76, 78, 80–81, 84
medical facilities 37
microloan lenders 13, 16–17
    nationwide listing 159–173
microloans 68–69
minority investments
    SBA assistance 8, 20
    SSBICs 219–232
Monthly Cash Flow Projection, Form 1100 9, 41–42, 57–59

N
National Association of Black Accountants 5
National Marine Fisheries Service (NMFS) 37
National Resources Sales Assistance Program 28
new business 89
non-bank lenders 13–16, 157

O
Office of Procurement Assistance 29
on-line service 8, 85

P

PASS Application, SBA Form 1167 28, 30–31
Personal Financial Statement, SBA Form 413 34, 41, 55–56, 91, 121
Pollution Control Loan Program 66, 68, 75
pre-business workshop 7, 9
Preferred Lenders Program (PLP) 66–68, 84
    nationwide listing 175–188
prime rate 38–39
probation or parole 38
processing time
    CLP and PLP 175
    IRS 41
    SBA loans 39
    7(a) Program 66–67
Procurement Assistance Programs 25
    bidding on a government contract 26
    Certificate of Competency (COC) Program 27–28
    helpful publications 29
    prime contracts 28
    Procurement Automated Source System (PASS) 28, 30–31
professional help 39
pro forma cash flow 91, 106
pro forma profit and loss 91, 104
purchase or construction of plant facilities 38
pyramid sales plans 36

R

real estate investment firms 35
recreational facilities and clubs 37
repayment ability 2, 80
Request for Counseling, SBA Form 641 5–6, 9–10, 22
Resource Directory for Small Business Management, Form 115C 5, 9
resumés 42, 113–114, 138–139
retail or service businesses 5, 33
Robert Morris & Associates' *Annual Statement Studies* 7

S

SBA Online 8
Schedule of Collateral, SBA Form 4 Schedule A 40, 53–54, 132
Seasonal Line of Credit Program 74
Service Corps of Retired Executives (SCORE) 4–7, 9, 20
7(a) Regular Loan Guarantee Program 66–68
Small Business Administration (SBA)
    counseling 4–6, 20
    equity guidelines 3–4
    field offices 147–154
    free advice 4–5
    history and background 2–3
    pre-business workshops 7, 9
    primary SBA lending programs 65–66
    Published Rules and Regulations 23
    SBA Online 8
Small Business Administration (SBA) loans
    business relocations 44–45
    close buyer/seller relationship 45
    closing costs 39
    collateral considerations 39
    construction loans 76
    contract loans 68
    direct loans 13, 38–39, 42–43, 66, 77–79
    eligibility requirements 33–38
    guaranty loans 42, 77, 81
    ineligible businesses 35
    interest rates 38–39, 68–85
    loan amounts 38–39, 65, 68–85
    processing time 39, 41, 66–67, 175
    terms 14, 38–39, 68–85
    7(a) Regular Loan Guarantee Program 66–68
    uses 65–66
Small Business Development Centers (SBDCs) 4, 6–7, 9, 21, 39, 44
Small Business Energy Loan Program 79
Small Business Innovation Research (SBIR) Program 85
Small Business Institute (SBI) Program 21
Small Business Investment Act of 1958 17
Small Business Investment Companies (SBICs) 14, 17–20
    eligibility 19
    equity-type investments 18
    history and background 17–18
    how SBIC financing works 18
    nationwide listing 189–232

SBICs (continued)
    response time 20
    straight loans 18–19
Small Business Sourcebook 7
Small General Contractor Loan Program 73
Small Loan Program 69
Specialized Small Business Investment Companies (SSBICs) 17
    nationwide listing 219–232
speculative activities 35
standard industrial classification or size standards 33
Starting Kit, The 5
start-up costs, how to estimate 11–12
Statement of Personal History, SBA Form 912 24, 38, 40, 52, 67, 91, 98, 121, 130–131
statewide programs 23
stockholders 35, 41–42
Surety Bond Guarantee (SBG) Program 23–25
surveys 39

T
terms 14, 38–39, 68–85
title reports 39
trade finance 23

U
use of proceeds 47
U.S. Department of Commerce 23, 37
U.S. Government Purchasing and Sales Directory 29

V
venture capital companies [See "Small Business Investment Companies (SBICs)"]
veterans 3, 8, 22, 42–43
    Defense Loan and Technical Assistance (DELTA) Program 22
    disabled 42–43
    veterans administration 43
    veterans affairs and the SBA 22

W
Wall Street Journal 39
wholesale businesses 33
women's business ownership 21–22
    Demonstration Training Program 21
    Network for Entrepreneurial Training 21
    Pre-Qualification Loan Program 21
working capital 38, 47, 90, 99–101, 112, 120, 137

Establish A Framework For Excellence With The Successful Business Library

Fastbreaking changes in technology and the global marketplace continue to create unprecedented opportunities for businesses through the '90s. With these opportunities, however, will also come many new challenges. Today, more than ever, businesses, especially small businesses, need to excel in all areas of operation to complete and succeed in an ever-changing world.

The Successful Business Library takes you through the '90s and beyond, helping you solve the day-to-day problems you face now, and prepares you for the unexpected problems you may be facing next. You receive up-to-date and practical business solutions, which are easy to use and easy to understand. No jargon or theories, just solid, nuts-and-bolts information.

Whether you are an entrepreneur going into business for the first time or an experienced consultant trying to keep up with the latest rules and regulations, The Successful Business Library provides you with the step-by-step guidance, and action-oriented plans you need to succeed in today's world. As an added benefit, PSI Research / The Oasis Press® unconditionally guarantees your satisfaction with the purchase of any book or software program in our catalog.

Your success is our success...

At PSI Research and The Oasis Press, we take pride in helping you and 2 million other businesses grow. It's the same pride we take in watching our own business grow from two people working out of a garage in 1975 to more than 50 employees now in our award-winning building in scenic southern Oregon.

After all, your business is our business.

OASIS PRESS
BOOKS & SOFTWARE

Call Toll Free To Receive A Free Catalog Or To Place An Order
1-800-228-2275
All Major Credit Cards Accepted

PSI Research, 300 North Valley Drive, Grants Pass, OR 97526 (800) 228-2275 (541) 479-9464 FAX (541) 476-14

Books that save you time & money

Now you can find out what venture capitalists and bankers really want to see before they will fund a company. This book gives you their personal tips and insights. The Abrams Method of Flow-Through Financials breaks down the chore into easy-to-manage steps, so you can end up with a fundable proposal.

Successful Business Plan: Secrets & Strategies   Pages: 339
Paperback: $24.95   *ISBN: 1-55571-194-4*
Binder Edition: $49.95   *ISBN: 1-55571-197-9*

Makes understanding the economics of your business simple. Explains the basic accounting principles that relate to any business. Step-by-step instructions for generating accounting statements and interpreting them, spotting errors, and recognizing warning signs. Discusses how creditors view financial statements.

Business Owners' Guide to Accounting and Bookkeeping   Pages: 145
Paperback $19.95   *ISBN: 1-55571-156-1*

From the editors at The Oasis Press comes this guide for the beginning business owner. This all-in-one business book lists the major requirements and issues a new business owner needs to know, including:
- Start-up financing
- Creating a business plan
- Marketing strategies
- Environmental laws

Checklists and Plans of Action ensure that you have all the bases covered.

Start Your Business: A Beginner's Guide   Pages: 198
Paperback $9.95   *ISBN: 1-55571-363-7*

Clearly reveals the essential ingredients of sound financial management in detail. By monitoring trends in your financial activities, you will be able to uncover potential problems before they become crises. You'll understand why you can be making a profit and still not have the cash to meet expenses. You'll learn the steps to change your business' cash behavior to get more return for your effort.

Financial Management Techniques   Pages: 262
Paperback: $19.95   *ISBN: 1-55571-124-3*
Binder Edition: $39.95   *ISBN: 1-55571-116-2*

ll toll free to order 1-800-228-2275   PSI Research   300 North Valley Drive, Grants Pass, OR 97526   FAX 541-476-1479

Books that save you time & money

Essential techniques to successfully identify, approach, attract, and manage sources of financing. Shows how to gain the full benefits of debt financing while minimizing its risks. Outlines all types of financing and carefully walks you through the process, from evaluating short-term credit options, through negotiating a long-term loan, to deciding whether to go public.

Financing Your Small Business **Pages: 214**
Paperback $19.95   ISBN: 1-55571-160-X

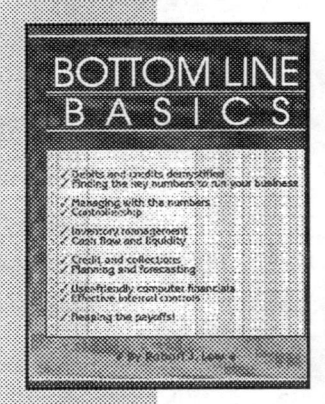

Guides you past the mechanics of accounting to an understanding of financial management allowing you to meet your business goals. This book provides immediate help to improve cash flow, reduce costs, and give you a clear idea of what is driving your business.

Bottom Line Basics   **Pages: 280**
Paperback: $19.95   ISBN: 1-55571-330-0
Binder Edition: $39.95 ISBN: 1-55571-329-7

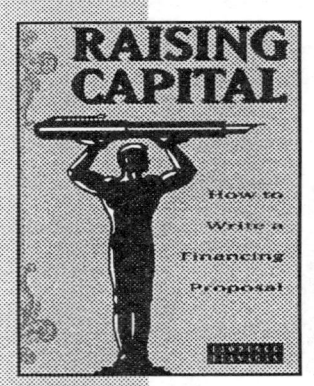

Valuable resource for writing and presenting a winning loan proposal. Includes professional tips on how to write the proposal. Presents detailed examples of the four most common types of proposals to secure venture capital and loans; private Placement Circular; Prospectus or Public Offering; Financing Proposal; and Limited Partnership Offering.

Raising Capital: How to Write a Financing Proposal   **Pages: 230**
Paperback: $24.95   ISBN: 1-55571-305-X
Binder Edition: $39.95 ISBN: 1-55571-306-8

Regularly Updated For Your State!
Our best seller for 13 years — still your best source of practical business information. Find out what new laws affect your business. Now there's an edition for every state in the U.S., plus the District of Columbia.

Starting & Operating a Business in... series
Paperback $24.95
Binder Workbook Edition $29.95
Specify which state you want.

Call toll free to order 1-800-228-2275   PSI Research   300 North Valley Drive, Grants Pass, OR 97526   FAX 541-476-

No matter what type of business or profession you're in, The Successful Business Library will help you find the solutions you need.

Call, Mail or Fax to: PSI Research, 300 North Valley Drive, Grants Pass, OR 97526 USA
Order Phone USA & Canada (800) 228-2275   **Inquiries and International Orders** (541) 479-9464   **FAX** (541) 476-1479

EXECARDS® Sampler (call for more information about this product) — ☐ $ 9.95

TITLE	✔ BINDER	✔ PAPERBACK	QUANTITY	COST
Bottom Line Basics	☐ $ 39.95	☐ $ 19.95		
The Business Environmental Handbook	☐ $ 39.95	☐ $ 19.95		
Business Owner's Guide to Accounting & Bookkeeping		☐ $ 19.95		
Buyer's Guide to Business Insurance	☐ $ 39.95	☐ $ 19.95		
California Corporation Formation Package and Minute Book	☐ $ 39.95	☐ $ 29.95		
Collection Techniques for a Small Business	☐ $ 39.95	☐ $ 19.95		
A Company Policy and Personnel Workbook	☐ $ 49.95	☐ $ 29.95		
Company Relocation Handbook	☐ $ 39.95	☐ $ 19.95		
CompControl: The Secrets of Reducing Worker's Compensation Costs	☐ $ 39.95	☐ $ 19.95		
Complete Book of Business Forms	☐ $ 39.95	☐ $ 19.95		
Customer Engineering: Cutting Edge Selling Strategies	☐ $ 39.95	☐ $ 19.95		
Doing Business In Russia		☐ $ 19.95		
Draw The Line: A Sexual Harassment Free Workplace		☐ $ 17.95		
The Essential Corporation Handbook		☐ $ 19.95		
The Essential Limited Liability Company		☐ $ 19.95		
Export Now: A Guide for Small Business	☐ $ 39.95	☐ $ 19.95		
Financial Management Techniques For Small Business	☐ $ 39.95	☐ $ 19.95		
Financing Your Small Business		☐ $ 19.95		
Franchise Bible: How to Buy a Franchise or Franchise Your Own Business	☐ $ 39.95	☐ $ 19.95		
Home Business Made Easy		☐ $ 19.95		
How to Develop & Market Creative Business Ideas		☐ $ 14.95		
Incorporating Without A Lawyer (Available for 32 States) SPECIFY STATES:		☐ $ 24.95		
The Insider's Guide to Small Business Loans	☐ $ 29.95	☐ $ 19.95		
InstaCorp – Incorporate In Any State Book & Software		☐ $ 29.95		
Keeping Score: An Insider Look at Sports Marketing		☐ $ 18.95		
Know Your Market: How to do Low-Cost Market Research	☐ $ 39.95	☐ $ 19.95		
Legal Expense Defense: How to Control Your Business' Legal Costs and Problems	☐ $ 39.95	☐ $ 19.95		
The Loan Package	☐ $ 39.95			
Location, Location, Location: How To Select The Best Site For Your Business		☐ $ 19.95		
Mail Order Legal Guide	☐ $ 45.00	☐ $ 29.95		
Managing People: A Practical Guide	☐ $ 39.95	☐ $ 19.95		
Marketing Mastery: Your Seven Step Guide to Success	☐ $ 39.95	☐ $ 19.95		
The Money Connection: Where and How to Apply for Business Loans and Venture Capital	☐ $ 39.95	☐ $ 24.95		
People Investment	☐ $ 39.95	☐ $ 19.95		
Power Marketing for Small Business	☐ $ 39.95	☐ $ 19.95		
Profit Power: 101 Pointers to Give Your Small Business A Competitive Edge		☐ $ 19.95		
Proposal Development: How to Respond and Win the Bid	☐ $ 39.95	☐ $ 19.95		
Raising Capital	☐ $ 39.95	☐ $ 19.95		
Retail In Detail: How to Start and Manage a Small Retail Business		☐ $ 14.95		
Safety Law Compliance Manual for California Businesses		☐ $ 24.95		
Company Illness & Injury Prevention Program Binder (or get a kit with book and binder $49.95)	☐ $ 34.95	☐ $ 49.95 kit		
Secrets to Buying & Selling a Business	☐ $ 39.95	☐ $ 19.95		
Secure Your Future: Financial Planning at Any Age	☐ $ 39.95	☐ $ 19.95		
Start Your Business (available in a book and disk package – see back)		☐ $ 9.95 (without disk)		
Starting and Operating A Business in... book INCLUDES FEDERAL section PLUS ONE STATE section—	☐ $ 29.95	☐ $ 24.95		
PLEASE SPECIFY WHICH STATE(S) YOU WANT:				
STATE SECTION ONLY (BINDER NOT INCLUDED) – SPECIFY STATES:	☐ $ 8.95			
FEDERAL SECTION SECTION ONLY (BINDER NOT INCLUDED)	☐ $ 12.95			
U.S. EDITION (FEDERAL SECTION – 50 STATES AND WASHINGTON, D.C. IN 11-BINDER SET)	☐ $295.00			
Successful Business Plan: Secrets and Strategies	☐ $ 49.95	☐ $ 24.95		
Successful Network Marketing for The 21st Century		☐ $ 14.95		
Surviving and Prospering in a Business Partnership	☐ $ 39.95	☐ $ 19.95		
Top Tax Saving Ideas for Today's Small Business		☐ $ 14.95		
Write Your Own Business Contracts	☐ $ 39.95	☐ $ 19.95		

BOOK SUB-TOTAL (FIGURE YOUR TOTAL AMOUNT ON THE OTHER SIDE)

IGBL196

OASIS SOFTWARE Please check Macintosh or 3-1/2" Disk for IBM-PC & Compatibles

TITLE	3-1/2" IBM Disk	Mac	Price	QUANTITY	COST
California Corporation Formation Package ASCII Software	☐	☐	$ 39.95		
Company Policy & Personnel Software Text Files	☐		$ 49.95		
Financial Management Techniques (Full Standalone)	☐		$ 99.95		
Financial Templates	☐	☐	$ 69.95		
The Insurance Assistant Software (Full Standalone)	☐		$ 29.95		
The Small Business Expert (Full Standalone)	☐		$ 34.95		
Start A Business (Full Standalone)	☐		$ 49.95		
Start Your Business (Software for Windows™)	☐		$ 19.95		
Successful Business Plan (Software for Windows™)	☐		$ 99.95		
Successful Business Plan Templates	☐	☐	$ 69.95		
The Survey Genie - Customer Edition (Full Standalone)	☐		$149.95		
The Survey Genie - Employee Edition (Full Standalone)	☐		$149.95		

SOFTWARE SUB-TOTAL

BOOK & DISK PACKAGES Please check Macintosh or 3-1/2" Disk for IBM-PC & Compatibles

TITLE	IBM	MAC	BINDER	PAPERBACK	QUANTITY	COST
The Buyer's Guide to Business Insurance w/ Insurance Assistant	☐		$ 59.95			
California Corporation Formation Binder Book & ASCII Software	☐	☐	☐ $ 69.95	☐ $ 59.95		
Company Policy & Personnel Book & Software Text Files	☐	☐	☐ $ 89.95	☐ $ 69.95		
Financial Management Techniques Book & Software	☐		☐ $129.95	☐ $119.95		
Start Your Business Paperback & Software (Software for Windows™)	☐			$ 24.95		
Successful Business Plan Book & Software for Windows™	☐		☐ $125.95	☐ $109.95		
Successful Business Plan Book & Software Templates	☐	☐	☐ $125.95	☐ $ 89.95		

BOOK & DISK PACKAGE TOTAL

AUDIO CASSETTES

TITLE	Price	QUANTITY	COST
Power Marketing Tools For Small Business	☐ $ 49.95		
The Secrets To Buying & Selling A Business	☐ $ 49.95		

AUDIO CASSETTE SUB-TOTAL

OASIS SUCCESS KITS Please call for more information about these book sets.

TITLE	Price	QUANTITY	COST
Start-Up Success Kit	☐ $ 39.95		
Business At Home Success Kit	☐ $ 39.95		
Financial Management Success Kit	☐ $ 44.95		
Personnel Success Kit	☐ $ 44.95		
Marketing Success Kit	☐ $ 44.95		

OASIS SUCCESS KITS TOTAL

COMBINED SUB-TOTAL (FROM THIS SIDE)

YOUR GRAND TOTAL

SUB-TOTALS (from other side) $
SUB-TOTALS (from this side) $
SHIPPING (see chart below) $
TOTAL ORDER $

SOLD TO: Please give street address
NAME
Title:
Company
Street Address
City/State/Zip
Daytime Phone   EMail

SHIP TO: If different than above give street address or P.O. Box
NAME
Title:
Company
Street Address
City/State/Zip
Daytime Phone

If your purchase is:	Then your shipping is:
$0 - $25	$5.00
$25.01 - $50	$6.00
$50.01 - $100	$7.00
$100.01 - $175	$9.00
$175.01 - $250	$13.00
$250.01 - $500	$18.00
$500.01+	4% of total merchandise

PAYMENT INFORMATION: Rush service is available. Call for details

☐ CHECK Enclosed payable to PSI Research   Charge ☐ VISA   ☐ MASTERCARD   ☐ AMEX   ☐ DISCOVER

Card Number: Expires:
Signature: Name On Card:

Call toll free to order 1-800-228-2275 PSI Research 300 North Valley Drive, Grants Pass, OR 97526 FAX 541-476-1479

Use this form to register for an advance notification of updates, new books and software releases, plus special customer discounts!

Please answer these questions to let us know how our products are working for you, and what we could do to serve you better.

The Insider's Guide To Small Business Loans

This book format is:
- ☐ Binder book
- ☐ Paperback book
- ☐ Book/Software Combination
- ☐ Software only

Rate this product's overall quality of information:
- ☐ Excellent
- ☐ Good
- ☐ Fair
- ☐ Poor

Rate the quality of printed materials:
- ☐ Excellent
- ☐ Good
- ☐ Fair
- ☐ Poor

Rate the format:
- ☐ Excellent
- ☐ Good
- ☐ Fair
- ☐ Poor

Did the product provide what you needed?
- ☐ Yes ☐ No

If not, what should be added?
_____
_____
_____

This product is:
- ☐ Clear and easy to follow
- ☐ Too complicated
- ☐ Too elementary

Were the worksheets (if any) easy to use?
- ☐ Yes ☐ No ☐ N/A

Should we include?
- ☐ More worksheets
- ☐ Fewer worksheets
- ☐ No worksheets

How do you feel about the price?
- ☐ Lower than expected
- ☐ About right
- ☐ Too expensive

How many employees are in your company?
- ☐ Under 10 employees
- ☐ 10 - 50 employees
- ☐ 51 - 99 employees
- ☐ 100 - 250 employees
- ☐ Over 250 employees

How many people in the city your company is in?
- ☐ 50,000 - 100,000
- ☐ 100,000 - 500,000
- ☐ 500,000 - 1,000,000
- ☐ Over 1,000,000
- ☐ Rural (Under 50,000)

What is your type of business?
- ☐ Retail
- ☐ Service
- ☐ Government
- ☐ Manufacturing
- ☐ Distributor
- ☐ Education

What types of products or services do you sell?
_____
_____
_____

What is your position in the company?
(please check one)
- ☐ Owner
- ☐ Administrative
- ☐ Sales/Marketing
- ☐ Finance
- ☐ Human Resources
- ☐ Production
- ☐ Operations
- ☐ Computer/MIS

How did you learn about this product?
- ☐ Recommended by a friend
- ☐ Used in a seminar or class
- ☐ Have used other PSI products
- ☐ Received a mailing
- ☐ Saw in bookstore
- ☐ Saw in library
- ☐ Saw review in:
  - ☐ Newspaper
  - ☐ Magazine
  - ☐ Radio/TV

Where did you buy this product?
- ☐ Catalog
- ☐ Bookstore
- ☐ Office supply
- ☐ Consultant

Would you purchase other business tools from us?
- ☐ Yes ☐ No

If so, which products interest you?
- ☐ EXECARDS® Communications Tools
- ☐ Books for business
- ☐ Software

Would you recommend this product to a friend?
- ☐ Yes ☐ No

Do you use a personal computer?
- ☐ Yes ☐ No

If yes, which?
- ☐ Macintosh
- ☐ IBM/compatible

Check all the ways you use computers?
- ☐ Word processing
- ☐ Accounting
- ☐ Spreadsheet
- ☐ Inventory
- ☐ Order processing
- ☐ Design/Graphics
- ☐ General Data Base
- ☐ Customer Information
- ☐ Scheduling

May we call you to follow up on your comments?
- ☐ Yes ☐ No

May we add your name to our mailing list? ☐ Yes ☐ No

If you'd like us to send associates or friends a catalog, just list names and addresses on back.

Is there anything we should do to improve our products?
_____

Just fill in your name and address here, fold (see back) and mail.

Name _____
Title _____
Company _____
Phone _____
Address _____
City/State/Zip _____
E Mail Address (Home) _____ (Business) _____

PSI Research creates this family of fine products to help you more easily and effectively manage your business activities:

The Oasis Press®
PSI Successful Business Library
PSI Successful Business Software
EXECARDS® Communication Tools

IGBL196

If you have friends or associates who might appreciate receiving our catalogs, please list here. Thanks!

Name_____ Name_____
Title_____ Title_____
Company_____ Company_____
Phone_____ Phone_____
Address_____ Address_____
Address_____ Address_____

FOLD HERE FIRST

BUSINESS REPLY MAIL
FIRST CLASS MAIL PERMIT NO. 002 MERLIN, OREGON

POSTAGE WILL BE PAID BY ADDRESSEE

PSI Research
PO BOX 1414
Merlin OR 97532-9900

NO POSTAGE
NECESSARY
IF MAILED
IN THE
UNITED STATES

FOLD HERE SECOND, THEN TAPE TOGETHER

Please cut
along this
vertical line,
fold twice,
tape together
and mail.